Mel Bay Presents

BLUEGRASS PICKER'S TUNE BOOK

Compiled by
Richard Matteson, Jr.

1 2 3 4 5 6 7 8 9 0

Photo Page

Matteson singing with Messengers at St. Mary's College.

Bluegrass Messengers photo for "Farther Along" CD.

Matteson backstage with Earl Skruggs, Doc Watson and Ricky Skaggs.

BLUEGRASS PICKER'S TUNE BOOK - TABLE OF CONTENTS

5

Appendix: Chords and Chord Diagrams

PREFACE

The purpose of this book is to give bluegrass pickers a book they can use in performances. Large type is used so that it can be read easily during a performance. I've arranged most of the songs in guitar and fiddle keys of G, A, E, and D. There are chord charts in the back of the book.

It was hard to limit the book to 213 tunes. The list of fiddle tunes and old-time tunes that could work for most bluegrass groups is enormous. Maybe I'll do Part II someday.

ABOUT THE AUTHOR

Richard L. Matteson Jr. is President of the Piedmont Guitar Society located in Winston-Salem NC. A resident of nearby Lexington, NC he lives in the heart of "bluegrass country" near some of the great festivals such as "Merle Watson Memorial Festival" in North Wilkesboro, NC; the "Mt Airy Fiddler's Convention" in Mt. Airy, NC and the "Galax Fiddler's Convention" in Galax, VA.

Matteson is a member of the High Lonesome Strings Bluegrass Assoc. and plays guitar and sings with his group, The Bluegrass Messengers, a group he created for his students. He teaches guitar, bass, fiddle, mandolin, dobro and banjo at Duncan Music Co, in Winston-Salem, NC.

Richard researches bluegrass and old-time music on his web-site: BluegrassMessengers.com and can be E-mailed from the site. His grandfather, Maurice Matteson, collected folk songs from Beech Mountain, NC and published several short books in the 1930's.

Matteson has performed and done workshops at the Merle Watson Memorial Festival in Wilkesboro and the Chet Atkins Festival in Nashville. He has played with or shared the stage with legendary guitarists Doc Watson, Roy Clark, Chet Atkins and Charlie Byrd. Matteson's other Mel Bay books, "Folk Songs from the Appalachian Mountains," "American Fiddle Tunes," and "Early American Hymns," reflect his deep interest in traditional music.

His bluegrass band, The Bluegrass Messengers, was started in the mid 1990's. Since he teaches guitar, fiddle, dobro, bass, and banjo, the band began as an opportunity for some of his talented students to perform "live" the music that they had been studying. The group has evolved through the last 7 years and four CD's. Although not a professional group, the Messengers enjoy playing and have had the fortune to perform with Doc Watson and other talented musicians. Some of the students that have played with the Messengers have gone on to become successful bluegrass musicians and have won top prizes in bluegrass competitions.

BLUEGRASS PICKER'S TUNE BOOK INTRODUCTION

INTRODUCTION, DEFINITIONS, ORIGIN, CATEGORIES

Bluegrass music has become popular again. There are more bluegrass pickers today than ever. With the popularity of the movie, "O Brother Where Art Thou?" and the hit crossover song from the movie, "Man of Constant Sorrow," bluegrass music has become a national and international phenomena.

Even though "O Brother" used the "hayseed" or "hillbilly" stereotype that was originally associated with early country and bluegrass (as portrayed in the 70's on TV show's like Hee Haw and the Beverly Hillbillies), the music today is a sophisticated concert music with virtuoso performers. There are many styles and categories within the "Bluegrass" label. Media and press sources often try to define parameters of "what is bluegrass" without understanding the origin or any definition of the word.

New progressive groups (including Alison Krauss and Union Station; Nickel Creek) have been labeled "Bluegrass" by the media. Many groups have evolved from traditional bluegrass that have become popular not only in the country market but also in the popular mainstream. Whether they are "bluegrass" or not depends on your definition of bluegrass.

MY JOURNEY: THE BLUEGRASS MESSENGERS

In the 1980's in South Carolina I learned some of the bluegrass repertoire while playing with Derrick Phillips. When I started my bluegrass band, The Bluegrass Messengers, in the mid 1990's, I renewed my love affair with bluegrass and old-time music. Since I teach guitar, fiddle, dobro, bass, and banjo, the band began as an opportunity for some of my talented students to perform "live" the music that they had been studying.

As one of the guitarists and singers for the Messengers I have seen the evolution of our group through the last 7 years and four CD's. Although we aren't a professional group, we enjoy playing and have had the fortune to perform with Doc Watson and other talented musicians.

Some of the students that have played with the Messengers have gone on to become successful bluegrass musicians and have won top prizes in bluegrass competitions. This has been the most rewarding aspect of organizing the Messengers.

For more information see the Bluegrass Messengers Online: BluegrassMessengers.com

WHAT IS (BLUE GRASS) BLUEGRASS?

The word, "bluegrass," or originally two words, "blue grass," is a species of grass (Poa pratensis) identified with "Kentucky blue grass," which has running rootstocks and spreads rapidly. It is valuable as a pasture grass, as it endures both winter and drought better than other kinds, and is very nutritious.

Bluegrass is not really blue-it's green, but in the spring, bluegrass produces bluish-purple buds that when seen in large fields give a rich blue cast to the grass. Early pioneers found bluegrass growing on Kentucky's rich limestone soil, and traders began asking for the seed of the "blue grass from Kentucky." The name stuck and today Kentucky is known as the "Bluegrass State."

Bill Monroe (1911-1996), the Father of Bluegrass Music, created the bluegrass genre. By the 1920's Monroe had settled on the mandolin as his instrument. After performing first with brothers Birch and Charlie (Monroe Brothers), then as a duet with Charlie, he formed his own band in 1938. Later that year in Atlanta he organized the first Blue Grass Boys, which he named in honor of his home state, a trio with guitar, fiddle, and mandolin.

The band's personnel changed much over the years, but the classic bluegrass group was formed by Bill Monroe in the winter of 1945, when a young banjo player named Earl Scruggs, and guitarist/vocalist Lester Flatt, joined the band. The origin of bluegrass music is generally attributed to Bill Monroe and his Blue Grass Boys' 1945-1946 band with Earl Scruggs featured playing three-finger style banjo. Many believe bluegrass music started that day that Earl Scruggs joined Bill Monroe, Lester Flatt, Chubby Wise, and Cedric Rainwater on the stage of the "Opry." His three-finger banjo roll style is what gives the bluegrass its "drive."

A DEFINITION

The term bluegrass is a nickname from the "Bluegrass State," (Kentucky) that is applied to the music of Bill Monroe and his Blue Grass Boys in the late 1940's. Bluegrass music is an acoustic ensemble music characterized by driving rhythms, improvised instrumental solos and close (high) harmony parts. The five primary concert instruments established by Bill Monroe are the guitar, the mandolin, the upright bass (or bass), the three-finger style banjo, the fiddle. Other instruments include the dobro (resophonic guitar played with a slide), electric bass, harmonica and sometimes percussion (drums, spoons etc.). Each instrument has developed a distinct role and style of playing within the bluegrass group.

Bluegrass music is considered a part of country music. Bill Monroe, the Father of Bluegrass, explained it this way: "To me bluegrass is really THE country music. It was meant for country people."

THE ORIGIN OF BLUEGRASS AND THE BLUEGRASS GENRE

While some fans of bluegrass music date the style back to 1939, when Monroe formed his first Blue Grass Boys band, most believe that the classic bluegrass sound began in winter of 1945, when Earl Scruggs, a 21 year old banjo player from North Carolina, joined the band. Scruggs played an innovative three-finger picking style on the banjo that energized audiences, and has since become simply, "Scruggs style" banjo. Equally influential in the classic 1945-46 line-up of the Blue Grass Boys were Lester Flatt, from Sparta, Tenn. on guitar and lead vocals against Monroe's tenor; Chubby Wise, from Florida, on fiddle; and Howard Watts, also known by his comedian name, "Cedric Rainwater," on acoustic bass. The bluegrass genre (it take two groups to create a genre) was created when Ralph Stanley's band played a cover of Monroe's "Molly and Tenbrooks" arrangement in 1948.

SOME CATEGORIES OF BLUEGRASS

Traditional Bluegrass- is the authentic bluegrass music as the founding fathers played it. If Bill Monroe, the Stanley Brothers or Flatt & Scruggs didn't play it, and if it isn't played exactly as they played it, then it isn't bluegrass. This the 'classic' bluegrass sound.

Contemporary Bluegrass isn't that far from traditional except it has more modern chord progressions with jazzier chords and some substitute chords. There are more distinct harmonies sometimes in three or four parts. Groups like the super group Seldom Scene or the Tony Rice Unit fit in the contemporary category.

Progressive Bluegrass- also known as newgrass, dawg music, jamgrass, and many other names, this type of music is often instrumental but always of a completely different arrangement than traditional or contemporary bluegrass. It commonly crosses genre borders by using electric instruments or fuses bluegrass with rock or jazz or other more mainstream music forms. Often younger with a varied music taste, the fans of progressive bluegrass don't care what you call it as long as it's good. Bela Fleck & The Flecktones (jazz), Leftover Salmon, and Nickel Creek are examples of what can be considered progressive bands.

ROOTS OF BLUEGRASS

Bluegrass music evolved from music indigenous to the Southern Appalachian region including fiddle tunes, folk songs and blues. Monroe called it, "the old Southern sound."

Music from the Southern Appalachian region draws heavily on older forms including:
 1) English ballads and songs brought to the US by the early settlers
 2) Fiddle and instrumental music both from overseas and the US
 3) Minstrel songs from the mid 1800's
 4) Gospel or shape-note hymns and tunes
 5) Popular songs and broadsides from the 19th Century

Around the turn of the century (1900) came the tin-pan alley songs, the medicine shows, ragtime, blues and jazz. Later in early 1920's the emergence of the rural string bands like the Leake County Revelers, Weem's Stringband, the Carter Brothers as well as solo performers like Fiddlin' John Carson, Doc Boggs, French Carpenter, Uncle Dave Macon and Clarence Ashley laid the foundation of bluegrass. These and the early country music artists like the Carter Family, Charlie Poole, the Mainer's, the Stoneman's, the Delmore's and the Blue Sky Boys played the old songs and old tunes now called "Old-time" music.

OLD-TIME MUSIC

Old-time music was the name given to mountain folk music. Old-time music is the main foundation for bluegrass music. Bill Monroe, Earl Scruggs, the Stanley Brothers and most rural people prior to the mid-nineteen twenties, were raised with traditional old-time music. It is the old unaccompanied English ballads like Barbara Allen, new American songs like Wild Bill Jones, old fiddle tunes like Devil's Dream, and newer banjo tunes like Cumberland Gap. It was played throughout rural America but has been identified with the rural Southeast, especially in the mountains. It is sung and played on a variety of acoustic instruments including the guitar and mandolin, which were newcomers to it in the early twentieth century. It was played by African-Americans as well as the English and Euro-Americans.

Generally music before the 1940's is called "Old-time" music. Old-time music is traditional folk music of the Southern Appalachians mixed with the influences of African-American musicians. The fiddle came over from Europe with the immigrants, the banjo came from Africa in primitive form and was refined and developed in the US cities in the minstrel era which started before the Civil War. The Civil War spread the banjo and the minstrel tunes into the remote Appalachian mountains, where they were adapted. So a general time frame for "old-time" music would be from the 1840's to the 1940's.

The term, "old-time music," can be traced back to 1923, when Georgia's Fiddlin' John Carson waxed "The Little Old Log Cabin in the Lane" for the OKeh label. Ralph Peer deemed Carson's performance "pluperfect awful," but enough rural Americans disagreed to make the record a hit, the first in the history of what's now called country music. Carson remarked at his first whiff of success: "I'll have to quit making moonshine and start making records." Carson's music appeared in OKeh's popular music catalog under the "old-time music" category.

Most of the "old-time" musicians were white rural agrarian Southerners. They had no formal music training and played primarily stringed instruments. Their song repertoire could be broadly divided between secular and sacred and further subdivided into categories of traditional, commercial (often of sufficient vintage to have entered oral tradition), and original (often topical and tragic) songs. These general elements are found equally in the commercial "old time music" recordings of the 1920s and in the performances captured decades later. Although identified with mountain and rural folk, some old-time musicians (jazz and blues) live in urban areas.

SIMILARITIES AND DIFFERENCES BETWEEN BLUEGRASS AND OLD-TIME MUSIC

Bluegrass has some of these characteristics of the old-time string bands from the 1920's and 30's. Certainly the vocal style is similar and some string bands sang a high harmony part. The vocal style is also similar the to the old gospel and shape-note singing found in rural churches in the south. The rhythm guitar style of the string bands with bass notes on the beat, off beat strums and bass runs is very similar to bluegrass rhythm guitar. The style of fiddling is also very similar.

The main difference between an old-time string band sound and the bluegrass sound is the banjo. Some bluegrass enthusiasts credit Earl Scruggs and the development of the three-finger or "Scruggs" style banjo playing as the origin of bluegrass. Most old-time bands have a claw-hammer or mountain style banjo player. Although other old-time performers like Charlie Poole played three-finger style, the banjo was usually used in an accompaniment or back-up role.

From the unified sound of old-time music, bluegrass music developed distinct styles for each instrument of the group. Today each member of the bluegrass group should be a soloist and provide specific rhythms and fills.

BLUEGRASS PICKER'S TUNE BOOK:
INTRODUCTION 2- INSTRUMENTATION

THE INSTRUMENTS

The five primary concert instruments established by Bill Monroe are the guitar, the mandolin, the upright bass (or bass), the three-finger style banjo, and the fiddle.
Other instruments include the dobro (resophonic guitar), electric bass, harmonica and sometimes percussion (drums, spoons etc.).

Bluegrass instrumentation was established by Bill Monroe's classic 1945-46 line-up of the Blue Grass Boys Band with Earl Scruggs of North Carolina on three-finger style banjo; Lester Flatt, from Sparta, Tenn. on guitar and lead vocals; Bill Monroe tenor harmony and mandolin; Chubby Wise, from Florida, on fiddle; and Howard Watts, also known by his comedian name, "Cedric Rainwater," on acoustic bass.

Monroe did not include the dobro (resophonic guitar) as one of the five essential instruments but it is now considered by many to be the sixth essential bluegrass instrument.

At the end of the book there is a section with chord diagrams for each instrument that you can use to play the songs in this book.

THE BANJO

"If you don't have a banjo playing, it ain't bluegrass!" The banjo is one of the essential elements of any bluegrass group. The banjo provides the drive with a series of fast rolls that imply the melody of the song or tune. Most bluegrass pickers use 2 metal fingerpicks on the right hand index and middle fingers and a plastic thumb pick for volume.

To play each song the banjo player needs to play a basic solo with the melody, a back-up or accompaniment part with or without fills and a more difficult solo usually played higher up the neck.

Back-up parts may be played:
1) staccato on the off-beat using chords played up the neck with no open strings. The staccato effect is achieved by gently lifting the left hand finger so they remain on the strings and dampen the sound.
2) staccato on and off the beat. The right hand will play the chords with an abbreviated roll/pinch pattern with the thumb playing on the beat: bum ti bum-pa-ti-ta (1 2 3+4+).
3) roll patterns can be played up or down the neck letting the chord ring.
4) fills may be added to the back-up part between or after the vocal or instrumental solos.

STYLES OF BLUEGRASS BANJO

The fundamental bluegrass style is the three-finger style developed at age 21 by Earl Scruggs when he played with Bill Monroe and his Blue Grass Boys in 1945-46. The melody is picked primarily with the thumb while the fingers add in a string of eight note chord tones that pause or stop only at the end of each phrase with a pinch or turnaround. The banjo turnaround (below) is as famous as the G-run on the guitar.

An important aspect of banjo playing is the alternation of the fingers when playing eighth notes.

VARIANTS OF SCRUGGS STYLE

Melodic Style: was developed to play fiddle tunes of melodies made up of eighth note scales. Melodic style uses open strings combined with fretted notes up the neck (V pos. and higher) to play scales in a roll pattern.

Melodic   Normal

Regular solos can be arranged melodic style. There's an overlapping of sound that gives the solos a hammer dulcimer-like ring.

Chromatic Style: This is used by progressive and contemporary style groups to spice up the traditional sound. Chromatic bluegrass music uses jazz chords and runs. Chord substitutes replace the standard bluegrass fare.

Banjo Tunings: Standard bluegrass tuning is standard open G: 1=D 2=B, 3=G, 4=low D, 5=high G. In the key of C the 4th string is tuned down one step to a C.

THE MANDOLIN

The mandolin is tuned the same as the fiddle but played like a miniature 12 string guitar. Its four strings are each doubled by another string giving it eight strings, amplifying the volume. The smaller scale of the neck (distance between the frets is smaller) affords the mandolin player the opportunity to cover a wide range of notes in one position. Bill Monroe, an under- rated mandolin player, helped establish the mandolin's role in the bluegrass group.

The mandolin is one of the most important rhythm instruments in the bluegrass group. Like the drummer, the mandolinist sets the rhythm with the bass player. The mandolinist provides the back-beat on off-beats 2 and 4. Bill Monroe not only set the rhythm with his punctuated off-beat attacks but pushed the rhythm (playing slightly ahead of the beat) creating the illusion of acceleration.

Since the mandolin doesn't have the sustain of the fiddle on longer tones during solos, a technique called tremolo (a rapid down and up strum on a single string or strings) is used to give the melody more volume.

Rhythm: Most mandolin players used closed chords (chords with no open strings) so that when they strum the back-beat their fingers can mute the strings making a punctuated staccato sound:

THE GUITAR

For many years the acoustic steel-string guitar was essentially a rhythm instrument, backing the singer with a steady bass-strum rhythm and playing bass runs and fills. Lester Flatt, the guitarist for Bill Monroe's 1946 group, played the bass part with a thumb-pick similar to the Carter family style. Although some guitarists (like Virginia guitarist Wayne Henderson) use the thumb pick, most guitarists today use the flatpick (plectrum).

One of the originators of the solo flatpick style used today is Doc Watson, who played with Jack Williams' western swing/rockabilly band in the 1950's. Because the band didn't have a fiddle player, Doc, at Williams' request, picked out tunes for square dance numbers on his guitar, thus developing what would become his trademark picking style.

The function of the guitar in bluegrass music is to play rhythm by playing bass notes on the strong beats (1 & 3) and strums on the off beats along with the mandolin. The guitar also plays bass runs between the chords, fills, and solos. The most famous guitar lick in bluegrass music is the famous G-Run below:

G-Run

Basic Guitar Rhythm

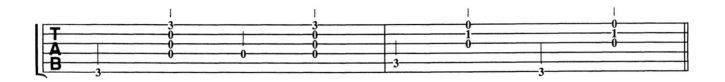

Bass Runs

Because the guitar has less volume than most of the bluegrass instruments, medium to heavy gauge strings are used to allow the guitar to be heard better during acoustic (unamplified) jam sessions.

THE FIDDLE

The fiddle (commonly known as the violin) is the lead voice in the bluegrass group. The fiddle is just a violin (from 1579, from It. *violino*, dim. of *viola)* played country or bluegrass style.

The word fiddle (O.E. *fidele*) is probably from M.L. *vitula* "stringed instrument," perhaps related to L. *vitularia* "celebrate joyfully," from *Vitula*, Roman goddess of joy and victory, who probably, like her name, originated among the Sabines. The word has been relegated to colloquial usage by its more proper cousin, *violin*, a process encouraged by phraseology such as *fiddlesticks* (originally "the bow of a fiddle," meaning "nonsense" is from 1600) and *fiddle-faddle*, which is unrelated, being a reduplication of obsolete *faddle* "to trifle."

Some differences in technique from classical violin technique including a shorter, vigorous bow stroke, sometimes holding the bow about a third of the way up from the frog with a wide variety of grips, resting the palm of the left hand against the neck, supporting the butt of the fiddle on the chest instead of under the chin, playing horizontally more in the first position, and using open strings and drone strings.

Some fiddlers prefer a flatter bridge does make it easier to rotate the bow to get to the next string and also to play both fingered open stops, and double fingered double stops. Some use the old-timey or folk style of supporting the butt of the fiddle on the chest instead of under the chin. This is a great advantage if you sing at the same time but is harder for the left hand.

Bluegrass fiddle is improvisational-the fiddler will have a basic solo and be expected to create variations. The bluegrass and country music fiddle style uses a different set of notes (modes) including the use of flatted 3rds and fifths and adding the flat sevenths and other blues notes in scales. Many bluegrass fiddlers use the pentatonic (5 note) scale and add in additional notes to spice up the scales.

The use of drone strings (an open string repeated with fretted notes) as well as unusual tunings (sawmill tuning etc.) are characteristics of bluegrass fiddling.

THE BASS

The stand up bass is the fundamental rhythm player for the bluegrass group because the bass player usually plays on the strong beats (beats 1 and 3). Typically on the first beat, the root of the chord is played, and on the third beat, the fifth of the chord is played. The strings are plucked with the right hand middle and index fingers using a rest stroke (appoyando, meaning to rest on the next adjacent string after following through).

Cedric Rainwater, who played for Bill Monroe classic 1946 band also used walking bass patterns familiar in blues and jazz music. Walking bass patterns usually are played on every beat and move diatonically or chromatically up the scale from the root of each chord.

Many bass players use a slap technique on the off-beat.

Traditional Bass Pattern

Walking Bass Patterns

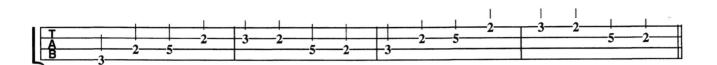

THE DOBRO OR RESOPHONIC GUITAR

The Dobro resonator guitar, an American instrument, has been around since the mid 1920's. The Dobro trademark is owned by Gibson. Guitars of this type, built by independent guitar makers, are referred to as *resonator*, or, *resophonic* guitars. Bill Monroe did not include the dobro as one of the original five instruments that make up bluegrass music.

Today the resonator guitar is popular in contemporary bluegrass music, adding a soulful, bluesy touch to the music. Jerry Douglas is one of the masters of the resophonic guitar. His speed and melodic taste make him a legend among steel guitarists. Modern *country* music has rediscovered the resonator guitar after abandoning the instrument for decades.

The instrument has either a *wooden* or *metal* body. *Square* necked guitars are played horizontally, similar to the *steel* guitar. The strings are elevated off the neck. The instrument is played with a bar called a *steel*. *Round* necked models are played *Spanish* style, with or without a slide.

A resophonic guitar is a type of guitar played horizontally. The guitar is fretted with a steel bar (the "steel") in the players left hand, and the strings are usually plucked using metal fingerpicks and a plastic thumbpick on the right hand.

RESOPHONIC GUITAR HISTORY

In his quest for a louder guitar, Los Angeles guitarist, George Beauchamp envisioned a mechanically amplified instrument whose volume could compete with the trumpets, saxophones and banjos dominating popular music of the day. Beauchamp took his idea to John Dopyera and his brother Rudy, Slovakian craftsmen who already held several patents for improving banjos. It was John who perfected a resonator design utilizing three aluminum cones while Rudy suggested using a metal body to further enhance amplification. Their collaborative efforts resulted in the 1927 National tri-cone resonator guitar.

John Dopyera left National the next year with an idea for developing a more affordable wooden bodied guitar. His new design, featuring a single cone with its bridge supported on an aluminium spiderweb base, was introduced late in 1928 under the name DOBRO (R). This clever contraction of "Dopyera Brothers" also forms the slavic translation of "good" —hence the slogan, "DOBRO(R) means GOOD in any language". All five brothers, John, Rudy, Emile (Ed), Robert, and Louis participated in the financing, production and everyday operations of the company. Eventually, even their sister, Gabriela would come to play a part in the continuing history of DOBRO(R).

Dobro Tuning: Traditional Dobro tuning is an open G chord: From the 6th string to the 1st string: G B D G B D.

A Beautiful Life

By William M. Golden; Old-Time Gospel Quartet **DATE:** 1918 **CATEGORY:** American Hymn **RECORDED BY:** Bill Monroe; Country Gentlemen; Jimmy Martin; Wade Mainer and the Sons of the Mountaineers; Stanley Brothers; Doyle Lawson and Quicksilver. **OTHER NAMES:** Beautiful Life **NOTES:** The bass takes the lead for the first half of the chorus.

     G **C**   **G**
Each day I do a golden deed
       D   **G**
By helping those who are in need
         C **G**
My life on earth is but a span
      D   **G**
And so I'll do   the best I can

              C
Chorus: Life's evening sun is sinking low
     D
A few more days and I must go
        G   **C**   **G**
To meet the deeds that I have done
         D   **G**
Where there will be no setting sun

To be a child of God each day
My light must shine along the way
I'll sing His praise while ages roll
And strive to help some troubled soul

While going down life's weary road
I'll try to lift some traveler's load
I'll try to turn the night to day
Make flowers bloom along the way

The only life that will endure
Is one that's kind and good and pure
And so for God I'll take my stand
Each day I'll lend a helping hand

A HUNDRED MILES

Traditional Bluegrass and Old-time Song **DATE:** Late 1800's; **CATEGORY:** Fiddle and Instrumental Tunes; **RECORDING INFO:** Fiddlin' John Carson; Hedy West; Flatt & Scruggs; Tommy Jarrell; Doc Watson; **OTHER NAMES:** One Hundred Miles; Five Hundred Miles; Nine Hundred Miles; Train 45; Reuben's Train; **NOTES:** This is a version of "Reuben's Train" and Grayson/Whitter "Train 45" family of songs.

   G   **Em**
If you miss the train I'm on, you could tell that I have gone
      Am   **D**   **G**
You could hear the whistle blow a hundred miles.
       G
A hundred miles, a hundred miles,
           Em
A hundred miles, a hundred miles,
     Am   **D**   **G**
You could hear the whistle blow a hundred miles.

Oh you oughta been uptown, and hear that train come down
You could hear the whistle blow a hundred miles.
A hundred miles, a hundred miles,
A hundred miles, a hundred miles
You could hear the whistle blow a hundred miles.

If that train runs right, I'll be home Saturday night
'Cause I'm five hundred miles away from home.
Away from home, away from home
Away from home, away from home
I'm five hundred miles away from home.

19

Ain't Gonna Work Tomorrow

Traditional Old-Time Song; **DATE:** Early 1900's; **CATEGORY:** Early Country and Bluegrass; **RECORDED BY:** Carter Family, Louvin Brothers, Wilma Lee Cooper and the Clinch Mountain Clan, Country Gentlemen, Flatt & Scruggs, Leftover Salmon. **OTHER NAMES:** I Ain't Gonna Work Tomorrow.

Chorus:

  G
I ain't gonna work tomorrow
C   **G**
I ain't gonna work today
C   **G**
I ain't gonna work tomorrow
        D
For it is my wedding day

I love my Mama and Papa, too
I love my Mama and Papa, too
I love my Mama and Papa, too
But I'd leave them both to go with you. *Chorus*

I've been all around this country
I've been all around this world
I've been all around this country, Lord
For the sake of one little girl. *Chorus*

I'm leaving you this lonesome song
I'm leaving you this lonesome song
I'm leaving you this lonesome song
Cause I'm gonna be long gone. *Chorus*

ALABAMA JUBLIEE

Traditional Old-Time, Bluegrass Jazz tune & Song. George L. Cobb, music; Jack Yellen, lyrics; **DATE:**1915; CATEGORY: Instrumental Tunes; **RECORDING INFO:** Tweedy Brothers; Roy Dark; Clark Kessinger; Clarence White; Wayne Henderson; **NOTES:** Recorded by many bluegrass pickers usually as an instrumental. Jack Yellen also composed the lyrics "Happy Days Are Here Again." Usually the chorus is the only part sung by bluegrass pickers. On Bluegrass Messengers CD "Bluegrass Boogie."

          A7

Chorus: You ought to see Deacon Jones When he rattles the bones

D   **G**

Old Parson Brown, foolin' round like a clown Aunt Jemima, who is past eighty three

C

Shoutin' I'm full o' pep! (Spoken) Watch your step! Watch your step!

A

One legged Joe danced aroun' on his toe,

Dm

Threw away his crutch and hollered, "Let 'er go!"

          C   **E**   **F**   **C**   **D**   **G**   **C**

Oh, honey, hail! Hail! The gang's all here, For the Alabama Jubilee.

ALL THE GOOD TIMES ARE PAST AND GONE

Traditional Waltz; **DATE:** 1936; **CATEGORY:** Classic Bluegrass; **RECORDED BY**: Monroe Brothers; Flat and Scruggs; Stanley Brothers; Kingston Trio; White Lightening; **OTHER NAMES:** All the Good Times **NOTES:** Uses Floating lyrics.

```
G                   C     G                 D
All the good times are past and gone, All the good times are o'er
G                   C     G                 D     G
All the good times are past and gone, Little darling don't you weep no more.
```

I wish to the Lord I'd never been born, Or died when I was young
I never would have seen your sparkling blue eyes, Or heard your lying tongue.

Don't you see that turtle dove, That flies from pine to pine?
He's mourning for his own true love, Just like I mourn for mine.

Don't you see that passenger train, Going around the bend?
It's taking away my own true love, To never return again.

Come back, come back my own true love, And stay a while with me
For if ever I've had a friend in this world, You've been a friend to me.

AMAZING GRACE

Traditional Tune, First Three Stanzas by John Newton (1715-1807) Stanza 4 Traditional; **DATE:** Lyrics appear in 1779; Lyrics and tune are combined in Southern Harmony-1855; **CATEGORY:** American Folk Hymn; **RECORDED BY:** Clarence Ashley; Buell Kazee; Seldom Scene; Stanley Brothers; Doc Watson; Osbourne Brothers; Don Reno; **SOURCES:** American Melody from Carrell's and Clayton's virginia Harmony (1831). **OTHER NAMES:** Called "New Britain" in Sacred Harp. **NOTES:** One of the favorite hymns.

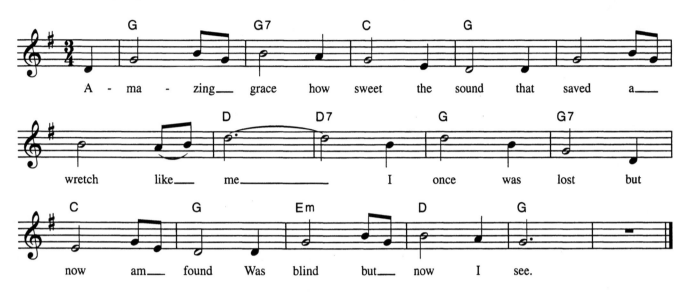

G   G7   C   G
Amazing grace, how sweet the sound
              D D7
That saved a wretch like me
G   G7   C   G
I once was lost, but now am found
     Em   D   G
Was blind, but now I see

Twas grace that taught my heart to fear
And grace my fears relieved
How precious did that grace appear
The hour I first believed

Through many dangers, toils, and snares
I have already come
Tis grace hath brought me safe thus far
And grace will lead me home

When we've been there ten thousand years
Bright shining as the sun
We've no less days to sing God's praise
Than when we first begun

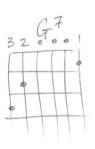

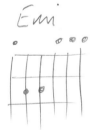

ANGEL BAND

By William Bradbury and Jefferson Hascal; **DATE:** First appears in J.D. Dadmun's "Melodian" in 1860. **CATEGORY:** American Hymn; **RECORDED BY;** Stanley Brothers; Flatt & Scruggs; Doyle Lawson and Quicksilver; Johnny Cash; Emmylou Harris; Hedy West and Bill Clifton; **NOTES:** Popularized by being included in the "0, Brother" soundtrack.

G   **C**   **G**
My latest sun is sinking fast
     D **G**
My race is nearly run
       C   **G**
My longest trials now are passed
    D **G**
My triumph has begun

    D   **G**
Chorus: Oh, come angel band
  D   **G**
Come and around me stand
C   **G**
Oh bear me away on your snow white wings
    D **G**
To my immortal home
C   **G**
Oh bear me away on your snow white wings
    D **G**
To my immortal home

Oh, bear my loving heart to him
Who bled and died for me
Whose blood now cleanses from all sins
And gives me victory *Chorus*

I've almost reached my heavenly home
My spirit loudly sings
The holy ones, behold they come
I hear the noise of wings *Chorus*

ARKANSAS TRAVELER

Old-Time, Bluegrass, American; Reel, universally known. **DATE:** The music was in print in 1847, Rosenberg states, and both the tune and the accompanying skit are presumed by him to have been in oral circulation at the time. **CATEGORY:** Fiddle and Instrumental Tunes; **RECORDING INFO:** Gid Tanner & Riley Pucket; Kenny Baker; Clark Kessinger; Roscoe Holcomb and Wade Ward; **NOTES:** One of the most popular bluegrass fiddle tunes.

D **Bm** **A7** **D**
Oh, once upon a time in Arkansas
A   **E**   **A7**
An old man sat in his little cabin door
D   **Bm**   **A7**   **D**
And fiddled a tune that he liked to hear
            G   **A7**   **D**
A jolly old tune that he played by ear.
D   **A**   **Bm**   **A**
It was raining hard, but the fiddler didn't care
D   **A**   **Bm**   **A**
He sawed a-way at the popular air
           D   **A**   **Bm** **A**
Though his rooftop leaked like a waterfall
D   **G**   **A7**   **D**
That didn't seem to bother the old man at all.

```
     D        Bm        A7       D
The cabin was afloat and his feet were wet
                       G      A7     D
But the old man still didn't seem to fret.
      D      A      Bm          A
So the stranger said "The way it seems to me
      D    A     Bm      A
You'd better mend your roof," said he
      D      A       Bm      A
But the old man said as he played away
   D           G        A7     D
I couldn't mend it now, it's a rainy day.
```

```
     D         Bm      A7      D
The traveler replied that's all quite true
   A7              E          A
But this I think is the thing for you to do
     D      Bm       A7      D
Get busy on a day that is fair and bright
                    G        A7       D
Then patch the old roof till it's good and tight
      D      A      Bm         A
But the old man kept on a-playing at his reel
      D      A         Bm     A
And tapped the ground with his leathery heel
      D      A      Bm        A
Get along said he for you give me a pain
      D      G        A7     D
My cabin never leaks when it doesn't rain.
```

As I Went Down in the Valley to Pray

(Down to the River to Pray)

Traditional Bluegrass, Gospel Tune; **DATE:** Mid 1800's; **CATEGORY:** Gospel Tunes **RECORDING INFO:** Alison Kraus O Brother Where Art Thou? Soundtrack; Tim and Molly O'Brien; Doc Watson; **OTHER NAMES:** The Good Old Way; Down to the River To Pray; **NOTES:** A gospel song from both a black and white sources. L.L. McDowell's Middle Tennessee *Songs of the Old Camp Ground;* White's Fisk *Jubilee Songs,* 1872.

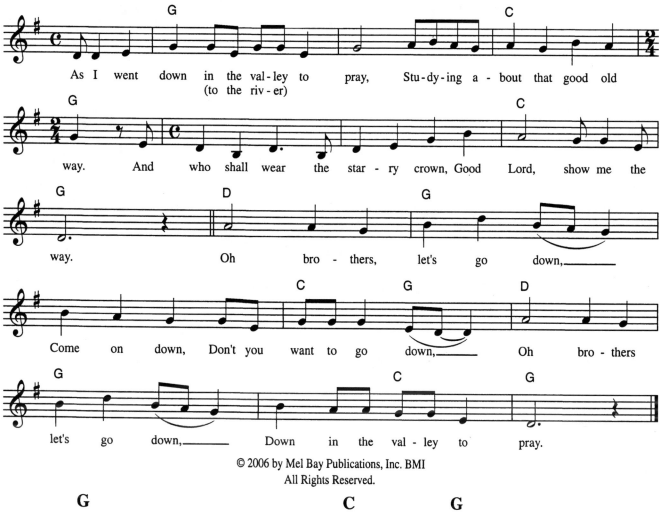

    G   **C**   **G**

1. As I went down in the valley to pray, Studyin' about that good old way.

                   C   **G**

And who shall wear the starry crown, Good Lord show me the way.

D   **G**   **C**   **G**

Oh brothers let's go down, Come on down, don't you want to go down.

D   **G**   **C**   **G**

Oh brothers let's go down, Down in the valley to pray.

2. Oh sisters let's go down...
3. Oh fathers let's go down...
4. Oh mothers let's go down...
5. Oh sinners let's go down...

BANKS OF THE OHIO

Traditional Folk Song; **DATE:** First appears around 1913; **CATEGORY:** Early Country; **RECORDED BY:** Monroe Brothers; Blue Sky Boys; Country Gentlemen; Tony Rice; Joan Baez; Doc Watson; **NOTES:** Was a hit for Blue Sky Boys in 1933.

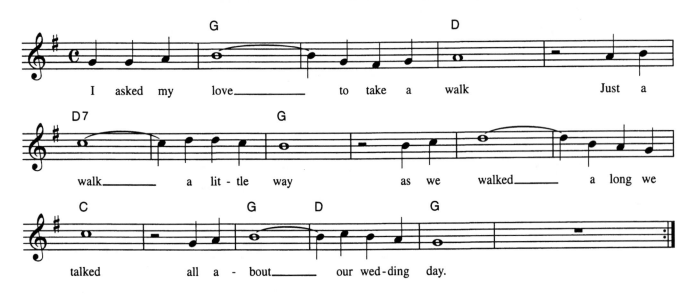

    G   **D**
I asked my love to take a walk
    D7   **G**
Just a walk a little way
            C
As we walked along we talked
 G   **D**   **G**
All about our wedding day.

And only say that you'll be mine
And our home will happy be
Down beside, where the waters flow
Down on the banks of the Ohio.

I held a knife close to her breast
As into my arms she pressed
She cried, "Oh, Willie, don't murder me,
I'm not prepared for eternity."

I took her by her lily white hand
Led her down where the waters stand
There I pushed her in to drown
And watched her as she floated down.

I started home tween twelve and one
I cried, "My God, what have I done."
I murdered the only woman I loved
Because she would not be my bride.

The very next morning about half-past four
The sheriff came knocking at my door
He said, "Young man, come with me and go
Down to the banks of the Ohio."

BATTLE OF NEW ORLEANS

Old-Time, Bluegrass; Breakdown. Widely known. Tune: Eighth of January, Lyrics: Jimmy Driftwood; **DATE:** Lyrics 1958; **CATEGORY:** Fiddle and Instrumental Tunes; **RECORDING INFO:** Johnny Horton; **NOTES:** On January 8, 1815, Major General Andrew Jackson led a small, poorly-equipped army to victory against eight thousand British troops at the Battle of New Orleans. The victory made Jackson a national hero and he was later elected President in 1970. In 1958, Jimmy Driftwood composed lyrics to the old tune and recorded it as "The Battle of New Orleans." In 1959, Johnny Horton recorded a version of Driftwood's song, and the song rose to the top of the hit parade that year.

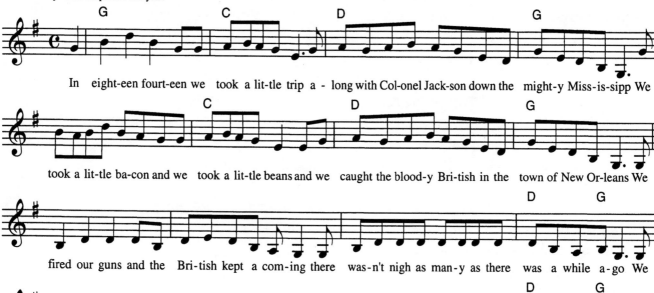

    G   **C**
In 1814 we took a little trip
    D   **G**
Along with Colonel Jackson down the mighty Mississipp
                   C
We took a little bacon and we took a little beans
    D   **G**
And we caught the bloody British in the town of New Orleans.

                  G
Chorus: We fired our guns but the British kept a coming
                   D   **G**
There wasn't nigh as many as there was a while ago

We fired once more and they began a running
                   D   **G**
Down the Mississippi to the Gulf of Mexico.

BATTLE OF NEW ORLEANS

We looked down the river and we seen the British come
And there must have been a hundred of them beating on the drums
They stepped so high and they made their bugles ring
We stood behind our cotton bales and didn't say a thing.   *Chorus*

Old Hickory said we could take em by surprise
If we didn't fire a musket till we looked em in the eyes
We held our fire till we seen their faces well
We opened up our squirrel guns and really gave em, well   *Chorus*

Bridge: Well, they ran through the briars and they ran through the brambles
And they ran through the bushes where the rabbits couldn't go
They ran so fast the hounds couldn't catch 'em
On down the Mississippi to the Gulf of Mexico.

We fired our cannon till the barrel melted down
Then we grabbed an alligator and we fought another round
We filled his head with cannonballs and powdered his behind
And when we touched the powder off the gator lost his mind.   *Chorus*

BILE THEM CABBAGE DOWN

Traditional Old-Time, Breakdown; **DATE:** Early 1900's; **CATEGORY:** Fiddle and Instrumental Tunes **RECORDED BY:** Charlie Monroe and the Kentucky Pardners; Gid Tanner and the Skillet Lickers;Flatt & Scruggs; **OTHER NAMES:** Boil Them Cabbage Down; Bake Them Hoecakes Brown; Raccoon and the Possum; **NOTES:** On Bluegrass Messengers' CD "Bluegrass Boogie."

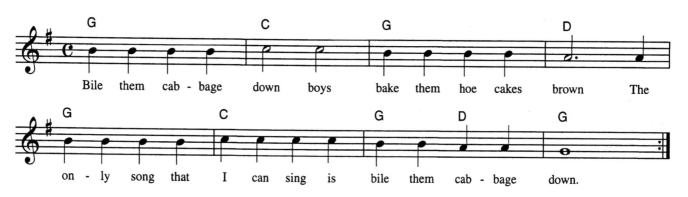

   G   C
Raccoon has a bushy tail
   G   D
Possum's tail is bare
    G   C
Rabbit's got no tail at all
     G   D   G
But a little bunch of hair

Chorus:
Bile them cabbage down boys
Bake that hoecake brown
The only song that I can sing is
Bile them cabbage down

Raccoon and the possum
Coming cross the prairie
Raccoon said to the possum
Did she want to marry *Chorus*

Raccoon up a 'simmon tree
Possum on the ground
Possum say to the raccoon
"Won't you shake them 'simmons down?"   *Chorus*

Jaybird died with the whooping cough
Sparrow died with the colic
Along came the frog with a fiddle on his back
Inquiring his way to the frolic   *Chorus*

BILL BAILEY, WON'T YOU PLEASE COME HOME?

American, Song Tune. By Hughie Cannon, **DATE:** Published in 1902; **CATEGORY:** Tin-Pan Alley and Jazz Song; **RECORDING INFO:** Louis Armstrong; Ella Fitzgerald; Big Bill Broonzy; Buddy Pendleton; Weavers; Johnny Whisnant; **NOTES:** This song was an instant hit when first introduced by John Queen, a minstrel. Often recorded and often associated with the great Louis Armstrong. Bobby Darin's version was a million seller. Most bluegrass groups play chorus only.

     G

Chorus: Won't you come home, Bill Bailey, Won't you come home?

          D

She moans the whole day long.

I'll do the cookin', darling, I'll pay the rent,

         G

I know I've done you wrong;

'Member that rainy evening that

              G7   **C**   **E Am**

I threw you out, With nothing but a fine-tooth comb?

C   **A7**   **G**   **E**

I know I'm to blame, Well, ain't that a shame

   A   **D**   **G**

Bill Bailey won't you please come home.

BLACK-EYED SUSIE

Traditional Old-Time, Breakdown; **DATE:** Early 1900's; **CATEGORY:** Fiddle and Instrumental Tunes; **RECORDING INFO:** Doc Roberts; Dillards; Roscoe Holcomb; Skillet Lickers; **OTHER NAMES:** "Pretty Little Black-Eyed Susie," "Green Corn," "(Hop Up) Kitty Puss," "Possum Sop and Polecat Jelly." **NOTES:** Composed of floater verses the New Lost City Ramblers call it "One of the most popular breakdown tunes." Bayard (1981) traces the history of the tune, beginning in the British Isles with a melody called "Rosasolis," set by Giles Farnaby (c. 1560- c.1600). Transported to the United States from various sources the melody developed into the old-time standard, "Black Eyed Susie," well known throughout the South and Midwest.

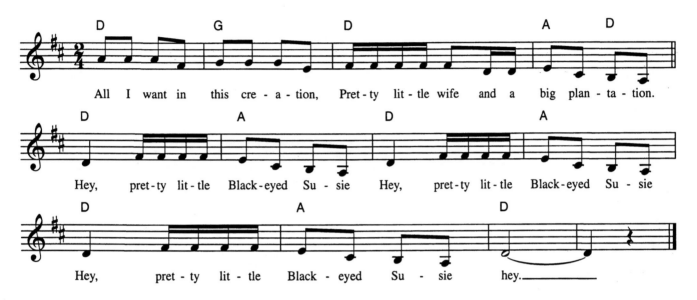

Verse:
D   G
All I want in this creation
D   A   D
Pretty little wife and a big plantation

Chorus:
D   A
Hey, pretty little black-eyed Susie
D   A
Hey, pretty little black-eyed Susie
D   A   D
Hey, little black-eyed Susie, Hey!

Verse 2: All I need to keep me happy
Two little boys to call me pappy

Verse 3: Up Red Oak and down salt water
Some old man gonna lose his daughter

Verse 4: I asked her to be my wife
She come at me with a barlow knife

Verse 5: Love my wife, love my baby
Love my biscuits sopped in gravy

BLUEGRASS BOOGIE

Bluegrass Song by Richard Matteson. **CATEGORY:** Fiddle and Instrumental Tunes **DATE:** 2002; **RECORDING INFO:** Bluegrass Messengers from "Bluegrass Boogie" CD; **NOTES:** Written with fiddle lyrics. Performed twice with Doc Watson.

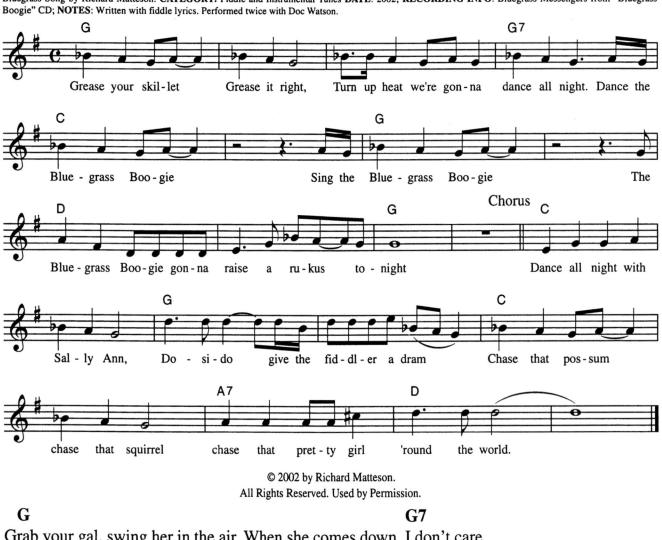

G   **G7**
Grab your gal, swing her in the air, When she comes down, I don't care
                C   **G**
Dance the Bluegrass Boogie, sing the Bluegrass Boogie
        D   **G**
The Bluegrass Boogie gonna raise a ruckus tonight
              C   **G**
Chorus: Dance all night with Sally Ann, Do-si-do give the fiddler a dram
C
Chase that possum, chase that squirrel
A7   **D**
Chase that pretty girl 'round the world ('round the world)

With a cornstalk fiddle and a shoestring bow
Pick up your feet and put 'em on the floor (Dance the Bluegrass Boogie...etc.)

Grab that possum, put 'im in the pan,
You know he's the best eatin' critter in the land. (Dance the Bluegrass Boogie...etc.)

BOWLING GREEN

American, Reel and Song Tune **DATE:** Early 1900's; **CATEGORY:** Fiddle and Instrumental Tunes; **RECORDING INFO:** Erik Darling; New Lost City Ramblers with Cousin Emmy; Mike Seeger and Alice Gerrard; **OTHER NAMES:** "Good Old Bowling Green;" **NOTES:** Originally a fiddle and fife tune.

C   **Am**
Wish I was in Bowling Green, sittin' in a chair
C
One arm round my pretty little gal
   G7   **C**   **G7**   **C**
The other 'round my dear, The other 'round my dear.
                          Am   **C** **G7**   **C**
Chorus: Bowling Green... Hey! Good old Bowling Green.

Goin' through this worried world, goin' through alone;
Goin' through this worried world,
I ain't got no home, I ain't got no home. *Chorus*

Wish I was a bumblebee, flyin' through the air
Take my true love by my side,
Touch her if you dare, Touch her if you dare. *Chorus*

Goin' back to Bowlin' Green, Don't know how or when;
When I get to Bowling Green,
I'll never leave again, I'll never leave again. *Chorus*

BROWN'S FERRY BLUES

Bluegrass, Old-time Blues Song; **CATEGORY:** Mountain Blues; **DATE:** Early 1900's; **RECORDING INFO:** Kenny Baker and Josh Graves; Callahan Brothers; Delmore Brothers; John Jackson; New Lost City Ramblers; Doc Watson; **OTHER VERSIONS:** Manhattan Blues; Them Ramblin' Blues; Oozlin' Daddy Blues; Rubber Neck Blues; Jackhammer John; **NOTES:** Similar to "Big River Blues" or "Deep River Blues." Named for an old ferry site on the Tennessee River.

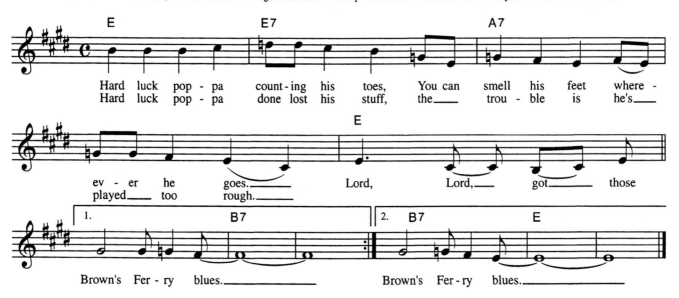

E   **E7**   **A7**
Hard luck poppa, a-countin' his toes, You can smell his feet wherever he goes,
E   **B7**
Lord, Lord, got those Brown's Ferry Blues.
E   **E7**   **A7**
Hard luck poppa done lost his stuff, The trouble with him he's played too rough.
E   **B7**   **E**
Lord, Lord, got those Brown's Ferry Blues.

Two old maids a-sitting in the sand, Each one wishing that the other was a man,
Lord, Lord, got those Brown's Ferry Blues
Two old maids done lost their style, If you want to be lucky you got to smile.
Lord, Lord, got those Brown's Ferry Blues

Early to bed and early to rise, And your girl goes out with other guys.
Lord, Lord, got those Brown's Ferry Blues
If you don't believe me try it yourself, Well I tried it and I got left.
Lord, Lord, got those Brown's Ferry Blues

Hard luck poppa standing in the rain, If the world was corn he couldn't buy grain.
Lord, Lord, got those Brown's Ferry Blues
Hardluck poppa standing in the snow, His knees knock together but he's raring to go.
Lord, Lord, got those Brown's Ferry Blues.

BUDDY WON'T YOU ROLL ON DOWN THE LINE?

Traditional Bluegrass Old-Time Song; **DATE:** 1880's; **CATEGORY:** Old-Time Song; **RECORDING INFO:** Allen Brothers, Carolina Tar Heels, Uncle Dave Macon, New Lost City Ramblers; **OTHER NAMES:** "Roll Down the Line," "Hey Buddy Won't You Roll Down the Line," "Brother Won't You Join in the Line." **NOTES:** Based on the Coal Creek, Tennessee labor wars.

BUDDY WON'T YOU ROLL ON DOWN THE LINE?

D
Way down yonder in Tennesee, they leased the convicts out
A7
To work in the coal mines, against free labor south;
    D
Free labor rebelled against it. To win it took some time.
A7   **D**
But while the lease was in effect, they made 'em rise and shine.

                          D
Chorus: Buddy, won't you roll down the line?

Buddy, won't you roll down the line?
                    A7
Yonder comes my darlin', comin down the line.

Buddy, won't you roll down the line?

Buddy, won't you roll down the line?
                         D
Yonder comes my darlin', comin down the line.

Early Monday morning they get you up on time,
Send you down to Lone Rock, just to look into that mine.
Send you down to Lone Rock, to look into that hole
Very last words the captain say "You better get your coal."

The beans they are half done, the bread is not so well.
The meat it is all burnt up and the coffee's black as heck.
But when you get your task done You're glad you come to call
Anything you get to eat, it tastes good- done or raw.

The bank boss he's a hard man, a man you all know well,
And if you don't get your task done, he's gonna give you hallelujah!
Carry you to the stockade, and it's on the floor you fall
Very last words you hear "You better get your coal."

Bury Me Beneath the Willow

Traditional Old-time Song; **DATE:** Early 1900's-RecordingKelleyHarrell 1925; **CATEGORY:** Early Country & Bluegrass; **RECORDED BY:** Kelly Harrell; Carter Family; Monroe Brothers; Lilly Brothers;Skaggs and Rice **OTHER NAMES** Weeping Willow Tree; Beneath the Weeping Willow Tree; Oh Bury Me Beneath the Willow; **NOTES:** This song was a hit for Kelley Harrell in 1925.

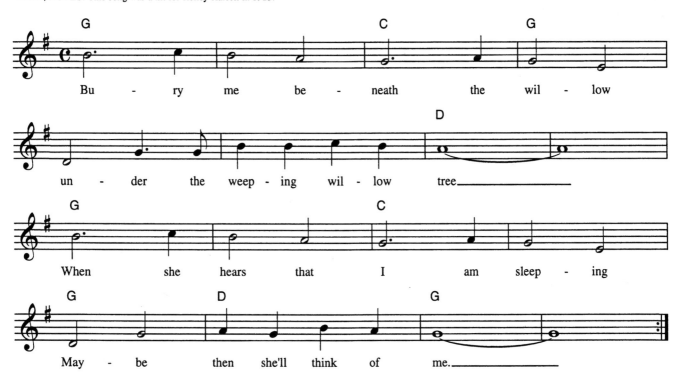

G   **C**   **G**
Bury me beneath the willow
                                D
Under the weeping willow tree
G   **C**
When she hears that I am sleeping
G   **D**   **G**
Maybe then she'll think of me.

G   **C**   **G**
My heart is sad and I'm in sorrow
                              D
Weeping for the one I love
G   **C**
When shall I see her, oh, no never
G   **D**   **G**
Till we meet in Heav'n above.

Tomorrow was to be our wedding
But Lord, oh Lord, where can she be?
She's gone, she's gone to find another
She no longer cares for me.

She told me that she did not love me
I couldn't believe it was true
Until an angel softly whispered,
"She no longer cares for you."

Place on my grave a snow white lily
To prove my love for her was true
To show the world I died of grieving
For her love I could not win.

CARELESS LOVE

Traditional Old-time Song; **DATE:** Early 1900's-Recording by Byrd Moore 1930; **CATEGORY:** Early Country & Bluegrass; **RECORDED BY:** Dock Boggs; Riley Puckett; Bill Monroe; Joan Baez; Big Bill Broonzy; Flatt & Scruggs with Doc Watson; Brownie McGhee; **NOTES:** This is an early white and black "blues" that has become a bluegrass standard. This version is the "male" lyrics.

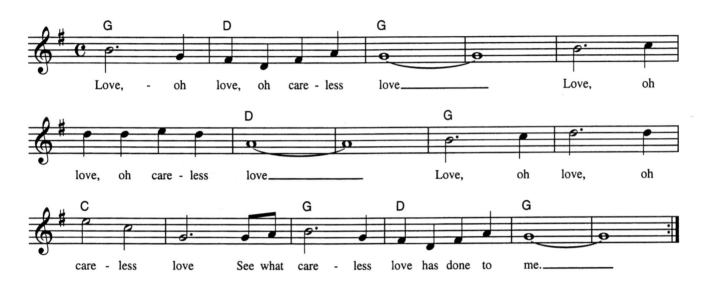

G   **D**   **G**
Love, oh love, oh careless love
                  D
Love, oh love, oh careless love
G   **C**
Love, oh love, oh careless love
        G   **D**   **G**
See what careless love has done to me.

G   **D**   **G**
Sorrow, sorrow to my heart,
                  D
Sorrow, sorrow to my heart,
G   **C**
Sorrow, sorrow to my heart,
        G   **D**   **G**
Since I and my true love did part.

G   **D**   **G**
How I wish that train would come,
                  D
How I wish that train would come,
G   **C**
How I wish that train would come,
        G   **D**   **G**
And take me back where I came from.

CHEWING GUM

Old-Time and Bluegrass Song; **DATE**: Randolph dates back to 1890's; **CATEGORY**: Fiddle and Instrumental Tunes; **RECORDING INFO**: Uncle Dave Macon; Carter Family; Legendary J. E. Mainer; New Lost City Ramblers; **NOTES**: This song is still popular in the Appalachian mountain regions.

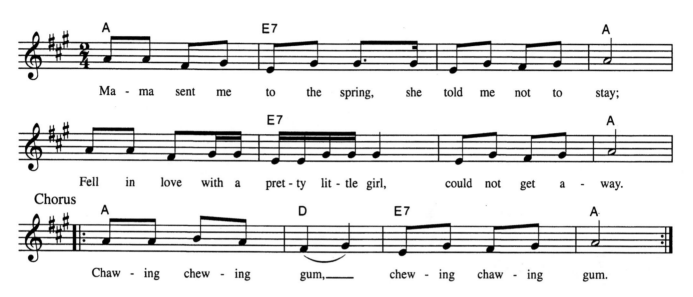

Ma - ma sent me to the spring, she told me not to stay;
Fell in love with a pret - ty lit - tle girl, could not get a - way.
Chorus
Chaw - ing chew - ing gum,___ chew - ing chaw - ing gum.

A   E7
Mama sent me to the spring
           A
She told me not to stay
           E7
I fell in love with a pretty little girl
           A
Could not get away

Chorus:
A   D E7   A
Chawin' chewin' gum, chewin' chawin' gum
A   D E7   A
Chawin' chewin' gum, chewin' chawin' gum

A   E7
First she give me peaches
           A
Then she give me pears
           E7
Then she give me fifty cents
           A
Kissed me on the stairs

Mama don't 'low me to whistle
Papa don't 'low me to sing
They don't want me to marry
I'll marry just the same

I wouldn't have a lawyer
I'll tell you the reason why
Every time he opens his mouth
He tells a great big lie

I wouldn't have a doctor
I'll tell you the reason why
He rides all over the country
Makes the people die

I took my girl to church last night
How do you reckon she done
She walked right up to the preacher's face
And chewed her chewing gum

CHILDREN GO WHERE I SEND THEE

Traditional Old-Time Song; **DATE:** Early 1900's- Recording by Kelley Pace in 1942. **CATEGORY:** Early Country & Folk; **RECORDINGS:** Kelley Pace; Ralph Stanley; Jean Ritchie; Johnny Cash; The Weavers; **OTHER NAMES:** "Holy Babe" **NOTES:** One of the best traditional mountain Christmas songs.

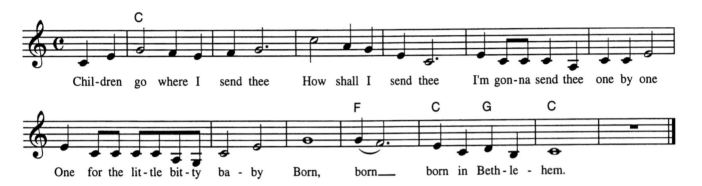

C
Children go where I send thee, how shall I send thee

I'm gonna send thee one by one

One for the little bitty baby
      F   **C**   **G**   **C**
Born, born, born in Bethlehem

C
Children go where I send thee, how shall I send thee

I'm gonna send thee two by two

Two for Paul and Silas, one for the little bitty baby
      F   **C**   **G**   **C**
Born, born, born in Bethlehem

(Add one line for each verse)
Three for the Hebrew children...
Four for the four that stood at the door...
Five for the gospel preachers.. .
Six for the six that never got fixed...
Seven for the seven that never went to Heaven...
Eight for the eight that stood at the gate...
Nine for the nine that dressed so fine...
Ten for the ten commandments...

CHILLY WINDS

Traditional Old-Time, Song and Breakdown; **DATE:** Early 1900's. **CATEGORY:** Fiddle and Instrumental Tunes; **RECORDING INFO:** Wade Ward- 1925; Tommy Jarrell; Cisco Houston, Kimble Family; **OTHER NAMES:** Goin' Down This Road Feelin' Bad; Lonesome Road Blues; Levee Moan; Honey Your Hair Grows Too Long; East Coast Blues. **NOTES:** Chilly Winds is a related version of "Goin' Down This Road Feelin' Bad." Both are frequently categorized under "Lonesome Road Blues."

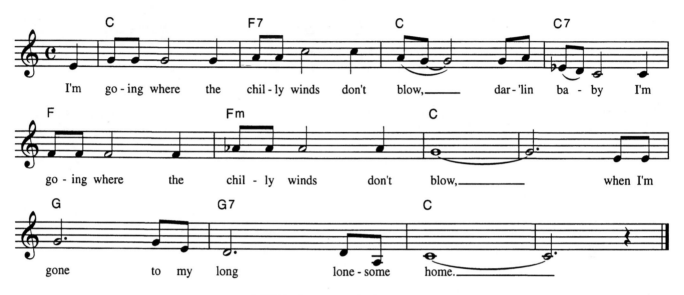

```
        C              F7         C         C7
1. I'm going where those chilly winds don't blow, darling baby
F              Fm         C
I'm going where those chilly winds don't blow
           G      G7         C
When I'm gone to my long lonesome home.


        C              F7         C         C7
2. Now who'll be your daddy when I'm gone, darling baby
F                  Fm         C
Now who'll be your daddy when I'm gone
           G      G7         C
When I'm gone to my long lonesome home.
```

3. Oh, who'll hoe your cotton when I'm gone...
4. Oh, it's way down in jail on my knees...
5. Oh they feed me on corn bread and beans...
6. Oh I'm going where the climate suits my clothes...
7. So make me a pallet on your floor...

CHURCH IN THE WILDWOOD, THE (WILLIAM P. PITTS)

Old-Time Bluegrass Gospel Song by James Rowe- words, William P. Pitts- music, **DATE:** 1857 Pitts; 1911 new lyrics by Rowe; **CATEGORY:** Gospel Song; **RECORDING INFO:** Carter Family; Johnny Cash; **OTHER NAMES:** Little Brown Church in the Vale; **NOTES:** The Little Brown Church in the Vale has become a famous tourist attraction in Iowa, and the song describing its beauty is still sung.

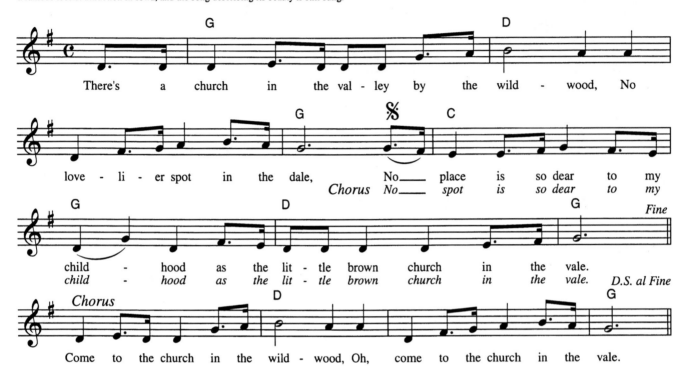

<pre>
        G   D   G
</pre>
There's a church in the valley by the wildwood, No lovelier spot in the dale;
<pre>
   C   G   D   G
</pre>
No place is so dear to my childhood, As the little brown church in the vale.
<pre>
                                    D   G
</pre>
Chorus: Come to the church in the wildwood, Oh, come to the church in the vale.
<pre>
   C   G   D   G
</pre>
No spot is so dear to my childhood as the little brown church in the vale.

Oh, come to the church in the vale, To the trees where the wild flowers bloom;
Where the parting hymn will be chanted, We will weep by the side of the tomb.   *Chorus*

How sweet on a clear Sabbath morning, To list to the clear ringing bell;
Its tones so sweetly are calling, Oh come to the church in the vale.   *Chorus*

From the church in the valley by the wildwood, When day fades away into night,
I would fain from this spot of my childhood, Wing my way to the mansions of light.   *Chorus*

Cindy

Traditional Old-Time Song and Breakdown; **DATE:** Early 1900's; **CATEGORY:** Fiddle and Instrumental Tunes; **RECORDING INFO:** The Hill Billies,- 1925; J. E. Mainer's Mountaineers; Coon Creek Girls; New Lost City Ramblers; **OTHER NAMES:** "Cindy in the Summertime," "Get Along Home, Cindy," "Cindy in the Meadows," "Get Along Home (Miss) Cindy," "Git Along Cindy," "Git Along," "Old Time Cinda," "Run Along Home, Cindy," "Whoop 'Em Up Cindy," "Old Time Cindy," **NOTES:** One of the great American folk songs and fiddle tunes.

G   **D**
She told me that she loved me, She called me her Sugar Plum
G   **C**   **G**   **D**   **G**
She throwed her arms around me, I thought my time had come.

                              C   **G**
Chorus: Get along home Cindy, Cindy. Get along home Cindy, Cindy.
              C   **G** **D**   **G**
Get along home Cindy, Cindy, I'll marry you someday.

She took me to her parlor, She cooled me with her fan
She told me I was the prettiest thing, In the shape of mortal man.

Oh where did you get your liquor, Where did you get your dram?
From an old moon shiner, Down in Rockingham.

Cindy got religion, She had it once before
And when she heard my old guitar, She danced across the floor.

CLUCK OLD HEN

Traditional Bluegrass and Old-Time breakdown; **DATE:** Early 1900's; **OTHER NAMES:** "Cluckin' Hen," "Snowbird in Ashbank;" "Knock-Kneed Nanny And Fare-Thee-Well" **RECORDING INFO:** Earliest recording is Fiddlin' Powers and Family; Wade Ward; Tommy Jarrell; **NOTES:** "Cluck Old Hen" is a well-known tune and song through the Appalachian South, quite distinct from "Cackling Hen." As an instrumental tune, it is popular on both fiddle and banjo. On the fiddle, one of the tune's special features is the "cluck" made by left-hand picking of the strings. Mt. Airy, North Carolina, fiddler Tommy Jarrell tells us that "Cluck Old Hen" is in the "old-timey tuning of A" also called the "sawmill key" (AEAE). On Bluegrass Messenger's CD "Don't Let Your Deal Go Down."

G		C	G		D	G

My old hen's a good ole hen, She lays eggs for the railroad men.

G		C	G		D	G

Sometimes eight, sometimes ten, And that's enough for the railroad men.

G		F	G		D	G

Cluck Old Hen, cluck and sing, Ain't laid an egg since way last spring.

G		F	G		D	G

Cluck Old Hen, cluck and squall, Ain't laid an egg since way last fall.

I had a little hen, she had a wooden leg, The best danged hen that ever laid eggs.
Laid more eggs than the hens around the barn, Another little drink wouldn't do me no harm.

Cluck old hen, cluck a lot, The next time you cluck, you'll cook in a pot.
Cluck old hen, cluck all night, Soon you will be Chicken Delight.

My old hen, she won't do, She lays eggs and taters too.
My old hen died, what'll I do, Guess I'll have some chicken stew.

Cluck old hen, cluck and sing, Cluck old hen, I got you by the wing.
Cluck old hen, cluck for your corn, Cluck old hen, your winter's all gone.

COLD RAIN AND SNOW (RAIN AND SNOW)

Traditional Bluegrass and Old-Time Breakdown and Song; **DATE:** Early 1900's; Collected by Sharp in Big Laurel, NC 1916; **CATEGORY:** Old-Time Song; **RECORDING INFO:** Dolly Parton; Arkansas Sheiks; Grateful Dead; **OTHER NAMES:** "Rain and Snow" **RELATES TO:** "Hundred Miles" songs- "Reuben's Train" **SIMILAR LYRICS AS:** "Red Apple Juice;" "Red Rocking Chair;" "Sugar Baby;" **NOTES:** The relationship of "Cold Rain and Snow" with the "Red Apple Juice/ Honey Babe Blues/Red Rocking Chair" group appears to be through lyrics only. This is a "white blues" from the same general region of the Appalachians that both Boggs and Poole lyrics sprang. This version is similar to Dillard Chandler's version on Classic Mountain Songs.

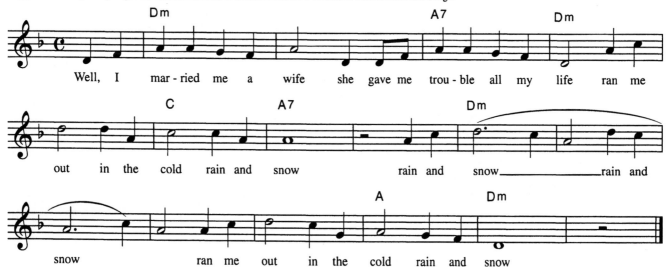

    Dm   **A7**   **Dm**
Well, I married me a wife, she gave me trouble all my life
    Dm   **C**   **A7**   **Dm**
Ran me out in the cold rain and snow, rain and snow — rain and snow
         A7   **Dm**
Ran me out in the cold rain and snow.

    Dm   **A7**   **G**
Well, she came down this path, combing back her long yellow hair
    Dm   **C**   **A7**   **Dm**
And her cheeks were as red as the rose, as the rose — as the rose
         A7   **Dm**
And her cheeks were as red as the rose.

Well, I did all I could do, to try to get along with you
And I'm not a gonna be treated this a way, this a way — this a way
And I'm not a gonna be treated this a way.

Well, she came in my room, where she met a painful doom
And I'm not gonna be treated this a way, this a way — this a way
And I'm not a gonna be treated this a way.

Columbus Stockade Blues-Major Key

Traditional Folk Blues; **DATE:** Early 1900's; **CATEGORY:** Blues Related; **RECORDED BY:** Woodie Guthrie; Bill Monroe; Doc Watson; J.E. Mainer's Mountaineers; Minnie Pearl; Country Gentlemen; Frank Profitt; **OTHER NAMES:** "Go and Leave Me If You Wish To," "Way Down in Columbus, Georgia" **NOTES:** Related to "Dear Companion" and a rework of an English love song, "Go and Leave Me." For a version in a minor key see page 49.

G	D	G

Way down in Columbus, Georgia wanna to be back in Tennessee

D	G	G7

Way down in Columbus stockade my friends all turned their backs on me.

C	G	C	D

Go and leave me if you wish to never let it cross your mind

G	D	G

If in your heart you love another, Leave me, Little Darling, I don't mind.

Last night as I lay sleeping, I dreamt I held you in my arms
When I awoke I was mistaken, I was peering through the bars.

Many a night with you I rambled, Many an hour with you I spent
Thought I had your heart forever, Now I find it was only lent.

COLUMBUS STOCKADE BLUES-MINOR KEY

Traditional Folk Blues; **DATE:** Early 1900's; **CATEGORY:** Blues; **RECORDED BY:** Bill Monroe, Doc Watson; **OTHER NAMES:** "Go and Leave Me If You Wish To," "Way Down in Columbus Stockade" **NOTES:** This version is in a minor key and is similar to the version played by my friend, Doc Watson. I like it best in this key with a Capo III.

Am   **E**   **Am**
Way down in Columbus, Georgia wanna to be back in Tennessee
       E   **Am**
Way down in Columbus stockade my friends all turned their backs on me.

Dm   **Am**   **Dm**   **E**
Go and leave me if you wish to never let it cross your mind
       Am   **E**   **Am**
If in your heart you love another, Leave me, Little Darling, I don't mind.

Last night as I lay sleeping, I dreamt I held you in my arms
When I awoke I was mistaken, I was peering through the bars.

Many a night with you I rambled, Many an hour with you I spent
Thought I had your heart forever, Now I find it was only lent.

Come All Ye Fair and Tender Ladies

Old-Time Ballad; **DATE:** Early 1900's; **RECORDED BY:** Roscoe Holcomb; Hedy West; Jean Ritchie; Mike Seeger; **OTHER NAMES:** Willow Tree; Young and Tender Ladies; Come All Fair Maids; Come All You Maidens Fair and Tender Ladies; Little Sparrow; **NOTES:** Once a popular Appalachian song. Cecil Sharp collected eighteen versions which appear in *English Folk Songs from the Southern Appalachians.*

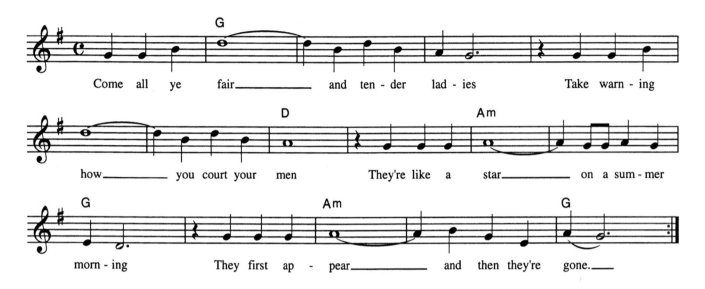

Come all ye fair___ and ten-der lad-ies Take warn-ing how___ you court your men They're like a star___ on a sum-mer morn-ing They first ap-pear___ and then they're gone.___

      G   **D**
Come all ye fair and tender ladies, Take warning how you court your men
      Am   **G**   **Am**   **G**
They're like a star on a summer morning, They first appear and then they're gone.

    G
They'll tell to you some loving story

              D
And they'll make you think that they love you well
    Am   **G**   **Am**   **G**
And away they'll go and court some other, And leave you there in grief to dwell.

I wish I was on some tall mountain, Where the ivy rocks were black as ink
I'd write a letter to my false true lover, Whose cheeks are like the morning pink.

I wish I was a little sparrow, And I had wings to fly so high
I'd fly to the arms of my false true lover, And when he'd ask, I would deny.

Oh love is handsome, love is charming, And love is pretty while it's new
But love grows cold as love grows old, And fades away like morning dew.

CORRINA, CORRINA

Traditional Bluegrass and Blues Song; **DATE:** Early 1900's; **CATEGORY:** Old-time Blues; **RECORDED BY:** Vassar Clements; Blue Sky Boys; Bob Wills; Blind Lemon Jefferson; Doc Watson; Mac Wiseman; **OTHER NAMES:** Corrine, Corrina; Alberta, Alberta; **NOTES:** A blues tune that has become a bluegrass standard.

    G   **D**   **G**   **G7**
Corrina, Corrina;   Where'd you stay last night?
        C   **G**
Corrina, Corrina; Where'd you stay last night?
        D   **G**
Your shoes ain't button'd gal; Don't fit you right.

Corrina, Corrina; Where've you been so long?
Corrine, Corrina; Where've you been so long?
Ain't had no lovin'; Since you've been gone.

I love Corrina; tell the world I do
I love Corrina; tell the world I do
Just a little more lovin'; Let your heart be true.

Got a bird that whistles, Got a bird that sings
Got a bird that whistles, Got a bird that sings
If I can't have Corrina; life don't mean a thing.

Corrina, Corrina; bye-bye, so long
Corrina, Corrina; bye-bye, so long
I'll have the blues Corrina, long as you are gone.

Cotton-Eyed Joe

Old-Time Breakdown; **CATEGORY:** Fiddle and Instrumental Tunes **DATE:** Late 1800's; **OTHER NAMES:** Miss Brown; Cotten-Eyed Joe; Red Dog; Sugar in My Coffee-O; Did You Ever See the Devil Uncle Joe?; **RECORDING INFO:** Fiddlin' John Carson; Skillet Lickers; Reno & Smiley; Bob Wills; **NOTES:** Marion Thede believes 'cotten-eyed' may refer to a person with very light blue eyes, while Alan Lomax suggests it was used to describe a man whose eyes were milky white from Trachoma. In Georgia, people with large whites to the eyes are called cotton-eyed. This usage is fairly common, as pointed out in the quote from a dictionary of slang (Gargoyle). Charles Wolfe (1991) writes that African-American collector Thomas Talley, in his manuscript of stories, *Negro Traditions*, related a story entitled "Cotton-Eyed Joe, or the Origin of the Weeping Willow." The story includes a stanza from the song, but more importantly details a bizarre tale of a well-known pre-Civil War plantation musician, Cotton Eyed Joe, who plays a fiddle made from the coffin of his dead son.

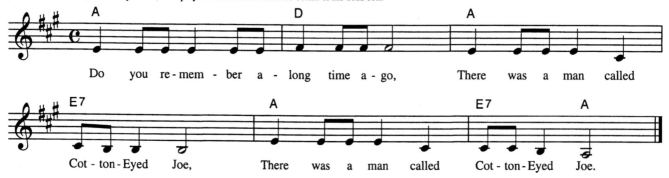

A   D
Do you remember a long time ago
A   E7
There was a man called Cotton-eyed Joe.
A   E7 A
There was a man called Cotton-eyed Joe?

I could have been married a long time ago
If it hadn't a-been for Cotton-eyed Joe. (etc.)

Old bull fiddle and a shoe-string bow
Wouldn't play nothing, but Cotton-eyed Joe. (etc.)

Play it fast or play it slow
Didn't play nothing but Cotton-eyed Joe. (etc.)

Where do you come from? Where do you go?
Where do you come from Cotton-eyed Joe? (etc.)

Cornstalk fiddle and shoestring bow,
Come down gals on Cotton-Eyed Joe. (etc.)

Wanna go to meeting and wouldn't let me go,
Had to stay home with Cotton-Eyed Joe. (etc.)

Come a little rain and come a little snow,
The house fell down on Cotton-Eyed Joe. (etc.)

CRAWDAD

Traditional Old-Time Breakdown and Song **DATE:** Early 1900's **CATEGORY:** Early Country and Bluegrass Song **RECORDING INFO:** Gus Cannon; Woody Guthrie; Doc Watson; Poplin Family **OTHER NAMES:** "You Get A Line and I'll Get a Pole;" "The Crow-Fish Man;" "Sweet Thing;" "Honey;" "Honey Babe;" "The Crawdad Song" **NOTES:** "Crawdad" is a "white blues" with three repeating lines and one answering line with the tag "honey babe/sweet child of mine". This 16 measure "blues" form is widely known and used in many variants.

E
Get up old man, you slept too late, honey
                            B7
Get up old man, you slept too late, babe
E   **E7**
Get up old man, you slept too late
A   **E**   **B7** **E**
Last piece of Crawdad's on your plate, Honey, sugar baby, mine.

Whatcha gonna do when the creek runs dry, honey
Whatcha gonna do when the creek runs dry, babe.
Whatcha gonna do when the creek runs dry
Sit on the banks and watch the crawdads die, Honey, sugar baby, mine.

Yonder comes a man with a sack on his back, honey
Yonder comes a man with a sack on his back, babe
Yonder comes a man with a sack on his back
He's got more crawdads than he can pack, Honey, sugar baby, mine.

CRIPPLE CREEK

Traditional Old-Time, Bluegrass; Breakdown. **DATE:** Early 1900's; **CATEGORY:** Fiddle and Instrumental Tunes; **RECORDING INFO:** The Hill Billies-1925; Doc Roberts-1925; Fiddlin' John Carson; Charlie Poole and the North Carolina Ramblers- "Shootin' Creek" 1928; J. E. Mainer & the Mountaineers; Flatt & Scruggs & the Foggy Mountain Boys; Fiddlin Cowan Powers; Stanley Brothers Doc Watson; **OTHER NAMES:** "Going Up/Down Cripple Creek," "Going Up/Down Shootin' Creek;" "Going Up/Down Brushy Fork," "Shootin' Creek;" "Buck Creek Girls (Gals)." **NOTES:** The tune had and still has wide currency throughout the South. There have been several suggestions about the origin of the title and tune, although no definitive information has been found. Folklorist Alan Jabbour, of the Library of Congress found that the oldest Appalachian fiddlers he collected from could recall the first time that they had heard "Cripple Creek," leading Jabbour to speculate that the title might have something to do with the Cripple Creek, Colorado, labor troubles. Gold had been discovered there in 1891 and the labor disputes date from 1903-1904. Many think the tune and title older however, and point out a likely candidate for the title origins include the Cripple Creek that flows through Grayson and Carroll Counties in Virginia, emptying into the New River. Below is the Bluegrass Messenger's version from "Live in Mt. Airy."

   G   **C**   **G**   **D**   **G**
I got a gal and she loves me, She's as sweet as she can be,
             C   **G**   **D**   **G**
She's got eyes of baby blue, Makes my gun shoot straight and true.
         G
Chorus: Goin' up Cripple Creek, goin' in a whirl,
        D   **G**
Goin' up Cripple Creek, to see my girl.

Goin' up Cripple Creek goin' in a run
             D   **G**
Goin' up Cripple Creek to have me some fun.

My gal lives at the head of the creek, I go up to see her 'bout twice a week.
She's got kisses sweet as any wine,
Wraps herself 'round me like a sweet pertater vine. *Chorus*

Cripple Creek's wide and Cripple Creek's deep,
I'll wade old Cripple Creek before I sleep
Roll my britches to my knees, I'll wade old Cripple Creek when I please. *Chorus*

CRYIN' HOLY

Traditional Old-Time, Bluegrass Gospel **DATE:** Early 1900's; CATEGORY: Early Gospel; **RECORDED BY:** Carter Family; Bill Monroe; J.D. Crowe and the New South; Flatt & Scruggs; **OTHER NAMES:** On the Rock Where Moses Stood; **NOTES:** In the chorus the other voices echo: Cryin' holy (Holy unto the Lord)... On that rock (Praise God) where Moses stood.

      G   **C**   **G**

Chorus: Cryin holy unto the Lord, Cryin holy unto the Lord

                         D   **G**

If I could I surely would, Stand on that rock where Moses stood.

      G

Sinners run and hide your face

      C   **G**

Sinners run and hide your face

Sinners run to that rock and hide your face

            D   **G**

The rock's dried out, no hiding place.   *Chorus*

      G

Lord I ain't no stranger now

      C   **G**

Lord I ain't no stranger now

I've been introduced to the Father and the Son

     D   **G**

And I ain't no stranger now.   *Chorus*

CUMBERLAND GAP

Traditional Old-Time, Breakdown; **DATE:** Early 1900's; **CATEGORY:** Fiddle and Instrumental Tunes. **RECORDING INFO:** Carter Family; Cockerham, Jarrell and Jenkins; McGee Brothers and Arthur Smith; J. E. Mainer**; OTHER NAMES:** "Tumberland Gap;" "Doggett's Gap" (Lunsford); "Riding a Buckin' Mule Through Cumberland Gap;" "Big Stone Gap;" **NOTES:** The Cumberland Gap is a pass in the Appalachians between upper Tennessee and Kentucky. Thomas Walker explored and named Cumberland Gap in 1750. The tune is derived from the Child ballad, "Bonnie George Campbell" (Child 210). A similar version called "Dogget's Gap" came from Lamar Bascom Lunsford. The lyrics to "Cumberland Gap" also have frequent lines about the Civil War.

    G   **Em**   **D**   **G**
Verse: Me and my wife and my wife's pap, We all live down in Cumberland Gap.

          G   **Em**   **D**   **G**
Chorus: Cumberland Gap, Cumberland Gap, Way down yonder in Cumberland Gap.

G   **Em**   **D**   **G**
Cumberland Gap is a noted place, Three kinds of water to wash your face.   *Chorus*

G   **Em**   **D**   **G**
The first white man in Cumberland Gap, Was Doctor Walker, an English chap.   *Chorus*

G   **Em**   **D**   **G**
Daniel Boone on Pinnacle Rock , He killed Injuns with his old flintlock.

G   **Em**   **D**   **G**
Lay down, boys, and take a little nap, Fo'teen miles to the Cumberland Gap.

G   **Em**   **D**   **G**
Cumberland Gap ain't my home, I'm gonna leave before too long.

G   **Em**   **D**   **G**
Lay down boys, take a little rest, We'll wake up in the whippoorwill's nest.

G   **Em**   **D**   **G**
When I die I'll make my will, I want to be buried on Cumberland Hill.

DANCE ALL NIGHT WITH A BOTTLE IN YER HAND

Traditional Old-Time, Breakdown; **DATE:** 1900's; **CATEGORY:** Fiddle and Instrumental Tunes; **RECORDING INFO:** Carter Brothers & Son; Gid Tanner and His Skillet Lickers; New Lost City Ramblers with Cousin Emmy; Tommy Jarrell; J. E. Mainer's Mountaineers; **OTHER NAMES:** "Danced All Night;" "Danced All Night With a Bottle in My Hand," "Give the Fiddler a Dram," "Give Me a Bottle of I Don't Care What." **NOTES:** Guthrie Meade thinks the tune has some relation to "Buffalo Gals." Rosenbaum (1989) points out that the recording by Gid Tanner and the Skillet Lickers for Columbia was very influential.

G
Old Aunt Peggy, won't you fill 'em up again,
D7   **G**
Fill 'em up again, fill 'em up again,

Old Aunt Peggy, won't you fill 'em up again,
D7   **G**
As we go marching along.

Dance all night with the fiddler's girl,
Swing her round the corner all around the world.
Swing that calico Sally Ann,
For we don't give a damn, gonna catch her if we can.

I left my jawbone sittin' on a fence,
I ain't seen nothin' of my jawbone since;
Walked on home and didn't get along,
In come Sally with her blue dress on.

Who's been here since I been gone?
Pretty little girl with the red dress on;
She took it off and I put it on,
In come Sally with her big boots on.

Daniel Prayed

Traditional Old-Time, Bluegrass Gospel **DATE:** 1800's; **CATEGORY:** Early Gospel; **RECORDED BY:** Stanley Brothers; Red Clay Ramblers; Patty Loveless (new release); Boone Creek (With Skaggs & Douglass); Doc Watson (with Price and Howard); **NOTES:** A great shaped-note version (unaccompanied vocals) was done by Doc Watson (Smithsonian Folkways).

G   D
They cast him in the lion's den because he would not honor men
G   A   D
When he prayed to God every morning, noon, and night
             G
Jaws were locked, it made him shout, God soon brought him safely out
                         D   G
Old Daniel prayed every morning, noon, and night. *Chorus*

Now brother let us watch and pray what Daniel did from day to day
He prayed to God every morning, noon, and night
Two can play deering do, things of God he'll take us through
Old Daniel prayed every morning, noon, and night. *Chorus*

DARK HOLLOW

Traditional Old-Time, Bluegrass; **DATE:** Early 1900's (1917 by Cecil Sharp); **CATEGORY:** Early Country and Bluegrass; **OTHER NAMES:** East Virginia Blues; Dark Holler Blues; Greenback Dollar; I Don't Want Your Millions Mister-tune; **RECORDED BY:** Buell Kazee; Stanley Brothers; Seldom Scene; Grateful Dead; Clarence "Tom" Ashley; **NOTES:** Dark Hollow is a variant of "East Virginia Blues." Later in the 1930's the song developed into the very popular "Greenback Dollar."

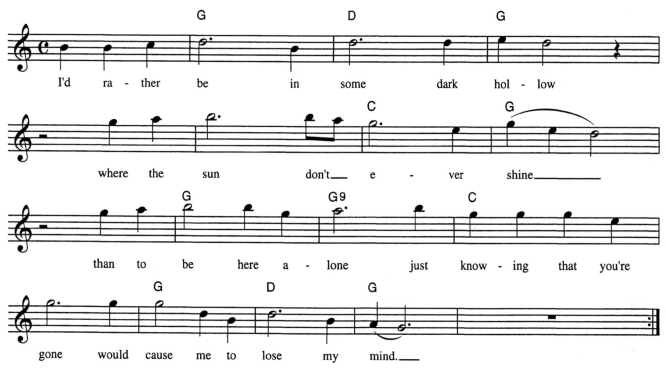

     G   **D**   **G**   **C** **G**
I'd rather be in some dark hollow, where the sun don't ever shine
     G   **G9**   **C**
Than to be here alone just knowing that you're gone,
     G   **D**   **G**
Would cause me to lose my mind.

     G   **D**   **G**   **C**   **G**
So blow your whistle freight train, carry me further on down the track
 G **G9**   **C**   **G**   **D**   **G**
I'm going away, I'm leaving today, I'm going but I ain't coming back.

     G   **D**   **G**   **C** **G**
I'd rather be in some dark hollow, where the sun don't ever shine
   G **G9**   **C**   **G**   **D**   **G**
Than to be in some big city, in a small room with your love on my mind.

DARLIN' COREY

Traditional Old-Time, Bluegrass; **DATE:** Early 1900's (1927 by Shelton and Kazee); **CATEGORY:** Early Country and Bluegrass Roots; **OTHER NAMES:** Darling Cora; Corey, Corey; Little Lulie; **RECORDED BY:** Buell Kazee (1927); Monroe Brothers (1936); Doc Watson; Seldom Scene; Kingston Trio; **NOTES:** Darlin' Corey is a recent "hit" for Bruce Hornsby.

   D   **A**   **D**
Wake up, wake up Darlin' Corey, What makes you sleep so sound?

                               C   **D**
The revenue officers are coming, They're gonna tear your still-house down.

   D   **A**   **D**
Well the first time I seen Darlin' Corey, She was sitting by the banks of the sea

                               C   **D**
Had a forty-four around her body, And a five string on her knee.

Go away, go away Darlin' Corey, Quit hanging around my bed
Your liquor has ruined my body, Pretty women gone to my head.

Dig a hole, dig a hole in the meadow, Dig a hole in the cold damp ground
Dig a hole, dig a hole in the meadow, We're gonna lay Darlin' Corey down.

Can't you hear them bluebirds a-singing, Don't you hear that mournful sound?
Dig a hole, dig a hole in the meadow, We're gonna lay Darlin' Corey down.

DAVY, DAVY

Traditional Old-Time Hoedown; **DATE:** Early 1900's; **CATEGORY:** Fiddle and Instrumental Tunes; **OTHER NAMES:** "Davy," "Goin' Down the River," "Sailing Down the River," "Paddy Won't You Drink Some Good Old Cider." **RECORDING INFO:** Weems String Band; Bob Carlin; New Lost City Ramblers; **NOTES:** "Davy" is a version of "Goin' Down the River," it resembles Green Corn/Black-Eyed Suzy.

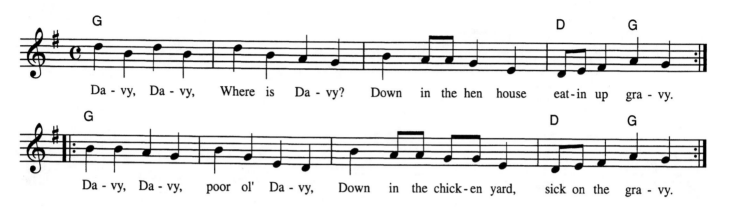

A Section:

G
Davy, Davy, Where is Davy?
      D   **G**
Down in the hen house eatin' up the gravy.

B Section:

G
Davy, Davy, poor ol' Davy.
      D   **G**
Down in the chicken yard sick on the gravy.

DEEP RIVER BLUES

Traditional Early Country and Bluegrass Song; **DATE:** Early 1900's; **CATEGORY:** Early Bluegrass Songs; **RECORDING INFO:** Delmore Brothers; Merle Travis; Doc Watson; **OTHER NAMES:** Big River Blues; **NOTES:** Based on *Big River Blues* by the Delmore Brothers, this tune has since become a signature piece of the great Doc Watson.

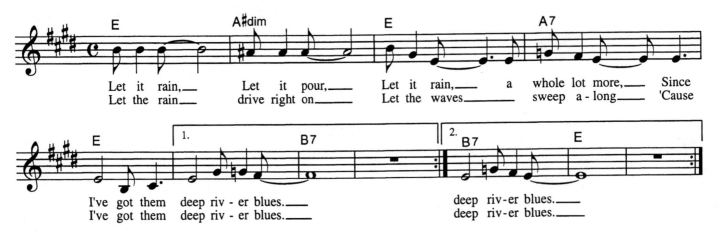

E   A♯dim
Let it rain, let it pour
E   A7
Let it rain a whole lot more, cause
E   B7
I got them deep river blues,
E   A♯dim
Let the rain drive right on
E   A7
Let the waves sweep along, cause
E   B7   E
I got them deep river blues.

E   A♯dim
My old gal's a good old pal,
E   A7
And she looks like a water fowl, when
E   B7
I get them deep river blues,
E   A♯dim
Ain't no one to cry for me,
E   A7
And the fish all go out on a spree when
E   B7   E
I get them deep river blues.

E   A♯dim
Give me back my old boat
E   A7
I'm gonna sail if she'll float, cause
E   B7
I got them deep river blues,
E   Asdim
I'm goin' back to Mussel Shoals,
E   A7
Times are better there I'm told, cause
E   B7   E
I got them deep river blues.

E   A♯dim
If my boat sinks with me
E   A7
I'll go down, don't you see, cause
E   B7
I got them deep river blues,
E   A♯dim
Now I'm gonna say good-bye
E   A7
'N if I sink, just let me die, cause
E   B7   E
I got them deep river blues.

Do Lord

Traditional Bluegrass and Old-Time Gospel Song; **DATE**: Early 1900's; **CATEGORY**: Early Bluegrass Gospel; **RECORDING INFO**: Mississippi John Hurt; **OTHER NAMES**: When My Blood Runs Chilly and Cold; Glory Land March; **NOTES**: One of the earliest popular praise choruses (one part song), the tune is based loosely on Battle Hymn of The Republic. Do Lord emerged in part in the 1920's and became popular at church meetings.

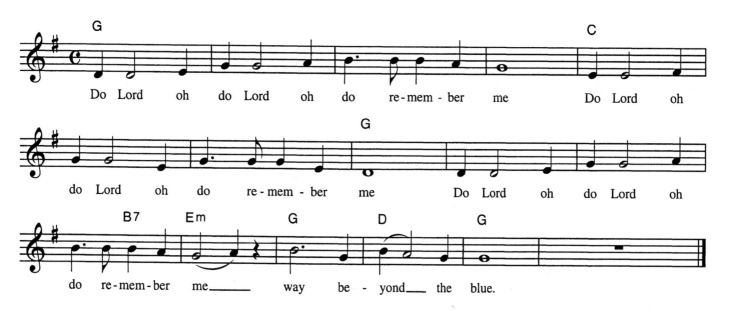

G
I've got a home in glory land that outshines the sun,
C   **G**
I've got a home in glory land that outshines the sun,
                                    B7   **Em**
I've got a home in glory land that outshines the sun,
G   **D**   **G**
Way beyond the blue.

                   G
Chorus: Do Lord, oh do Lord, oh do remember me,
C   **G**
Do Lord, oh do Lord, oh do remember me,
                                    B7   **Em**
Do Lord, oh do Lord, oh do remember me,
G   **D**   **G**
Way beyond the blue.

I take Jesus as my Savior, you take him too (repeat 3 times)
Way beyond the blue.   *Chorus*

If you will not bear the cross, you cannot wear the crown (repeat 3 times)
Way beyond the blue.   *Chorus*

DOGGET'S GAP

Traditional Old-time and Bluegrass Breakdown; **DATE:** Early 1900's; **CATEGORY:** Fiddle and Instrumental Tunes; **RECORDING INFO:** Bascom Lamar Lunsford of South Turkey Creek, NC, at Swannanoa NC 1946; Bluegrass Messengers on "Bluegrass Boogie" CD; **OTHER NAMES:** Similar to "Cumberland Gap" **NOTES:** The fiddle tune from Western North Carolina is fairly obscure. Dogget's Gap is located in Madison County, NC just above Spring Creek on Hwy 63, near an area called Sliding Knob.

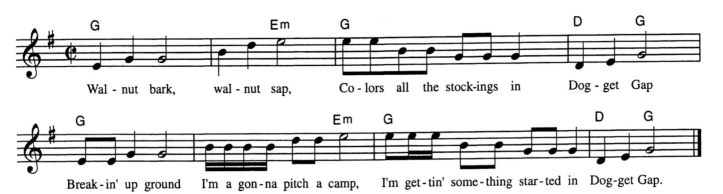

G **Em G** **D G**
Walnut bark, walnut sap, Colors all the stockings in the Dogget Gap.
G **Em**
Breaking up ground and I'm a gonna pitch a camp,
G **D G**
I'm getting something started in the Dogget Gap.

G **Em**
Jerked on the boots and pulled on the strap,
G **D G**
With both socks missing in the Dogget Gap.
G **Em**
They went to the buggy and they raised up the flap,
G **D G**
Stole all my liquor in the Dogget Gap.

Oh, they took off a wheel and they throwed away a tap,
When I went a courtin' in the Dogget Gap.
I reined up my filly and I give a little slap,
And I run like the devil through the Dogget Gap.

I've got a girl in the Dogget Gap,
She don't mind sittin' in her sweetheart's lap.
Ask your pappy to send you back,
Send all the children to the Dogget Gap.

DON'T LET YOUR DEAL GO DOWN

Traditional Old-Time Breakdown; **DATE:** Early 1900's; **CATEGORY:** Fiddle and Instrumental Tunes; **SIMILAR SONGS:** "Last Gold Dollar;" "High Top Shoes;" "Don't Let My Deal Go Down," "No Low Down Hanging Around;" "Lynchburg Town (Tune);" "Black Dog Blues;" **CATEGORY:** Fiddle and Instrumental Tunes; **RECORDING INFO:** Charlie Poole and the North Carolina Ramblers; Bob Wills & his Texas Playboys; Flatt And Scruggs; Wade Ward; Doc Watson; **NOTES:** One of the standard "white blues" from the piedmont region. "Don't Let Your Deal Go Down" was performed initially by Charlie Poole and Fiddlin' John Carson. It was also adapted by black Piedmont blues artists like Etta Baker and John Jackson. There are many great fiddle versions including those by Bob Wills, Benny Thomasson and later Mark O'Conner. Most bluegrass versions are in the Key of D, starting on an F chord.

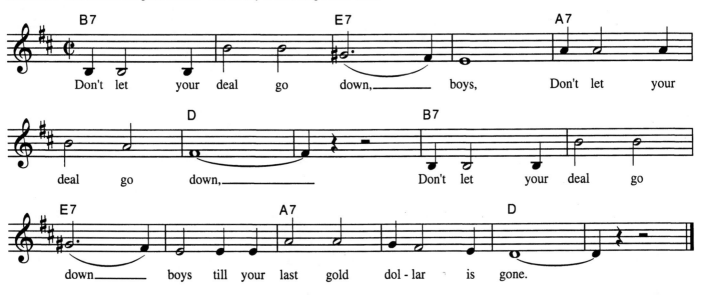

B7　　　　　　　　**E7**
Chorus: Don't let your deal go down boys ,
A7　　　　　　　**D**
Don't let your deal go down
B7　　　　　　　**E7**
Don't let your deal go down boys,
　　　　　　A7　　　　　**D**
'Till your last gold dollar is gone.

Now I've been all around this whole wide world
Down to Memphis, Tennessee
Any old place I hang my hat
Looks like home to me.

Now I left my little girl crying
Standing in the door
Throw'd her arms around my neck
Saying "Honey, don't you go."

Now where did you get them high heeled shoes?
Dress you wear so fine?
Got my shoes from a railroad man
And my dress from a driver in the mine

Who's gonna shoe your pretty white feet?
Who's gonna glove your hand?
Who's gonna kiss your lily white cheeks?
Who's gonna be your man?

Now Papa may shoe my pretty white feet
Mama can glove my hand
She can kiss my lily-white cheeks
'Till you come back again

DON'T THIS ROAD LOOK ROUGH AND ROCKY

Traditional Bluegrass and Old-Time Song; **DATE:** Early 1900's; **CATEGORY:** Fiddle and Instrumental Tunes; **RECORDING INFO:** Flatt and Scruggs; Osborne Brothers; Seldom Scene; Ricky Skaggs; J. D. Crowe & Friends; **OTHER NAMES:** Rough and Rocky; **NOTES:** The Flatt and Scruggs version is based the Blue Sky Boys song "Can't You Hear That Night Bird Crying." Meade categorizes the song with "Little Bunch of Roses" in a large group of songs on Lovers Parted. "Last Gold Dollar" by Murphy Brothers Harp Band has similar lyrics.

G   C   G
Darling, I have come to tell you
                           G
Though it almost breaks my heart
G   C   G
That before the morning, darling
D   G
We'll be many miles apart.

C   G
Don't this road look rough and rocky
                         D
Don't that sea look wide and deep
G   C   G
Don't my baby look the sweetest
D   G
When she's in my arms asleep.

G   C   G
Don't you hear the nightbirds calling
                         G
Far across the deep blue sea?
D   C   G
While of others you are thinking
D   G
Won't you sometimes think of me?

G   C   G
One more kiss before I leave you
                         G
One more kiss before we part
D   C   G
You have caused me lots of trouble
D   G
Darling, you have broke my heart.

DON'T YOU HEAR JERUSALEM MOAN

Traditional Old-Time and Bluegrass Songs; **DATE**: Early 1900's; **CATEGORY**: Old-Time Gospel Song; **RECORDING INFO**: Gid Tanner and His Skillet Lickers; Don Reno and Red Smiley; **OTHER NAMES**: Jerusalem Mourn; Hear Jerusalem Mourn; Preacher Blues; **NOTES**: Gid Tanner and His Skillet Lickers, a prolific Georgia string band of the 1920s and 30s, did a classic version of this old gospel/novelty song which manages to poke fun at several of the major religions.

    G
Well, I got a home on the other shore (Don't you hear Jerusalem moan)
          D   **G**
I know I'll live there forever more (Don't you hear Jerusalem moan)
    G
Chorus: Don't you hear Jerusalem moan? Don't you hear Jerusalem moan?

Thank God there's a heaven and a ringing in my soul
          D   **G**
And my soul set free, don't you hear Jerusalem moan?

It's a high road to walk and a might long way
(Don't you hear Jerusalem moan)
But your feet are just a flying when your soul is saved
(Don't you hear Jerusalem moan) *Chorus*

Well, a Baptist preacher sure knows his bible
(Don't you hear Jerusalem moan)
He's on a first name basis with the Saints inside us
(Don't you hear Jerusalem moan) *Chorus*

DOWN THE ROAD

Traditional Old-Time Breakdown and Song; **DATE:** Early 1900's; **CATEGORY:** Fiddle and Instrumental Tunes; **RECORDING INFO:** Flatt & Scruggs; Tony Rice; Greenbriar Boys. **RELATED TO:** "Ida Red," "Over the Road I'm Bound To Go," "Letter from Down the Road," "On the Road Again," "Kassie Jones," (Furry Lewis's version); **OTHER NAMES:** "Down the Road Just a Mile or Two" **NOTES:** Part of the "Ida Red/Over the Road I'm Bound To Go/Feather Bed" group of songs.

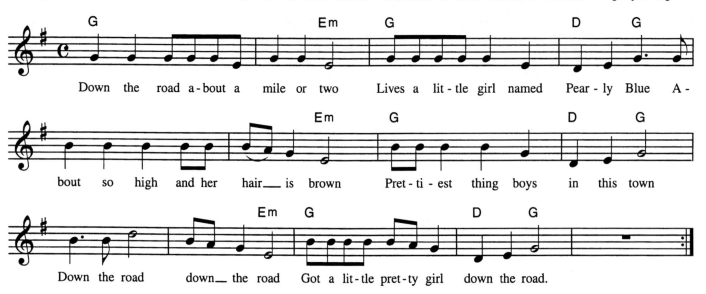

G   **Em G**   **D**   **G**
Down the road just a mile or two, Lives a little girl named Pearly Blue
                 Em   **G**   **D**   **G**
About so high and hair is brown, Prettiest thing boys in this town.

       G   **Em G**   **D**   **G**
Chorus: Down the road, down the road, Got a little pretty girl down the road.

G   **Em G**   **D**   **G**
Now any time you wanna know, Where I'm heading is down the road
     Em G   **D**   **G**
See that girl on the line, You'll find me there most any old time.   *Chorus*

Now every day and Sunday, too, I go to see my Pearly Blue
Before you hear the rooster crow,
You'll see me headed down the road.   *Chorus*

Clemny Rakestraw owns a farm, From the hog wash to the barn
From the barn to the rail, Made his living by carrying the mail.   *Chorus*

Now every time I get the blues, I walk the soles right off my shoes
Now every time I get the blues
I walk the soles right off my shoes. *Chorus*

DRIFTING TOO FAR FROM THE SHORE

Bluegrass and Old-Time Gospel Song; Charles E. Moody, words and music; **DATE**: 1923; **CATEGORY:** Early Gospel Song; **RECORDING INFO**: Monroe Brothers; Roy Acuff; Country Gentlemen; **NOTES**: Charles E. Moody was a member of the Georgia Yellow Hammers. The song appeared in a Stamps-Baxter Songbook and was first recorded by Carolina Gospel Singers in 1929.

```
     G    D    G          D         G
Out on the perilous deep, where danger silently creeps
                   C        G      D      G
And storm so violently sweeping, you're drifting too far from the shore.
```

```
        C            G        D              G
Chorus:  Drifting too far from the shore, you're drifting too far from the shore
                              C      G     D       G
Come to Jesus today let him show you the way, you're drifting too far from the shore.
```

```
  G    D    G      D           G
Today the tempest rose high, and clouds o'er shadow the sky
                    C      G      D       G
Sure death is hovering nigh, you're drifting too far from the shore.     Chorus
```

EAST VIRGINIA BLUES

Traditional Bluegrass Song and "Blues" **DATE:** 1917 (collected by Cecil Sharp); **CATEGORY:** Early Country and Bluegrass Song; **OTHER NAMES:** "East Virginia;" "Old Virginny" (Ritchie); "In Old Virginny" (Sharp); **RELATED TO:** " Dark Holler Blues" (Ashley); "I Don't Want Your Millions, Mister;" "Greenback Dollar;" "Dark Hollow" (Browning); "Man of Constant Sorrow" "Darling Think of What You've Done;" "Oh Molly Dear (Go Ask Your Mother)" "Silver Dagger;" **RECORDING INFO:** First recorded by Buell Kazee, 1927; The Bray Brothers; Flatt and Scruggs (When I Left East Virginia); The Country Gentlemen; The Stanley Brothers; **NOTES:** One of the first published versions of "East Virginia" is "In Old Virginny" from *Sharp's English Folk Songs from the Southern Appalachians.*

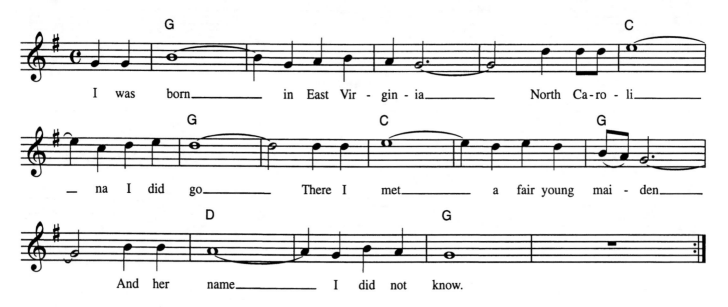

    G   **C**   **G**
I was born in East Virginia, North Carolina I did go
    C   **G**   **D**   **G**
There I met a fair young maiden, And her name I did not know.

Oh her hair was dark and curly, And her cheeks were rosy red
On her breast she wore white lilies, Where I longed to lay my head.

I don't want your greenback dollar, I don't want your watch and chain
All I want is your heart darling, Say you'll take me back again.

The ocean's deep and I can't wade in, And I have no wings to fly
I'll just get me a blue eyed boat man, For to row me over the tide.

I'll go back to East Virginia, North Carolina ain't my home
I'll go back to East Virginia, Leave them North Carolineans alone.

ENGINE 143

Traditional Old-Time and Bluegrass Ballad; **DATE**: late 1800's; **CATEGORY:** Fiddle and Instrumental Tunes; **RECORDING INFO**: Carter Family; Johnny Cash; Flatt and Scruggs; **OTHER NAMES**: George Allen's Engine 143; The F.F.V.; George Allen; George Alley's F.F.V.; **NOTES**: George Alley was killed on Oct. 23, 1890 near Hilton, W. Va., when his engine overturned from a landslide.

G		C	G

Along came the FFV, the swiftest on the line

	A7	D7

Running o'er the C&O road just 20 minutes behind

G		C	G

Running into Seville headquarters on the line

C	G	D7	G

Receiving their strict orders from a station just behind.

ENGINE 143 (ADDITIONAL VERSES)

Running into Hampton, the engineer was there
George Allen was his name, with curling golden hair
His fireman, Jack Dixon, was standing by his side
Awaiting for strict orders while in the cab to ride

Georgie's mother came to him with a bucket on her arm
Saying, my darling son, be careful how you run
For many a man has lost his life in trying to make lost time
And if you run your engine right you'll get there just on time

Mother, I know your advice is good and later I'll take heed
I think my engine is all right, I'm sure that she will speed
O'er this road I need to go at the rate of a cannonball
And when I blow for the stockyard gate I'm sure they'll hear my call

Up the road she darted, against the rocks she crashed
Upside-down the engine turned, poor Georgie's breast it smashed
His head was against the firebox door, the flames were rolling high
I'm glad I was born for an engineer, on the C&O road to die

The doctor said to Georgie, my darling boy, be still
Your life may yet be saved if it is God's blessed will
Oh, no, said Georgie, that will not do, I want to die so free
I want to die for the engine I love, one hundred and forty-three

The doctor said to Georgie, your life cannot be saved
Murdered upon the railroad and laid in a lonesome grave
His face was covered up with blood, his eyes you could not see
And the very last words poor Georgie said was nearer, my God, to Thee

FADED LOVE

Bluegrass and Old-Time Song. By Bob Wills and Johnny Wills; **DATE:** 1950; **CATEGORY:** Fiddle and Instrumental Tunes; **RECORDING INFO:** Bob Wills and the Texas Playboys; Vassar Clements; Mark O'Connor; Tony Rice; Larry Sparks and the Lonesome Ramblers; **NOTES:** Featuring one of the classic fiddle solos in the (key of) D section. Lyrics are sung in the second part (Key A). Sometimes called, "Soldier's March."

Verse: **A**   **D**
As I look at the letters That you wrote to me,
     A   **E**   **A**
It's you that I'm thinking of, As I read the lines
          D   **A**   **E**   **A**
That to me were so sweet, I remember our faded love.

Chorus:

I miss you, darling, more and more every day,
As heaven would miss the stars above,
With every heartbeat
I still think of you,
And remember our faded love.

Verse:

I think of the past, And all the pleasures we had
As I watch the mating of the dove,
It was in the springtime, That you said good-bye,
I remember our faded love.   *Chorus*

(And remember our faded love.)

FARTHER ALONG

Southern Gospel Song by W.B. Stevens and J.R. Baxter, Jr. © 1937 **CATEGORY:** Early Gospel Songs; **DATE:** 1937; **RECORDING INFO:** Bill Monroe; Elvis Pressley, Johnny Cash, Emmylou Harris-Linda Ronstadt-Dolly Parton; Doc Watson; **NOTES:** One of the great Southern Gospel songs. On the Bluegrass Messengers "Farther Along" CD.

	D	G	D		E7	A7

Tempted and tried we're oft made to wonder, Why it should be thus all the day long;

	D	G	D		A7		D

While there are others living about us, Never molested, though in the wrong.

Chorus: Farther along we'll know all about it. Farther along we'll understand why.
Cheer up my brothers, live in the sunshine; We'll understand it all bye and bye.

"Faithful to death" saith our loving Savior, Only a while to labor and wait.
All of our toils will soon be forgotten, As we sweep through that beautiful gate.

When we see Jesus coming in glory; When He comes from His home in the sky.
Then we shall meet Him in that bright mansion; We'll understand it all bye and bye.

Often I wonder why I must journey, Over a road so rugged and steep;
While there are others living in comfort; While with the lost I labor and weep.

FLY AROUND MY PRETTY LITTLE MISS

Traditional Old-Time Breakdown; **DATE:** Early 1900's; **CATEGORY:** Fiddle and Instrumental Tunes; **OTHER NAMES:** Blue-Eyed Girl; Fly Around My Pretty Little Miss; Blue-Eyed Girl; Susannah Gal; Blue Eyed Miss; Fly Around My Pretty Little Pink; **RELATED TO:** Shady Grove; Weevily Wheat (floating lyrics); Say, Darling, Say; Where Are You Going; Washing Mama's Dishes; Black Jack Davy (Tune); Betty Ann; **RECORDING INFO:** Samantha Bumgarner- 1924; Gid Tanner and His Skillet Lickers; Frank Blevins & His Tar Heel Rattlers; Joel Mabus; Charlie Moore; **NOTES:** The "Fly Around My Pretty Little Miss" text is related to the branch of the "I'll be Sixteen/Seventeen Next Sunday" songs which can be traced to England. There are many floater fiddle tune lyrics from "Shady Grove" and other songs.

G

Chorus: Fly around, my pretty little Miss, Fly around, my daisy

                                                      D7   **G**

Fly around, my pretty little Miss, You almost drive me crazy.

G

The higher up the cherry tree, The riper grows the cherries

                                                   D7   **G**

The more you hug and kiss the girls, The sooner they will marry   *Chorus*

G

Coffee grows on white oak trees, The river flows with brandy

                                      D7   **G**

If I had my pretty little miss, I'd feed her sugar candy.   *Chorus*

G

Going to get some weevily wheat, I'm going to get some barley

                                      D7   **G**

Going to get some weevily wheat, And bake a cake for Charlie.   *Chorus*

Foggy Mountain Top

Traditional Old-Time and Bluegrass Song; **DATE:** Early 1900's; **CATEGORY:** Early Country and Bluegrass Song; **OTHER NAMES:** The Rocky Mountain Top; **RECORDING INFO:** Monroe Brothers; Carter Family; Flatt & Scruggs; New Lost City Ramblers; **NOTES:** This mountain song, first recorded by Samantha Bumgarner in 1924, is composed of mainly floating lyrics which can be traced to other sources.

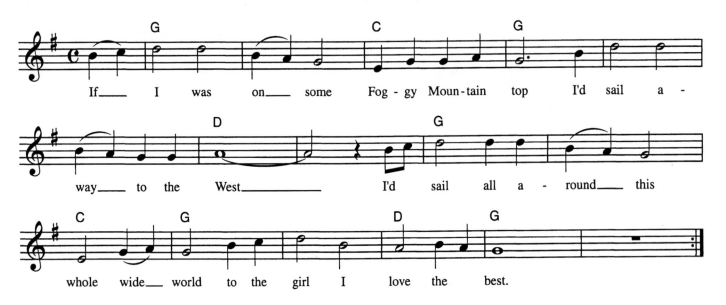

    G   **C**   **G**
Chorus: If I was on some Foggy Mountain top
        D
I'd sail away to the West
  G   **C** **G**
I'd sail all around this whole wide world
    D **G**
To the girl I love the best

If I'd have listened to what Mama said
I would not be in here today
Lying around this old jailhouse
Just wasting my poor life away. *Chorus*

Oh, she caused me to weep, she caused me to mourn
She caused me to leave my home
Oh, the lonesome pines and the good old times
I'm on my way back home. *Chorus*

FOOTPRINTS IN THE SNOW

Bluegrass and old-Time Song; Harry Wright- Words and Music 1880's; G. R Jackson wds. and CW Bennett m. 1886; **CATEGORY:** Early Country and Bluegrass Song; **DATE:** 1880's; **RECORDING INFO:** Bill Monroe and his Bluegrass Boys; Hylo Brown; Doc Watson, Clint Howard & Fred Price; Don Reno, Bill Harrell and the Tenn. Cutups; Mac Wiseman; **OTHER NAMES:** I Traced Her Little Footsteps; Only Girl I Ever Loved; Little Foot Prints; **NOTES:** The tune is similar, especially in the beginning, to "Little Stream of Whiskey."

C
Some folks like the summer time, When they can walk about
G   **C**
Strolling through the meadow green, There's comfort there no doubt
                                                           F
But give me the winter time, When snow is on the ground
 G   **C**
I found her when the snow is on the ground

 C   **G**   **C**
Chorus: I traced her little foot prints in the snow, I found her little footprints in the snow
                                      F
Bless that happy day, when my Nellie lost her way,
 G   **C**
I found her when the snow lay on the ground

I went out to see her, there was a big round moon
Her mother said she just stepped out but would be returning soon
I found her little footprints and traced them through the snow
I found her when the snow lay on the ground

Now she's up in Heaven with that angel band
I know I'm going to meet her in that promised land
Every time the snow falls it brings back memories
I found her when the snow lay on the ground.

THE FOX

d Bluegrass Song; **DATE**: 1810 (Gammer Gurton's Garland); **CATEGORY**: Songs From Overseas; **RECORDING INFO**: Burl Ives; Pete Nickel Creek; **OTHER NAMES**: Daddy Fox; Old Mother Hippletoe; Fox Went Out on a Chilly Night; **NOTES:** The earliest version of this piece app... ...en a Middle English poem found in a British Museum dating from the fifteenth century. It has become popular in some bluegrass circles after a recording by Nickel Creek.

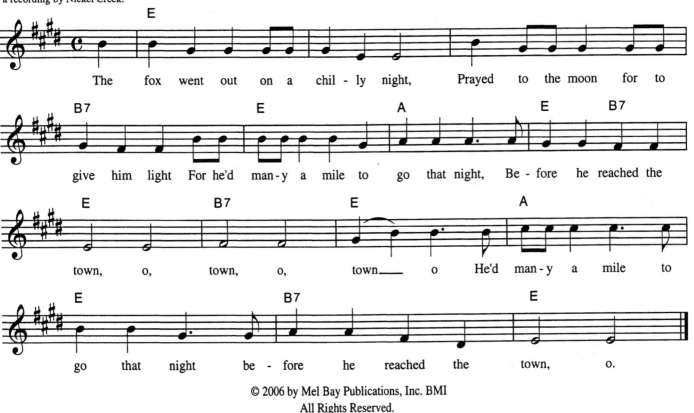

     E
The fox went out on a chilly night
                        B7
And he prayed for the moon to give him light
         E   **A**
He had a many a mile to go that night
E   **B7**   **E**   **B7**   **E**
Before he reached the town, o, town, o, town, o,
    A   **E**   **B7**   **E**
He'd a many a mile to go that night before he reached the town, o.

     E
Well the fox he ran till he came to the pen
                            B7
Where the ducks and the geese were kept there in
            E   **A**
He said a couple of you are gonna grease my chin
E   **B7**   **E**   **B7**   **E**
Before I leave this town, o, town, o, town, o,
    A   **E**   **B7**   **E**
A couple of you are gonna grease my chin before I leave this town, o.

THE FOX (ADDITIONAL VERSES)

Well he grabbed the old grey goose by the neck
Swung her up and across his back
He didn't mind her quacky quack quack,
And her legs all hanging down, o, down, o, down, o,
He didn't mind her quacky quack quack, and her legs all hanging down, o.

Old mother Flipper Flopper jumped out of bed
Looked out the window and cocked her head
She said John the grey goose is gone,
And the fox is on the town, o, town, o, town, o.
She said John the grey goose is gone, and the fox is on the town, o.

So John he scampered to the top of the hill
Blew his horn both loud and shrill
The fox said heel I better flee with my keel
Cause they'll soon be on my trail, o, trail, o, trail, o.
The fox said heel I better flee with my keel, cause they'll soon be on my trail, o.

Well the fox he ran till he came to the den
There were the little ones 8, 9, and 10
They said daddy better go back again
'Cause it must be a mighty fine town, o, town, o, town, o.
They said daddy better go back again, 'cause it must be a mighty fine town, o.

FREE LITTLE BIRD

Old-Time Song and Breakdown; Original words by L. V. H. Crosby **DATE:** 1853; **CATEGORY:** Fiddle and Instrumental Tunes; **OTHER NAMES:** Little Birdie; Katy Cline; **RELATED TO:** Willie Dear; Katy Cline; Careless Love; **RECORDING INFO:** Dykes Magic City Trio-1927; Clarence Ashley & Fred Price; Roscoe Holcomb; Bascam Lamar Lunsford; New Lost City Ramblers; Hedy West; **NOTES:** "Free Little Bird" is an adaptation of "Kitty Clyde," written and composed by L. V. H. Crosby and published in 1853.

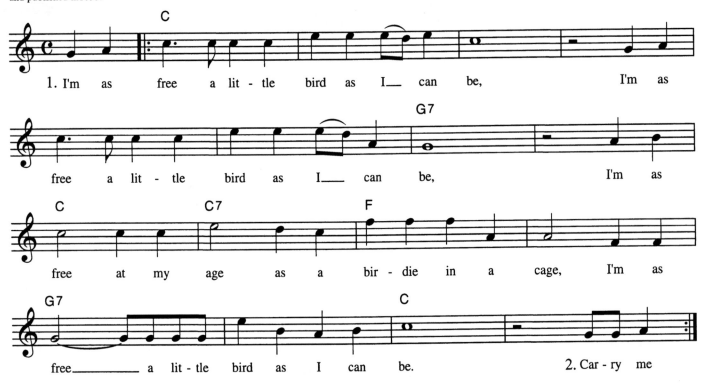

    C   **G7**
I'm as free a little bird as I can be, I'm as free a little bird as I can be,
    C   **C7**   **F**   **G7**   **C**
I'm as free at my age as a birdie in a cage, I'm as free a little bird as I can be.

      C
Carry me home little birdie, carry me home,
                       G7
Carry me home little birdie, carry me home,
    C   **C7**   **F**
Carry me home to my wife, she's the joy of my life,
  G7   **C**
Carry me home little birdie, carry me home.

     C   **G7**
I'll never build my nest on the ground, Neither in the forks of a tree.
    C   **C7**   **F**   **G7**   **C**
I'll build my nest in the ruffles of her dress, Where the bad boys can never bother me

FREIGHT TRAIN

Old-Time Instrumental and Song; Words and tune by Elizabeth Cotton; **DATE:** Early 1900's; **CATEGORY:** Instrumental Tunes; **RECORDING INFO:** Joan Baez; Norman Blake and Red Rector; Elizabeth Cotton; New Lost City Ramblers; Doc Watson; **NOTES:** The singing and playing of Elizabeth Cotten, from Chapel Hill, North Carolina is well known to anyone interested in traditional guitar styles. She had a very individual sound; because she played the guitar left-handed, with a right-handed guitar held upside down. "Freight Train" is Libba Cotten's most well known song. She composed it when she was about twelve years old, wondering where the train that ran past her farm might be headed and what the people there might be like.

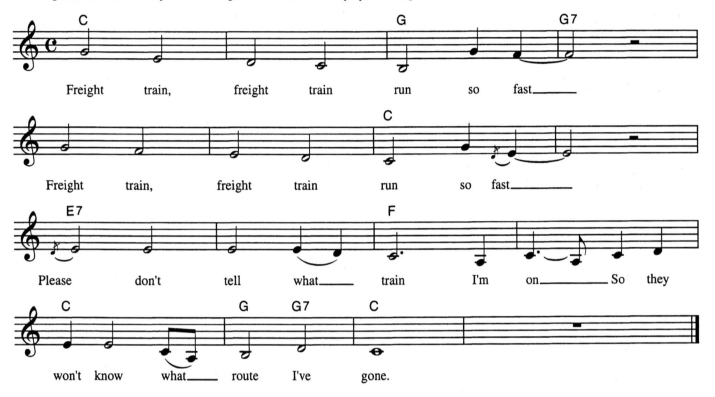

Freight train, freight train run so fast

Freight train, freight train run so fast

Please don't tell what train I'm on So they

won't know what route I've gone.

	C	G	G7	C
Chorus:	Freight train, freight train run so fast,	Freight train, freight train run so fast,		

E7   **F**   **C**   **G**   **G7**   **C**
Please don't tell what train I'm on, So they won't know what route I've gone.

     C   **G**   **G7**   **C**
1. When I die Lord bury me deep,   Way down on old Chesnut Street,
     E7   **F**   **C**   **G** **G7** **C**
    So I can hear old Number Nine, As she goes rolling by.   Chorus

     C   **G**   **G7**   **C**
2. When I'm dead and in my grave,   No more good times here I'll crave,
     E7   **F**   **C**   **G** **G7** **C**
    Place the stones at my head and feet, And tell them all that I've gone to sleep.

Chorus

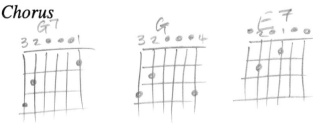

Froggie Went A-Courtin'

Appalachian and Old English Ballad; **DATE:** First appears in 1549 (Wedderburn's "Complaynt of Scotland"); **CATEGORY:** English Ballad; **OTHER NAMES:** Frog Went A-Courting; A Frog He Would A-Wooing Go; The Frog's Courtship; The Frog and the Mouse; It was a frog in a well; There Was a Puggie in a Well; There Lived a Puddie in the Well; The Frog's Wooing; **RECORDING INFO:** John Jacob Niles; Peggy Seeger; McLain Family; Bluegrass Messengers; Doc Watson; **NOTES:** Horace M. Belden believes this is the most widely known song in the English language. The exchange of lyrics with "Froggie" and many other folk songs and fiddle tunes in the US has caused some confusion. Fiddle tunes often borrow short rhyming lines that make little sense as a narrative. Presumably some of the nonsense rhymes could have traveled from songs like "Froggy" and "Martin Said to His Man," to the related "Kemo Kimo" and "Kitty Alone" songs. Lyrics from Bluegrass Messengers on "Diggin' Up Roots" CD.

C
Froggie went a-courtin' and he did ride, Uh-huh,
                                          G
Froggie went a-courtin' and he did ride, Uh-huh,
C
Froggie went a-courtin' and he did ride,
  F   **C**   **G**   **C**
A sword and a pistol by his side, Uh-huh, Uh-huh, Uh-huh.

Well he rode up to Miss Mousey's door, Uh-huh,
Well he rode up to Miss Mousey's door, Uh-huh,
Well he rode up to Miss Mousey's door.
He hit it loud and made it roar, Uh-huh, Uh-huh, Uh-huh.

He took Miss Mousey on his knee, Uh-huh,
Took Miss Mousey on his knee, Uh-huh,
Took Miss Mousey on his knee.
Said, "Miss Mousey, will you marry me?" Uh-huh, Uh-huh, Uh-huh.

"Without my uncle Rat's consent, Uh-huh
"Without my uncle Rat's consent, Uh-huh
"Without my uncle Rat's consent,
I wouldn't marry the president, Uh-huh, Uh-huh, Uh-huh.

FROGGIE WENT A-COURTIN'
(ADDITIONAL VERSES)

Uncle Rat laughed and he shook his fat sides, Uh-huh,
Uncle Rat laughed and he shook his fat sides, Uh-huh,
Uncle Rat laughed and he shook his fat sides,
To think his niece would be a bride, Uh-huh, Uh-huh, Uh-huh.

Oh where will the wedding party be? Uh-huh,
Where will the wedding party be? Uh-huh,
Where will the wedding party be?
Way down yonder in a holler tree, Uh-huh Uh-huh, Uh-huh.

The first to come were two little ants, Uh-huh,
First to come were two little ants, Uh-huh,
First to come were two little ants,
Fixin' around to have a dance, Uh-huh Uh-huh, Uh-huh.

Next to come in was a bumble bee, Uh-huh
Next to come in was a bumble bee, Uh-huh
Next to come in was a bumble bee.
Bouncin' a fiddle on his knee, Uh-huh, Uh-huh, Uh-huh.

Next to come was a big bull-frog, Uh-huh,
Next to come was a big bull-frog, Uh-huh,
Next to come was a big bull-frog,
He jumped up high and started to clog, Uh-huh Uh-huh, Uh-huh.

Mr. Frog went swimmin' across the lake, Uh-huh,
Mr. Frog went swimmin' across the lake, Uh-huh,
Mr. Frog went swimmin' across the lake, (pause)
And he got swallowed up by a big black snake, Uh-huh Uh-huh, Uh-huh.

THE GAL I LEFT BEHIND ME

Old-Time, American, Irish, Scottish, English March and Song; **DATE:** As "Brighton Camp" 1600's; As "Maggie Walker" early 1900's. **CATEGORY:** Fiddle and Instrumental Tunes; **OTHER NAMES:** "Maggie Walker's Blues" "Brighton Camp," "The Girl I Left Behind Me," "Peggy Walker's Blues;" "My Parents Reared Me Tenderly;" **RECORDING INFO:** Grayson and Whitter-1928; Dock Boggs, as "Peggy Walker;" New Lost City Ramblers; Red Clay Ramblers; Hobart Smith; Bob Wills; Norman Blake and Red Rector; Doc Watson. **NOTES:** "The Girl I Left behind Me" has a history in both the British Isles and America as a song and a march, but it has become an item of general repertory for many fiddlers. In addition to this ballad form, there is a song with this title (indexed as "The Girl I Left Behind Me (lyric)"). The two have cross-fertilized (often sharing the latter's tune "Brighton Camp"). In the US, "Peggy Walker Blues" has become a significant branch with early recordings by Dock Boggs and others.

```
    C          F         C          G
```
I struck the trail in seventy nine, The herd strung out behind me.
```
    C          F                 G7         C
```
As I jogged along, my mind ran back, To the gal I left behind me.

```
              C                              D7  G
```
Chorus: That sweet little gal, that true little gal, The gal I left behind me.
```
    C          F                 G7         C
```
That sweet little gal, that true little gal, The gal I left behind me.

The wind did blow, the rain did fall, The hail did fall and blind me.
I thought of the gal, that sweet little gal, The gal I left behind me.   *Chorus*

If I ever get off the trail, and the Indians they don't find me.
I'll make my way back again, to the gal I left behind me.   *Chorus*

When we sold out I took the train, I knew that I would find her.
When I got back we had a smack, and I'm no golderned liar.   *Chorus*

GEORGIA PINEYWOODS

Bluegrass Song by B. & F. Bryant; **DATE:** 1971; **CATEGORY:** New Bluegrass Songs; **RECORDING INFO:** Osborne Brothers; Bottle Hill; **NOTES:** One of many songs written by Bryant/Bryant, who also penned Rocky Top. Osborn's play in G with a capo IV (Key of B).

```
         E   B    A   E        B    A    B
Chorus: Miss those Georgia Pineywoods, wonder if they miss me
 E      B  A    E
Thoughts of all those Pineywoods
                    B7      (E)   B    E
 Ancient home of the Creek and the Cherokee   and me.
 E           A                E                    B7
I was born in the Georgia Pineywoods, fifteen miles from a grocery store
 E                       E        B7    E
No T.V., no gold plate shiny goods, cracked linoleum on the floor
 E           A                E                  B7
We had cows in the back fields a grazin, chickens clucking out in the pen
 E           A                E      B7    E
Life was good but it's amazin' tho', how I couldn't see it back then.   Chorus
```

When I'd look for Indian arrowheads, I was as happy as Borden's cow.
I've lost all my Indian arrowheads, They're no good to me here no-how.
I get paid now by the hour And lead my typical suburban life,
Credit cards and buyin' power, And owe more money than Caesar's wife.   *Chorus*

GIVE ME THE ROSES WHILE I LIVE

Old-Time and Bluegrass Gospel Song by James Rowe and R.H. Cornelius; **DATE:** Early 1900's; **CATEGORY:** Bluegrass Gospel Song; **RECORDING INFO:** Coon Creek Girls; Carter Family; Blue Sky Boys; Jimmy Martin and Roy Lee Centers; Red Clay Ramblers; **OTHER NAMES:** Give Me The Roses Now; **NOTES:** This is one of the classic bluegrass gospel waltzes.

G   **D**   **G**
Wonderful things of folks are said, When they have passed away
                              D   **G**
Roses adorn the narrow bed, Over the sleeping clay.
C   **G**   **D**
Give me the roses while I live, Trying to cheer me on
G   **D**   **G**
Useless are flowers that you give, After the soul is gone.

Let us not wait to do good deeds, Till they have passed away
Now is the time to sow good seeds, While here on earth we stay. *Chorus*

Kind words are useless when folks lie, Cold in a narrow bed
Don't wait till death to speak kind words, Now should the words be said. *Chorus*

GLORY LAND WAY

Old Time Bluegrass and Gospel Song by J. S. Torbett; **DATE:** Late 1800's- exact date unknown; **CATEGORY:** Early Sounthern Gospel song; **RECORDING INFO:** Jenkins Family- 1934; J.E. Mainer and his Mountaineers; Bill Monroe; **OTHER NAMES:** I'm in the Gloryland Way; **NOTES:** James S. Torbett was born in Alabama in 1868; He was a singing school teacher for thirty-five years. His most popular song, Glory Land Way is a bluegrass favorite after being performed by Bill Monroe. The Chuck Wagon Gang also recorded the song in 1966.

    G   **C**   **G**   **D**

1. I'm in the way, the bright and shining way, I'm in the glory-land way;

G   **C**   **G**   **D**   **G**

Telling the world that Jesus saves today, Yes, I'm in the glory-land way.

         C   **G**   **D**

Chorus: I'm in the glory-land way, I'm in the glory-land way;

G   **C**   **G**   **D**   **G**

Heaven is nearer and the way groweth clearer, For I'm in the glory-land way.

   G   **C**   **G**   **D**

2. List to the call, the Gospel call today, Get in the glory-land way;

G   **C**   **G**   **D**   **G**

Wanderers come home, Oh, hasten to obey, For I'm in the glory-land way. *Chorus*

  G   **C**   **G**   **D**

3. Onward I go rejoicing in His love, I'm in the glory-land way;

G   **C**   **G**   **D**   **G**

Soon I shall see Him in that home above, Oh, I'm in the glory-land way. *Chorus*

GO LONG MULE

Bluegrass Song- Written by Richard L. Matteson Jr. **DATE:** 1993; **CATEGORY:** New Bluegrass Songs; **RECORDING INFO:** Matteson Blues "True Blue;" Bluegrass Messengers "Diggin' Up Roots;" **NOTES:** New music by Richard Matteson. Lyrics based on Uncle Dave Macon's song, Go Long Mule.

```
     C      F    C        F    C      F      G
1. I got a mule, he's such a fool, He never pays no heed.
     C      F    C     F      G              C
I built a fire beneath his tail, And then he showed me some speed.
           F                             G
Chorus: Go 'long mule, don't you roll them eyes
           C      F       C     F      G        C
You can change a fool but a doggone mule, Is a mule until he dies.
```

2. I drove down to the graveyard late last night, Some peaceful rest to find,
But when a black cat crossed my path, I sure did change my mind.

3, I bought some biscuits for my dog, And I laid them on the shelf
Times got so hard, I shot the dog, And ate that bread myself.

4. A cowslip aint no kind of slip, To slip upon a cow.
That's why a catfish never answers, To a cat's meow.

5. I'm goin' down to that Muddy River, To lay me down and die,
And if I find the water's wet, I'll wait until it's dry.

GOD MOVES IN A WINDSTORM

Traditional Bluegrass Gospel; **DATE**: Early 1900's; **CATEGORY:** Early Gospel Songs; **RELATED TO**: On the Hallelujah Strand; **RECORDING INFO**: Sarah Ogan Gunning; Blue Highway; **NOTES**: God Moves in a Windstorm was recorded first by Sarah Ogan Gunning and was a hit for Blue Highway.

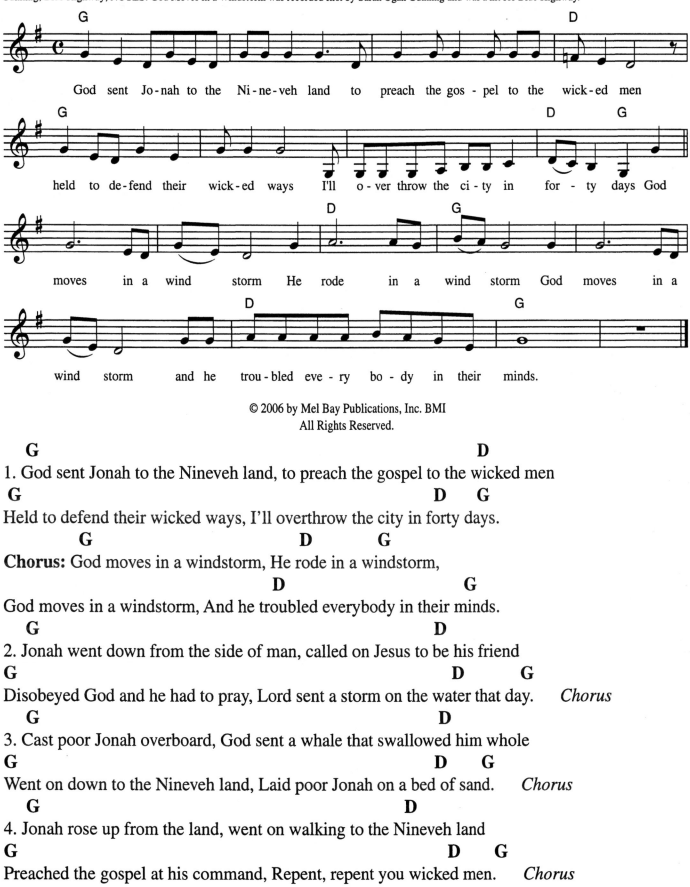

God sent Jo-nah to the Ni-ne-veh land to preach the gos-pel to the wick-ed men
held to de-fend their wick-ed ways I'll o-ver throw the ci-ty in for-ty days God
moves in a wind storm He rode in a wind storm God moves in a
wind storm and he trou-bled eve-ry bo-dy in their minds.

   G   **D**

1. God sent Jonah to the Nineveh land, to preach the gospel to the wicked men

  G   **D**   **G**

Held to defend their wicked ways, I'll overthrow the city in forty days.

       G   **D**   **G**

Chorus: God moves in a windstorm, He rode in a windstorm,

                       D   **G**

God moves in a windstorm, And he troubled everybody in their minds.

  G   **D**

2. Jonah went down from the side of man, called on Jesus to be his friend

G   **D**   **G**

Disobeyed God and he had to pray, Lord sent a storm on the water that day. *Chorus*

  G   **D**

3. Cast poor Jonah overboard, God sent a whale that swallowed him whole

G   **D**   **G**

Went on down to the Nineveh land, Laid poor Jonah on a bed of sand. *Chorus*

  G   **D**

4. Jonah rose up from the land, went on walking to the Nineveh land

G   **D**   **G**

Preached the gospel at his command, Repent, repent you wicked men. *Chorus*

GOD'S GONNA SET THIS WORLD ON FIRE

Traditional Spiritual and Bluegrass Gospel song; **DATE:** early 1900's; **CATEGORY:** Fiddle and Instrumental Tunes; **RECORDING INFO:** Zwan; Old Reliable String Band; Moses Hogan Chorale; Clint Howard and Fred Price; Hylo Brown; Carter Family; **OTHER NAMES:** Some of These Days; River of Jordan; I'm Gonna Tell God How You Treat Me; **NOTES:** Included in Sandburg's book, American Songbag, this spiritual has been performed by the rock group Zwan, African-American gospel quartets and old-time/bluegrass groups. Known as one of the "Some of These Days" group of songs which date back to 1915, a related version has been recorded by the Carter Family as "River of Jordan."

G
God's gonna set this world on fire
C   **G**
God's gonna set this world on fire one of these days Hallelujah
                              Em
God's gonna set this world on fire
G   **D**   **G**
God's gonna set this world on fire one of these days.

I'm gonna sit at the welcome table
I'm gonna sit at the welcome table one of these days Hallelujah
I'm gonna sit at the welcome table
I'm gonna sit at the welcome table one of these days.

I'm gonna eat and never get hungry
I'm gonna eat and never get hungry one of these days Hallelujah
I'm gonna eat and never get hungry
I'm gonna eat and never get hungry one of these days.

I'm gonna drink and never get thirsty
I'm gonna drink and never get thirsty one of these days Hallelujah
I'm gonna drink and never get thirsty
I'm gonna drink and never get thirsty one of these days.

GOIN' 'CROSS THE MOUNTAIN

Traditional Bluegrass Song; **DATE:** 1800's; **CATEGORY:** Early Country and Bluegrass Songs; **RECORDING INFO:** Frank Proffitt; Pete Seeger; **OTHER NAMES:** Going Across the Mountain; **NOTES:** A Civil War era song that Frank Proffitt learned from his father, Wiley. There being little political connection between mountain folk and the "secesh" south, many southern Appalachian men opted to join the union forces. Wiley's father, John Proffitt, was a member of the 13th Tennessee Cavalry, USA. John's brother was conscripted, and fought for the Confederacy.

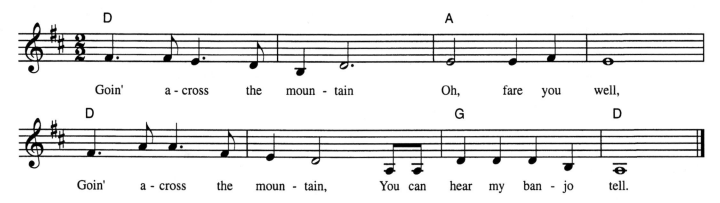

D   A
I'm goin' across the mountain, oh, fare you well
D   G   D
Goin' 'cross the mountain, you can hear my banjo tell
D   A
Got my rifle on my back, my powder it is dry
D   G   D
Goin' 'cross the mountain, Chrissy, don't you cry.

D   A
Goin' across the mountain to join the boys in blue
D   G   D
When the war is over, I'll come back to you
D   A
Goin' across the mountain if I have to crawl
D   G   D
Give old cap's men some of my rifle ball.

Waitin' for it's good n' daylight, if nothin' happens to me
I'll be wary down yonder in old Tennessee
I'll expect you'll miss me when I'm gone, but I'm goin' through
When this fightin's over, I'll come back to you.

Got my own waist coat, got my mountain dew
Chrissy, don't you worry 'cause I'll come back to you
I'm goin' across the mountain, oh fare you well
Goin' 'cross the mountain, you can hear my banjo tell.

GOIN' DOWN THIS ROAD FEELIN' BAD

Traditional Bluegrass Song;. **DATE:** Early 1900's; **CATEGORY:** Early Country and Bluegrass Songs; **RECORDING INFO:** Bill Monroe; Ralph Stanley; Tommy Jarrell; Wade Ward; **OTHER NAMES:** Lonesome Road Blues; Levee Moan; Honey Your Hair Grows Too Long; East Coast Blues. **NOTES:** Chilly Winds is a related version of "Goin' Down This Road Feelin' Bad". Both are frequently categorized under "Lonesome Road Blues." The title appears in a list of traditional Ozark Mountain fiddle tunes compiled by musicologist/folklorist Vance Randolph, published in 1954. Mt. Airy, North Carolina, fiddler and banjo player Tommy Jarrell learned the tune in early in the 20th century and played it in AEAE tuning. Skillet Lickers included it in their skit "A Corn Likker Still in Georgia" in about 1930, and it was present before then. A bluegrass favorite recorded by Bill Monroe to Doc Watson.

G   **C**   **G**
Going down that road feeling bad, Going down that road feeling bad
C   **G**   **D**   **G**
Going down that road feeling bad, And I ain't gonna be treated this a way

Got me way down in jail on my knees, This jailer, he sure is hard to please
Feed me on corn bread and peas, And I ain't gonna be treated this a way

Sweet mama won't buy me no shoes, She's left with these lonesome jail house blues
My sweet Mama won't buy my no shoes, And I ain't gonna be treated this a way

These two dollar shoes they hurt my feet, The jailer won't give me enough to eat
These two dollar shoes they hurt my feet, And I ain't gonna be treated this a way

I'm going where the climate suits my clothes, I'm going where these chilly winds don't blow
I'm going where the climate suits my clothes, And I ain't gonna be treated this a way.

GRANDFATHER'S CLOCK

Old-Time Breakdown and Song. Words and Music by Henry Clay Work, Dedicated to his Sister Lizzie; **DATE:** 1876; **CATEGORY:** Fiddle and Instrumental Tunes; **RECORDING INFO:** Country Gentlemen; Homer and the Barnstormers; Sons of the Pioneers; Doc Watson; **NOTES:** Famous bluegrass instrumental and song tune by Henry Clay Work, usually in the key of G.

C	G	C	F	C	G	C

My grandfather's clock was too large for the shelf, So it stood ninety years on the floor;

	G	C	F	C	G	C

It was taller by half than the old man himself, Though it weighed not a pennyweight more.

C	E7	Am	F	G	C		D7	G

It was bought on the morn of the day that he was born, And was always his treasure and pride.

C	G	C	F		C	G	C

But it stopp'd short, never to go again, When the old man died.

GRANDFATHER'S CLOCK (ADDITIONAL VERSES)

Chorus:

       C   F   C
Ninety years without slumbering
Tick, tock, tick, tock,
                       F   C
His life seconds numbering,
Tick, tock, tick, tock
    C   G   C   F
It stopp'd short, never to go again
           C   G   C
When the old man died.

In watching its pendulum swing to and fro,
Many hours had he spent while a boy;
And in childhood and manhood the clock seemed to know,
And to share both his grief and his joy.
For it struck twenty-four when he entered the door,
With a blooming and beautiful bride.
But it stopp'd short, never to go again,
When the old man died.   *Chorus*

My grandfather said, that of those he could hire,
Not a servant so faithful he found:
For it wasted no time, and had but one desire,
At the close of each week to be wound.
And it kept in its place, not a frown upon its face,
And its hands never hung by its side;
But it stopp'd short, never to go again,
When the old man died.   *Chorus*

It rang an alarm in the dead of the night,
And alarm that for years had been dumb;
And we know that his spirit was pluming its flight,
That his hour of departure had come.
Still the clock kept the time, with a soft muffled chime,
As we silently stood by his side;
But it stopp'd short, never to go again,
When the old man died.   *Chorus*

GREAT SPECKLED BIRD

Traditional Southern Gospel; **CATEGORY:** Fiddle and Instrumental Tunes; **DATE:** Early 1900's; **RECORDING INFO:** Roy Acuff; Wade Mainer; Monroe's Boys; **SAME MELODY:** "Wild Side Of Life;" "It Wasn't God Who Made Honky Tonk Angels;" "I'm Thinking Tonight Of My Blue Eyes;" **OTHER NAMES:** Great Speckle Bird; **NOTES:** Roy Acuff began his recording career in 1936, when William R. Calaway of the American Radio Corporation heard him singing The Great Speckled Bird. Set to the melody of the popular song "I'm Thinking Tonight of My Blue Eyes," Speckled Bird came to Acuff through the performances of a Knoxville radio group, Charlie Swain and the Black Shirts. The authorship of this famous song will probably always remain unknown, although it has been attributed to a Rev. Gant and to Rev. Guy Smith. The song, which pictures the church as a group of persecuted individuals who ultimately will gain eternal salvation as a reward for their earthly travail, is based upon the ninth verse of the twelfth chapter of Jeremiah: 'Mine heritage is unto me as a speckled bird, the birds round about are against her.'

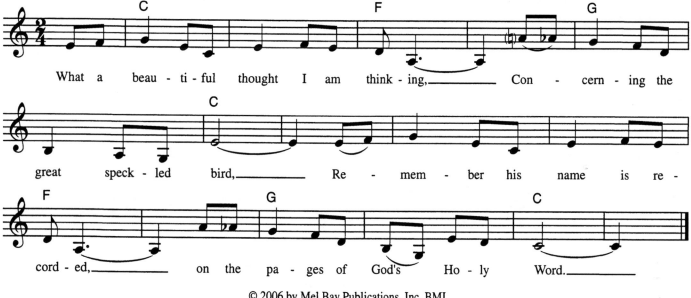

         C   **F**
What a beautiful thought I am thinking
         G   **C**
Concerning the great speckled bird
                                F
Remember her name is recorded
         G   **C**
On the pages of God's Holy Word.

There are many who'd lower her standards
And they watch ev'ry move that she makes;
They just want to find fault with her teachings,
Tho' they search, they can find no mistakes.

I am glad I have learned of her meekness
I am proud that my name is in the book
For I want to be one never fearing
On the face of my Savior to look

When He comes on a cloud in the morning,
And His voice 'round the earth shall be heard;
Oh, I want to be ready to meet Him
And go up on that Great Speckled Bird.

GREEN PASTURES

Traditional Southern Gospel based on a hymn composed by Isaac Watts; **DATE:** 1709; **CATEGORY:** Fiddle and Instrumental Tunes; **RECORDING INFO:** Emmylou Harris with Gillian Welch and David Rawlings on Down From The Mountain from the movie, *O Brother, Where Art Thou?* **NOTES:** This graceful hymn dates back to 1709, being composed by Isaac Watts. Its original title was "The Hopes of Heaven Our Support Under Trials on Earth " which was shortened to the title in the hymnal, "Saints Delight." Among the folk song community, the song is probably better known as "Green Pastures." Congregations in Southern Appalachia have sung this song for well over 200 years, following the melody and harmony in their "shape-note" hymnals.

```
G                    C           G         D
```
Troubles and trials   often betray those, Out in the weary body to stray
```
             G           C           G    D     G
```
But we shall walk beside the still waters, With the Good Shepherd leading the way.

Those who have strayed were sought by the Master
He who once gave His life for the sheep
Out on the mountain still He is searching
Bringing them in forever to keep.

Going up home to live in green pastures
Where we shall live and die never more
Even the Lord will be in that number
When we shall reach that heavenly shore.

We will not heed the voice of the stranger
For he would lead us to despair
Following on with Jesus our Saviour
We shall all reach that country so fair.
(Repeat 3rd verse)

GROUND HOG

Traditional Old-Time Song Tune and Breakdown. **DATE:** Circa 1850's; **CATEGORY:** Fiddle and Instrumental Tunes; **OTHER NAMES:** Groundhog; The Ground-Hog Song; Whistle-Pig; **RECORDING INFO:** Cockerham, Jarrell and Jenkins; Dillards; Doc Watson; Tommy Jarrell; Frank Proffit; **NOTES:** A well-known Appalachian folk song, nursery and fun song, and banjo tune. Brown says, "Its appearence in the Ozarks is doubtless due to immigration from Kentucky. It has not been found in the northern states, nor is it a Negro song." From Tommy Jarrell (solo fiddle) to Flatt and Scruggs, "Groundhog" is a bluegrass favorite. February 2nd (Groundhog Day) is the date when farmers and other folk congregate to see if the groundhog casts a shadow. This forecasts an early or late spring.

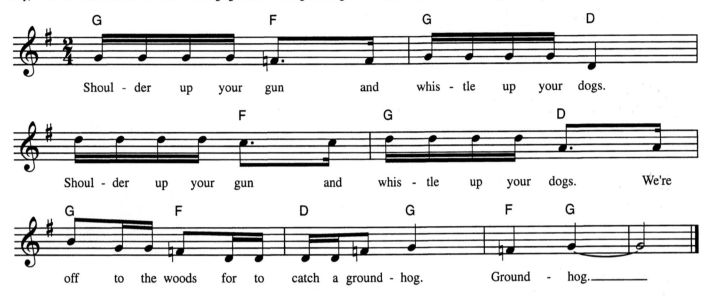

```
G              F    G       D
```
Shoulder up your gun and whistle up your dog,
```
                  F    G       D
```
Shoulder up your gun and whistle up your dog,
```
     G     F     D       G  F  G
```
We're off to the woods to catch a groundhog, groundhog.

Children all around, they screamed and cried,
Children all around, they screamed and cried;
They love a groundhog stewed and fried, and fried.

Yonder comes Rhody with a very big pole,
Yonder comes Rhody with a very big pole,
To run these groundhogs outta their hole, their hole.

I skin his hide and I tan his hide;
I skin his hide and I tan his hide;
Lordy, Lordy, Mammy, I got my pride, my pride.

Yonder comes sister with a twinkle and a grin,
Yonder comes sister with a twinkle and a grin,
Groundhog grease all over her chin, her chin.

HALLELUJAH I'M READY

Traditional Bluegrass Gospel; Additional verse by Susan O. Hinton; **DATE:** Early 1900's; **CATEGORY:** Early Southern Gospel Songs; **RECORDING INFO:** Bill Monroe; Bob Dylan; Ricky Skaggs; **OTHER NAMES:** Hallelujah I'm Ready To Go; **NOTES:** One of the popular call and response style traditional Southern gospel songs. On Bluegrass Messenger's "Bluegrass Boogie" CD.

Chorus: Hallelujah (I am ready), I am ready (hallelujah!)
        C   **G**

                                D
I can hear the voices singing soft and low.
       C   **G**   **D**   **G**
Hallelujah (I am ready), I am ready (hallelujah!) Hallelujah, I'm ready to go!
                          C   **G**
1. In the darkness of night not a star was in sight,
                   D
On the highway that leads down below.
G   **C**   **G**   **D**   **G**
But Jesus came in and saved my soul from sin, Hallelujah, I'm ready to go!

2. When He comes on that cloud with a great mighty shout,
I'll be caught up with the saints of old;
As I meet Him in the air, all my friends will be there, Hallelujah, I'm ready to go!

3. Oh now sinners don't wait until it's too late,
He's a wonderful Savior you know.
Well I fell on my knees and He answered my pleas, Hallelujah, I'm ready to go!

Hallelujah We Shall Rise

Bluegrass Gospel- Words and Music by John E. Thomas; **DATE:** 1904; **CATEGORY:** Early Southern Gospel; **RECORDING INFO:** Cranford and Thompson (Red Fox Chasers) NC; Sauceman Brothers; Stanley Brothers; **OTHER NAMES:** We Shall Rise (Carter Family); **NOTES:** John E. Thomas was born in Calhoun Co. Arkansas in 1860. He studied with T.E. Bridges and helped found the Trio Music Co. in Fort Worth, Texas.

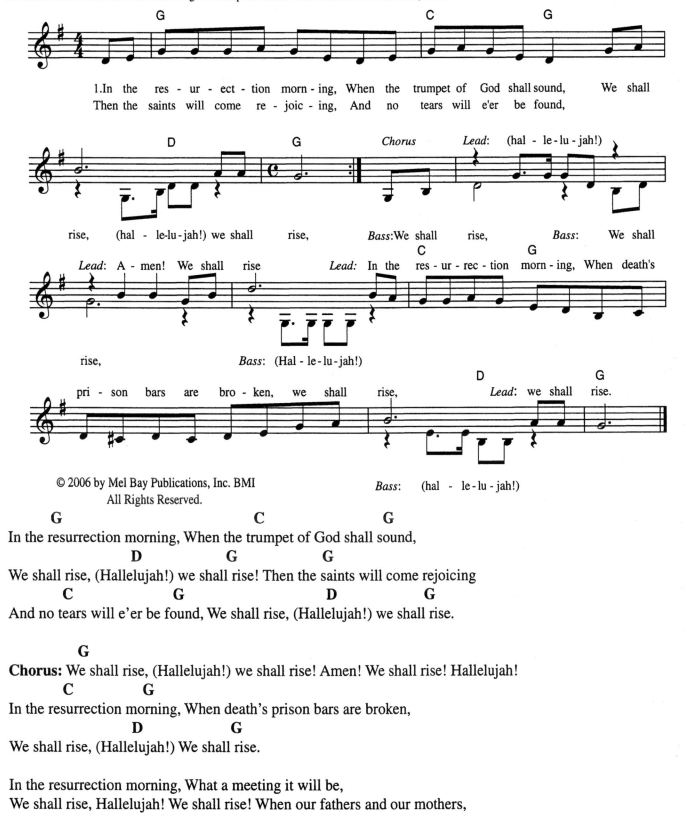

G   C   G
In the resurrection morning, When the trumpet of God shall sound,
            D   G   G
We shall rise, (Hallelujah!) we shall rise! Then the saints will come rejoicing
     C   G   D   G
And no tears will e'er be found, We shall rise, (Hallelujah!) we shall rise.

       G
Chorus: We shall rise, (Hallelujah!) we shall rise! Amen! We shall rise! Hallelujah!
    C   G
In the resurrection morning, When death's prison bars are broken,
      D   G
We shall rise, (Hallelujah!) We shall rise.

In the resurrection morning, What a meeting it will be,
We shall rise, Hallelujah! We shall rise! When our fathers and our mothers,
And our loved ones we shall see, We shall rise, Hallelujah! we shall rise!   *Chorus*

In the resurrection morning, Blessed thought it is to me,
We shall rise, Hallelujah! we shall rise! I shall see my blessed Savior,
Who so freely died for me, We shall rise, Hallelujah! we shall rise!   *Chorus*

HANDSOME MOLLY

Traditional Old-Time Song; Widely known **DATE:** 1927 recording, Grayson & Whitter; **CATEGORY:** Fiddle and Instrumental Tunes; **RECORDING INFO:** Doc Watson & Gaither Carlton; Country Gentlemen; New Lost City Ramblers; Stanley Brothers; Norman Blake; Flatt & Scruggs; **NOTES:** Handsome Molly is a version of the "Irish Girl/Farewell Ballymoney" branches of tunes. Farewell Ballymoney branch includes the titles "Black-Eyed Mary" "Lovely Molly" and "Loving Hannah." This version is based on the Grayson and Whitter recording.

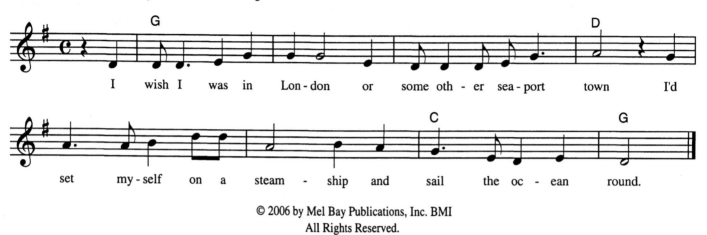

    G   **D**
Well I wish I was in London or some other seaport town
    D   **C**   **G**
I'd set my foot on a steamboat sail the ocean round
    G   **D**
Sailin' around the ocean, sailin' around the sea
    D   **C**   **G**
I'd think of handsome Molly wherever she may be

Her hair was black as a raven's, her eyes were bright as coal
Her teeth shone like lilies out in the morning cold
Sailin' around the ocean, sailin' around the sea
I'd think of handsome Molly wherever she may be

Do you remember Molly when you give me your right hand
Said if you ever married that I would be your man
Saw her in church last Sunday she passed me on by
I could tell her mind was changing by the roving of her eye

Well I wish I was in London or other seaport town
I'd set my foot on a steamboat sail the ocean round
Sailin' around the ocean, sailin' around the sea
I'd think of handsome Molly wherever she may be.

HE WILL SET YOUR FIELDS ON FIRE

Southern Gospel, H.M. Ballew words, Mrs. L.L. Brackett music; **DATE:** Unknown, circa early 1900's; **CATEGORY:** Early Southern Gospel Songs; **RECORDING INFO:** Johnson County Ramblers, Monroe Brothers- Bill Monroe; Charlie Moore and the Dixie Partners; Reno & Smiley. **NOTES:** A favorite Southern gospel song from the early 1900's.

      G   **C**   **G**
There's a call that rings from the throne it springs to those have gone astray
                              A   **D**
Saying, "Come ye men and your load of sin there at the alter lay."
     G   **C**   **G**
You don't seem to heed for the chain of greed your conscience never tires
  C   **G**   **E**   **A**   **D** **G**
Be assured my friend if you still offend, He will set your world on fire.

HE WILL SET YOUR FIELDS ON FIRE

```
        G                                      C            G
There's a call that rings from the throne it springs to those have gone astray
                                        A        D
Saying, "Come ye men and your load of sin there at the alter lay."
        G                                      C            G
You don't seem to heed for the chain of greed your conscience never tires
        C              G      E      A      D      G
Be assured my friend if you still offend, He will set your world on fire.
```

```
            G                                          D
Chorus: If you  don't from sin retire, He will set your fields on fire
                                                  G
You have heard Jesus call and in death your soul must fall
                                                  C
But my friend if you desire, you may join the Heavenly Choir
                          G      E      A      D      G
And rejoice with Him, free from every sin when He sets this world on fire.
```

```
        G                                  C            G
Take a friend's advice, make the sacrifice, completely turn from sin
                                      A          D
Taking up the cross, counting earth as dross, let Jesus live within
        G                                  C        G
When temptations come keep on facing home, to Satan never hire
        C              G      E      A      D      G
But rejoice and pray on the last great day when He sets this world on fire.
```

HESITATION BLUES

Traditional Old-Time Blues Song; **DATE:** Early 1900's, W.C. Handy- 1915; **CATEGORY:** Old-Time Blues Songs; **RECORDING INFO:** Jerry Garcia and David Grisman; Kenny Hall and the Sweets Mill String Band; Holy Modal Rounders; Bascam Lamar Lunsford; Charlie Poole and the North Carolina Ramblers; Doc and Merle Watson; Old Crowe Medicine Show; **OTHER NAMES:** If the River Was Whiskey; The Hesitating Blues; **NOTES:** There are many different sources and versions of this blues song. The main versions are: WC Handy's "Hesitating Blues"; Charlie Poole's "If the River Was Whiskey"; Rev. Gary Davis's "Hesitation Blues." The lyrics from Hesitation Blues are generally floaters from other songs, especially the "Rye Whiskey/Jack O'Diamonds" group.

D
1. If the river was whiskey and I was a duck
                         D7
I'd dive to the bottom and I'd never come up
                 G   **D**
Chorus: Oh, tell me how long have I got to wait
          A7   **D**
       Oh, can I get you now, must I hesitate?

2. If the river was whiskey and the branch was wine
    You would see me in bathing just any old time.   *Chorus*
3. I was born in England, raised in France
    I ordered a suit of clothes and they wouldn't send the pants.   *Chorus*
4. I was born in Alabama, I's raised in Tennessee
    If you don't like my peaches, don't shake on my tree
5. I ain't no doctor but the doctor's son
    I can do the doct'rin' till the doctor comes
6. Got the hesitation stockings, the hesitation shoes
    Believe to my Lord I've got the hesitation blues

HOG-EYE MAN

Traditional Old-Time Breakdown and Song; **DATE:** Hog Eye-Jigg 1853; From Cecil Sharp's EFSSA, sung by Miss Lizzie Abner Oneida School, Clat County, KY Aug, 18 1917; Pope's Arkansas Mountaineers 1928 recording; **CATEGORY:** Fiddle and Instrumental Tunes. **RECORDING INFO:** Arkansas Sheiks; New Lost City Ramblers; Hollow Rock String Band; Luther Strong; **OTHER NAMES:** Hog-Eye; Hog Eye and' a 'Tater; Hog-Eyed Man; Sally in the Garden; Granny Will Your Dog Bite; Fire on the Mountain; **NOTES:** "Hog-Eyed Man" is a well-known fiddle tune in the older repertory of the South. A nineteenth-century set in Winner's Collection of Music for the Violin, p. 75 "Hog Eye-Jigg" suggests that the song may have had some circulation on the popular stage. "Jigs" of this sort were a mid-nineteenth-century American genre in 2/4 time often associated with the minstrel stage or other popular entertainment. Modern song and fiddle versions suggest that it was widespread in Southern tradition and may have gone from there to the popular stage, not the other way around. There may be an African-American connection to the song; it is certain that a sailor's shanty, with associated lyrics but a different tune, turns up in older sea shanty collections. The words to the song are typically bawdy.

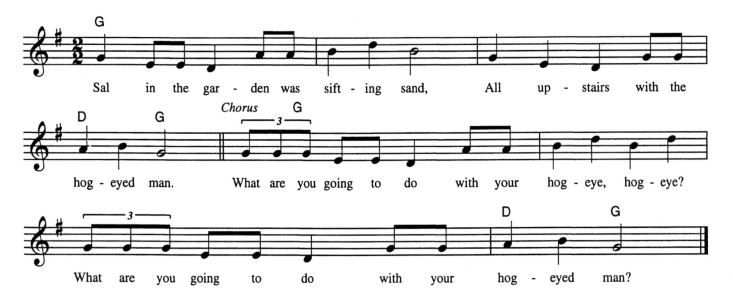

G
Sal's in the garden sifting sand,
                    D   **G**
All upstairs with the hog-eyed man.

               G
Chorus: What are you going to do with your hog-eye, hog-eye?
                      D   **G**
What are you going to do with your hog-eye man?

Chicken in the bread pan peckin' out dough
Sally will your dog bite No, child, no.   *Chorus*

I went down to hog-eye town, Dey sot me down to table
I et so much dat hog-eye grease, Till the grease run out my nabel.   *Chorus*

HOLD TO GOD'S UNCHANGING HAND

Southern Gospel; Jennie Wilson- words, F. L. Eiland- music; **DATE:** 1905; **CATEGORY:** Early Gospel Songs; **RECORDING INFO:** Vaughan Quartet-1926; Smith's Sacred Singers; EC and Orna Ball; Rev. Gary Davis; Cockman Family; **NOTES:** Born in 1857 on a farm in South Whitley Indiana, Jennie Wilson was stricken with spinal sickness and spent most of her 56 years in a wheelchair. She studied music at home and wrote over 2,200 poems.

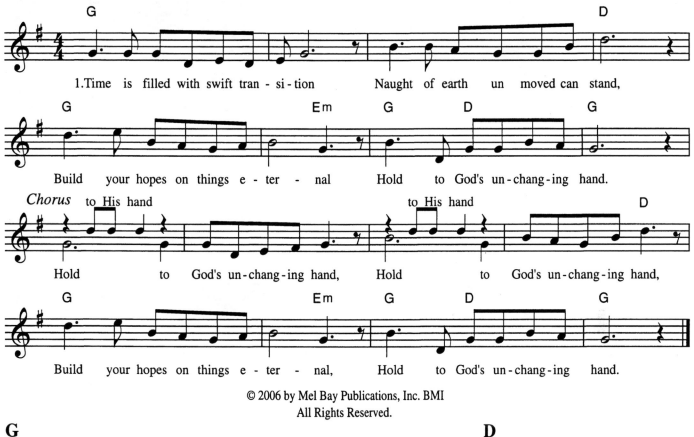

G   **D**
Time is filled with swift transition, 'Naught of earth unmoved can stand
G   **Em G**   **D**   **G**
Build your hopes on things eternal, Hold to God's unchanging hand.

                        G
Chorus: Hold (to His hand) to God's unchanging hand
                                      D
Hold (to His hand) to God's unchanging hand
G   **Em G**   **D**   **G**
Build your hopes on things eternal, Hold to God's unchanging hand.

Trust in Him who will not leave you, What so ever years may bring
If by earthly friends forsaken, Still more closely to him cling.   *Chorus*

Covet not this world's vain riches, That so rapidly decay
Seek to gain the Heavenly treasures, They will never pass away.   *Chorus*

When your journey is completed, When the valley you pass through
Fair, and bright the Home in glory, Your enraptured soul will view.   *Chorus*

HOME! SWEET HOME!

Bluegrass Breakdown and Song- words by John Howard Payne, music by Henry Rowley Bishop. Revised bluegrass lyrics by Richard L. Matteson Jr. 2002; **DATE:** Published 1823; **CATEGORY:** Fiddle and Instrumental Tunes; **RECORDING INFO:** Elizabeth Cotton; Flatt & Scruggs & the Foggy Mountain Boys; Don Reno; Red Smiley and the Tennessee Cut Ups; Skillet Lickers; **NOTES:** The home that Payne wrote of was a little cottage in East Hampton, Long Island. The song was first heard in London in his play "Clari" in 1823. The air had appeared in an early collection of Bishop's as a Sicilian tune. The theme of the song and the beauty of the melody have given it world-wide fame. Most bluegrass groups play "Home Sweet Home" as an instrumental. Recording is available on bluegrassmessengers.com. The melody of the chorus is the same as the second half of the verse.

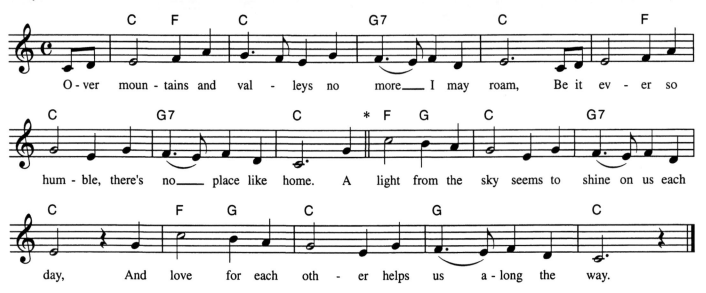

```
        C      F         C      G7          C
Over mountains and valleys no more we may roam
          F      C          G7            C
Be it ever so humble, there's no place like home
    F   G      C          G7          C
A light from the sky seems to guide us each day
        F   G      C        G          C
And love for each other helps us along the way.


                 F  G      C              G          C
Chorus: Home ! Sweet Home. There's no place like home.
              F  G      C              G          C
        Home ! Sweet Home. There's no place like home.
```

Repeat Verse

Repeat Chorus

* Melody of chorus

HOP UP, MY LADIES (HOP HIGH LADIES)

Traditional Old-Time Breakdown and Song (Miss McCleod's Reel/ McCloud's Reel). **DATE:** The British Isles at the beginning of the nineteenth century (Early 1800's). **CATEGORY:** Fiddle and Instrumental Tunes; **RECORDING INFO:** Uncle Dave Macon-1927; Fiddlin' Powers & Family; New Lost City Ramblers; Holy Modal Rounders; Clark Kessinger; Doc Roberts, Charlie Poole and the North Carolina Ramblers; Skillet Lickers; **OTHER NAMES:** "Uncle Joe," "Hop Light Lady," "Hop High Ladies, the Cake's All Dough," "Did You Ever See The Devil, Uncle Joe?," "Hop Up Ladies," "Miss McCloud's/McCloud's Reel" "(Miss) McCloud's Reel," "Miss McLeod's Reel," "Did You Ever Go To Meetin' Uncle Joe, Uncle Joe?" "Do You Want to go to Heaven, Uncle Joe?" **NOTES:** An American 'old-time' version of the Scottish "Miss McCloud's/Miss McLeod's Reel," the main difference being that the old-time version resolves to the tonic on the cadence, while the Scottish tune generally ends on the dominant. Lomax included collection Our Singing Country. That set is from the playing and singing of Fields and Wade Ward of Galax, Virginia, and Aaron Copland took the tune from the Lomax book (as Ruth Crawford Seeger had transcribed it) to use as the second instrumental tune in the "Hoedown" of Aaron Copland's music for Rodeo. The tune was also used in the world of popular music for another song, "Uncle Joe" ("Do you want to go to heaven, Uncle Joe?"), so some fiddlers know it by that title. Outside of the South, the tune is usually called either "McLeod's Reel" or "Miss McCloud's Reel."

    A
Did you ever go to meetin', Uncle Joe, Uncle Joe?
    E
Did you ever go to meetin', Uncle Joe, Uncle Joe?
    A
Did you ever go to meetin', Uncle Joe, Uncle Joe?
  D   **A**   **E7**   **A**
Don't mind the weather so the wind don't blow.

HOP UP, MY LADIES (ADDITIONAL VERSES)

        A
Chorus: Hop up, my ladies, three in a row,
               B7   **E7**
Hop up, my ladies, three in a row,
A
Hop up, my ladies, three in a row,
         D   **A**   **E7**   **A7**
Don't mind the weather so the wind don't blow.

Would you rather own a pacer, Uncle Joe, Uncle Joe
Would you rather own a pacer, Uncle Joe, Uncle Joe
Would you rather own a pacer, Uncle Joe, Uncle Joe
Don't mind the weather so the wind don't blow.   *Chorus*

Will your horse carry double, Uncle Joe, Uncle Joe
Will your horse carry double, Uncle Joe, Uncle Joe
Will your horse carry double, Uncle Joe, Uncle Joe
Don't mind the weather so the wind don't blow.   *Chorus*

Say, you don't want to gallop, Uncle Joe, Uncle Joe
Say, you don't want to gallop, Uncle Joe, Uncle Joe
Say, you don't want to gallop, Uncle Joe, Uncle Joe
Don't mind the weather so the wind don't blow.   *Chorus*

Is your horse a single-footer, Uncle Joe, Uncle Joe
Is your horse a single-footer, Uncle Joe, Uncle Joe
Is your horse a single-footer, Uncle Joe, Uncle Joe
Don't mind the weather so the wind don't blow.   *Chorus*

Say, you might take a tumble, Uncle Joe, Uncle Joe
Say, you might take a tumble, Uncle Joe, Uncle Joe
Say, you might take a tumble, Uncle Joe, Uncle Joe
Don't mind the weather so the wind don't blow.   *Chorus*

Well, we'll get there soon as t'others, Uncle Joe, Uncle Joe
Well, we'll get there soon as t'others, Uncle Joe, Uncle Joe
Well, we'll get there soon as t'others, Uncle Joe, Uncle Joe
Don't mind the weather so the wind don't blow.   *Chorus*

HOT CORN, COLD CORN

Traditional Old-Time Song Tune; **DATE:** Earliest report-1859; **CATEGORY:** Fiddle and Instrumental Tunes; **RECORDING INFO:** New Lost City Ramblers; Holy Modal Rounders; Don Reno and Bill Harrell with the Tennesse Cutups; Flatt and Scruggs; **OTHER NAMES:** "Green Corn," "Green Corn, Come Along Charlie," "I'll Meet You in the Evening," "Barnyard Banjo Pickin';" **NOTES:** A nonsense song popular with both blacks and whites, according to Charles Wolfe. It is attributed by a least one source to singer and guitarist Asa Martin of Estill County, Kentucky, although his version seems to be from tradition. The famous bluegrass duo Flatt and Scruggs performed it under this title. African-American collector Thomas Talley, in his book *Negro Folk Rhymes*, published a version under the title "Bring on Your Hot Corn," apparently the first time it appeared in print, although Randolf (2:342-343) has a version called "I'll Meet You in the Evening." Wolfe points out it was recorded by Leadbelly as "Green Corn, Come Along Charlie."

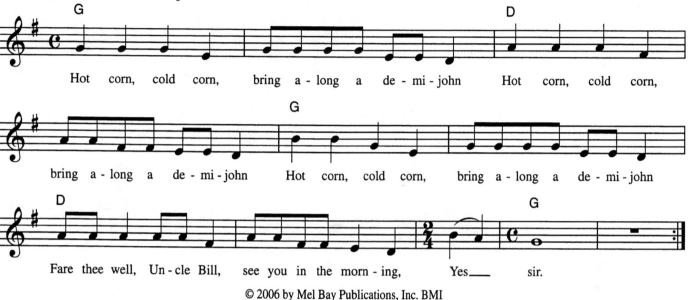

G
Hot corn, cold corn, bring along a demijohn
D
Hot corn, cold corn, bring along a demijohn
G
Hot corn, cold corn, bring along a demijohn
D   **G**
Fare thee well, Uncle Bill, see you in the morning, Yes sir.

Upstairs, downstairs, down in the kitchen
Upstairs, downstairs, down in the kitchen
Upstairs, downstairs, down in the kitchen
See Uncle Bill, he's a raring and pitching, Yes sir.

Old Aunt Peggy won't you fill 'em up again
Old Aunt Peggy won't you fill 'em up again
Old Aunt Peggy won't you fill 'em up again
Ain't had a drink since I don't know when, Yes sir.

Yonder comes the preacher and the children are a crying
Yonder comes the preacher and the children are a crying
Yonder comes the preacher and the children are a crying
Chickens are a hollering, toenails are a flying, Yes sir.

HOUND DOG SONG (GOTTA QUIT KICKIN' MY DOG AROUND)

Traditional Old-Time, Breakdown; **DATE:** Late 1800's. Popularized in 1912 as a campaign song. **CATEGORY:** Fiddle and Instrumental Tunes; **RECORDING INFO:** Gid Tanner and His Skillet Lickers; **OTHER NAMES:** Gotta Quit Kickin My Dog Around; Every Time I Go To Town; **NOTES:** This was the campaign song of Champ Clark, senator from Missouri, during his campaign for President of the United States. He lost. Randolph heard a story which based this on a pre-Civil War incident in Forsyth, Missouri. Proof is, of course, lacking. "They Gotta Quit Kickin' My Dog Aroun'" was a comedy favorite for James Bland's minstrel troupe. The melody of "The Hound Dog Song" is similar to "Sally Ann" and "Great Big Taters."

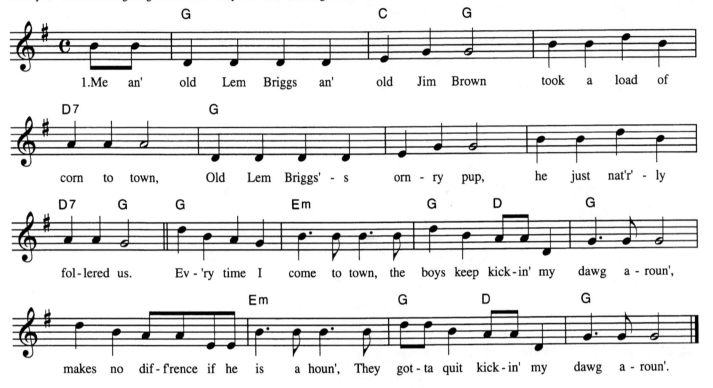

　　　　　　　G　　　　　**Em**　　　　　　**G**　　　**D**　　　**G**

Chorus: Well, everytime I go to town, The boys keep kickin' my dog around.

　　　　　　　　　　　　　　Em　　　　　　**G**　　　**D**　　　**G**

It makes no diff'rence if he is a hound, They've gotta quit kickin' my dog around.

　　　　G　　　　　　　　**C**　　　**G**　　　　　　　**D7**

Me an' ol' Lem Briggs and ol' Bill Brown, Took a load of corn to town

G　　　　　　　　　　　　　　　　　　　**D7**　　　**G**

Ol' Lem Briggs's ornery pup, He just naturally follered us.

They tied a can to old Jim's tail; An' run him a-past the county jail;
That just naturally made us sore, Lem, he cussed an' Bill he swore.

As we passed by Johnson's store, A passel of yaps came out the door.
It made my Jim hide under a box, With all of them fellers a throwin' rocks.

Me an' Lem Briggs an' old Bill Brown, Lost no time a-gittin' down;
We wiped them fellers on the ground, For kickin' my old Jim dawg around.

HOUSE OF THE RISING SUN

Traditional Old-Time Song; **DATE:** Early 1900's; **CATEGORY:** Early Country and Bluegrass Songs; **RECORDING INFO:** Tom Ashley and Gwen Foster recorded Rising Sun Blues on September 6, 1933 on Vocalion 02576; Texas Alexander recorded "The Risin' Sun" on November 15, 1928 [OK 8673]; Homer Callahan recorded "Rounder's Luck" on 11 April 1935 - issued on ARC in February 1936; Recorded by E. Tubb in 1936 (both he and Acuff where on Grand Old Opry); Roy Acuff recorded 'Rising Sun' on November 3, 1938 - issued as Vo/OK 04909 in August 1939.: Recorded by Josh White in 942, copyrighted by Leeds Music Corp., N.Y.; Mike Auldridge; Joan Baez; Bob Dylan; Country Gentlemen; Roscoe Holcomb and Wade Ward (Rising Sun); Leadbelly; Doc Watson; Seldom Scene; **OTHER NAMES:** In New Orleans; Rising Sun Blues; **NOTES:** In 1905 "House of the Rising Sun" is said to have been known by miners. Clarence Ashley said he taught "Rising Sun Blues" or "House of the Rising Sun" to Roy Acuff after 1924, when Acuff graduated from high school in Knoxville and joined Dr Hauers Medicine Show. Ashley has said that he thought he recalled his grandmother, Enoch Ashley, singing it to him when he was a young boy. R. Shelton has in the *Josh-White-Songbook* the following information: "He (J. White) learned "Rising Sun" from a white hillbilly singer in N.C. His only time in North Carolina was in 1923 and early 1924, when he had been leased out by Arnold to Blind Lemmon Jefferson whom he led through the major cities of N.C., the same area Clarence Ashley toured with a medicine show since 1911. Ashley might have been the "white hillbilly singer." In 1937 a "ragged Kentucky Mountain girl" sang it to A. Lomax.

There is   a___   house   in   New   Or - leans,   They   call   the

Ris - ing___   Sun._____   It's   been   the   ru - in   of   man - y   a   poor___

boy,   and   me,   oh   Lord,___   I'm___   one.   If   Sun.

| Am | C | D | F | **Am** | C | E7 E7 |

There is a house in New Orleans, they call the Rising Sun.

| Am | C | D | F | Am | E | Am |

It's been the ruin of many a poor boy, and me, O Lord, I'm one.

My mother, she's a tailor; she sold those new blue jeans.
My father was a gamblin' man way down in New Orleans.

The only thing a drunkard needs is a suitcase and a trunk.
The only time he's satisfied is when he's on a drunk.

Fills his glasses to the brim, pass them around.
Only pleasure he gets out of life is hoboin' from town to town.

One foot is on the platform and the other one on the train,
I'm going back to New Orleans to wear that ball and chain.

Going back to New Orleans, my race is almost run.
Going to spend the rest of my days beneath that Rising Sun.

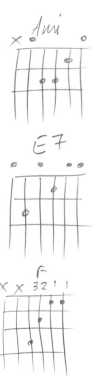

How Beautiful Heaven Must Be

Bluegrass Southern Gospel-Mrs. A. B. Bridgewater and A.P. Bland; **DATE:** Unknown-circa early 1900's; **CATEGORY:** Early Southern Gospel; **RECORDING INFO:** First recorded by Eva Quartet in 1927; Monroe Brothers; Uncle Dave Macon; **OTHER NAMES:** "We Read of a Place Called Heaven;" **NOTES:** Chosen by Grand Ole Opry star Uncle Dave Macon as his theme song, it was also carved on his tombstone.

G
We read of a place that's called Heaven,
               D
It's made for the pure and the free;
  G
These truths in God's Word He hath given,
        D   **G**
How beautiful Heaven must be.

     G   **C**   **G**
Chorus: How beautiful Heaven must be,
         A7   **D**
Sweet home of the happy and free;
 G
Fair haven of rest for the weary,
        D   **G**
How beautiful Heaven must be.

In Heaven no drooping nor pining,
No wishing for elsewhere to be;
God's light is forever there shining,
How beautiful Heaven must be. *Chorus*

Pure waters of life there are flowing,
And all who will drink may be free;
Rare jewels of splendor are glowing,
How beautiful Heaven must be. *Chorus*

The angels so sweetly are singing,
Up there by the beautiful sea;
Sweet chords from their gold harps are ringing,
How beautiful Heaven must be. *Chorus*

I Ain't Broke But Brother I'm Badly Bent

Traditional Old-Time and Bluegrass Song; **DATE:** Early 1900's; **CATEGORY:** Early Country and Bluegrass Songs; **RECORDING INFO:** Ricky Skaggs; IIIrd Time Out; Flatt and Scruggs; Delaney Brothers; The (almost) Original New South; **OTHER NAMES:** "I Ain't Broke;" **NOTES:** One of the earliest versions of "I Ain't Broke" is "The Panic Is On " by Hezekiah Jenkins who recorded it for Columbia [Co 14585-D] in 1931. The lyrics include: All the landlords done raised the rent/Folks that ain't broke is badly bent. Paul Oliver has noted that Jenkins' song was "a remodeling of an earlier theme" and therefore it is possible that the expression did not originate with him. Willie Dixon also used the expression in the chorus of his "Dead Presidents."

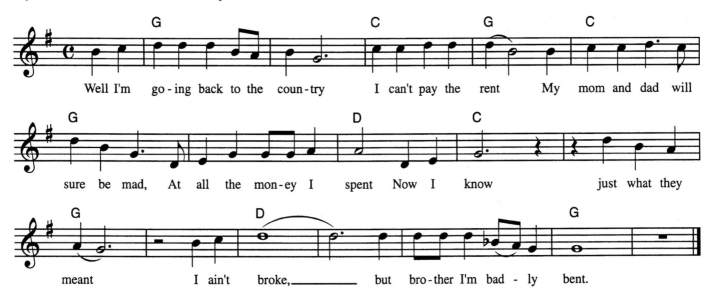

     G   **C**   **G**
Well I'm going back to the country, I can't pay the rent
  C   **G**   **D**
My mom and dad will sure be mad, at all the money I spent
    C   **G**   **D**   **G**
Now I know just what they meant I ain't broke, but brother I'm badly bent.

Well I had a lot of money, But to the city I went
I met a lot of good-looking girls, And that's where my money went.
Now I know just where it went, I ain't broke, but brother I'm badly bent.

Well when I get back to the country, I'll be living in a tent
My mom and dad will sure be mad, At all the money I spent.
They won't understand just where it went, I ain't broke, but brother I'm badly bent.

I Am A Girl of Constant Sorrow/Man Of Constant Sorrow

Traditional Old-Time Song and "Blues;" **DATE:** 1913 Burnett; 1917 Sharp; 1936 Gunning; **CATEGORY:** Early Country and Bluegrass Songs; **RECORDING INFO:** Sarah Ogan Gunning; Barbara Dane; Bonnie Dobson; **OTHER NAMES:** "Farewell Song;" "I Am a Man of Constant Sorrow;" "Maid of Constant Sorrow;" **NOTES:** Sarah Ogan Gunning reworked Emry Arthur's version of "Man of Constant Sorrow" in 1936 with the title, "Girl of Constant Sorrow." Since that time the "Girl" song has entered the folk tradition, with different lyric versions sung by women.

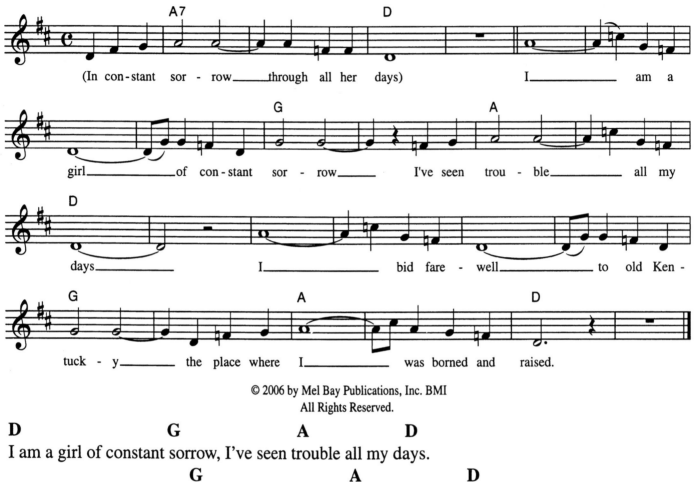

(In con-stant sor-row_____through all her days) I_____ am a girl_____of con-stant sor-row_____ I've seen trou-ble_____ all my days_____ I_____ bid fare-well_____ to old Ken-tuck-y_____ the place where I_____ was borned and raised.

D   G   A   D
I am a girl of constant sorrow, I've seen trouble all my days.
                G   A   D
I bid farewell to old Kentucky, The place where I was born and raised.

My mother, how I hated to leave her, Mother dear who now is dead.
But I had to go and leave her, So my children could have bread.

Perhaps, dear friends, you are wonderin', What the miners eat and wear.
This question I will try to answer, For I'm sure that it is fair.

For breakfast we had bulldog gravy, For supper we had beans and bread.
The miners don't have any dinner, And a tick of straw they call a bed.

Well, we call this hell on earth, friends, I must tell you all goodbye.
Oh, I know you all are hungry, Oh, my darlin' friends, don't cry.

I Am A Pilgrim

Traditional Gospel Song; **DATE:** 1862; **CATEGORY:** Early Southern Gospel; **RECORDING INFO:** Merle Travis on Capitol "Folk Songs of the Hills," 1947; Country Gentlemen; Bill Monroe, Stanley Brothers; Doc Watson; **RELATED TO:** "Wayfaring Stranger;" "Going Over Jordan;" **NOTES:** The origins of this song are entwined with "Poor Wayfaring Stanger" which appears in the Sacred Harp 1844; "I'm a Pilgrim" appears in *The Southern Zion's Songster* printed in Raleigh, NC in 1864 and in *Hymns For the Camp*, in1862 and begins: "I'm a pilgrim and I'm a stranger/I can tarry but a night." This hymn seems to have been a favorite in the South during the Civil War. The current song is similar to Merle Travis's version, who first heard a version of this song from Lyman Rager, who learned it while he was in the Elkton, Kentucky jail.

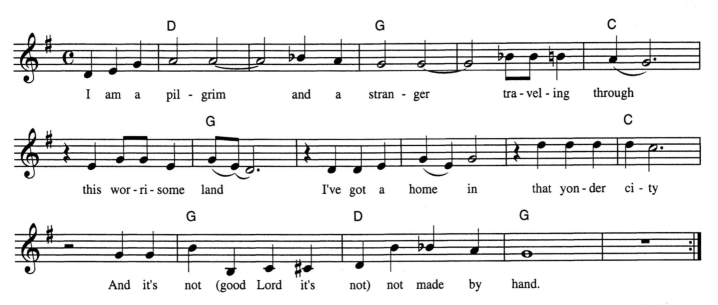

    D   **G**
I am a pilgrim and a stranger
               C   **G**
Traveling through this worrisome land
                  C
I've got a home in that yonder city
    G   **D**   **G**
And it's not (Good Lord it's not), not made by hand

I've got a mother, a sister, and a brother
Who have gone on before
And I'm determined to go and meet them, Good Lord
Over on that other shore *Chorus*

I'm going down to the river of Jordan
Just to cleanse my weary soul
If I could touch but the hem of his garment, Good Lord
I do believe it would make me whole *Chorus*

I Can't Feel At Home In This World Anymore

Traditional Gospel Song; **DATE:** 1919; **CATEGORY:** Early Gospel Songs; **RECORDING INFO:** Carter Family; J.E. Mainer's Mountaineers; The Morris Brothers with Wade Mainer; Monroe Brothers; Blue Sky Boys; **OTHER NAMES:** "I Can't Feel At Home;" "This World Is Not My Home;" **NOTES:** This gospel song was a 'hit' record by the Prairie Ramblers in 1935.

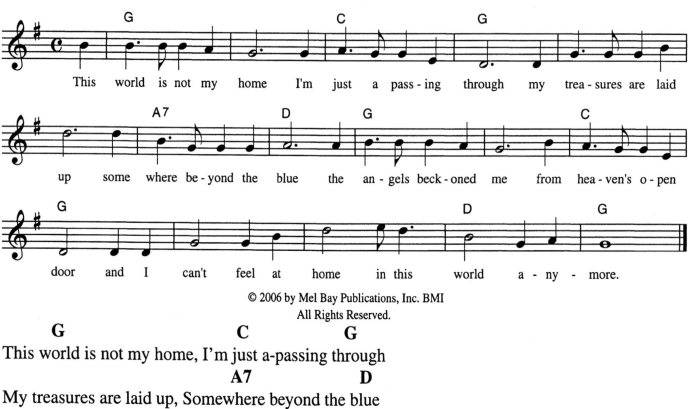

G   **C**   **G**
This world is not my home, I'm just a-passing through
          A7   **D**
My treasures are laid up, Somewhere beyond the blue
G   **C**   **G**
The angels beckon me from Heaven's open door
          D   **G**
And I can't feel at home in this world any more.

Chorus: O Lord, you know, I have no friend like you
If Heaven's not my home, then Lord what will I do?
The angels beckon me from Heaven's open door
And I can't feel at home in this world any more.

They're all expecting me, and that's one thing I know;
My Savior pardoned me and now I onward go
I know he'll take me through, though I am weak and poor
And I can't feel at home in this world any more.

Just up in Gloryland we'll live eternally,
The saints on every hand are shouting victory;
Their song of sweetest praise drifts back from Heaven's door
And I can't feel at home in this world any more.

I FEEL LIKE TRAVELING ON

Southern Gospel Song-William Hunter words; **DATE:** 1912; **CATEGORY:** Early Gospel Songs; **RECORDING INFO:** Frank Welling and John McGee-1928; Reno & Smiley; Hymns, Sacred Gospel Songs, King 693, LP-cut#B.04; Jim & Jesse; Charlie Waller and the Country Gentlemen; **NOTES:** One of the all-time great Southern gospel songs.

     G   **D**

Chorus: Yes I feel like traveling on, I feel like traveling on

     G   **D**   **G**

My heavenly home is bright and fair, I feel like traveling on.

     G   **D**

My heavenly home is bright and fair, I feel like traveling on.

     G   **D**   **G**

Nor pain nor death can enter there, I feel like traveling on

Its glitt'ring tow'rs the sun outshine, I feel like traveling on
That heavenly mansion shall be mine, I feel like traveling on.

Let others seek a home below, I feel like traveling on
Which flames devour or waves o'erflow, I feel like traveling on.

The Lord has been so good to me, I feel like traveling on
Until that blessed home I see, I feel like traveling on.

I HAVE FOUND THE WAY

Bluegrass Gospel; Words and music: Adgar M. Pace and L. A. Green; **DATE**: Early 1900's; **CATEGORY**: Fiddle and Instrumental Tunes; **RECORDING INFO**: Doyle Lawson & Quicksilver on Kept and Protected (1997); Flatt & Scruggs & the Foggy Mountain Boys; Louvin Brothers; Blue Sky Boys; **NOTES**: Adgar M. Pace from South Carolina was born in 1882 and became an important contributor to gospel music. A singer, composer and singing-school teacher, he also served as music editor for Vaughn Publishing Company and was the first president of the National Singing Convention.

    G   **C**   **G**   **D**
I have found the way that leads to endless day, Yonder in the Glory-land.

    G   **C**   **G**   **D**   **G**
And the road is bright for Jesus is the light, And I'll hold His guiding hand.

        C   **G**
Chorus: I have found the way (found the glory way).

          D
I have found the way (found the gospel way).

C   **G**   **D**   **G**
Glory hallelujah (hallelujah), I have found the way.

I will never fear while Jesus is so near, I will bravely meet the foe.
Happy songs I'll sing in honor to the King, And to glory onward go. *Chorus*

To the journey's end led by the Faithful Friend, Never more in sin to roam
By the way called straight I'll reach the Golden Gate Of the soul's eternal home. *Chorus*

I Never Will Marry (Laws K17)

Traditional Old-Time and Bluegrass Ballad; **DATE**: Early 1900's; **CATEGORY:** Early Country and Bluegrass Songs; **RECORDING INFO:** Carter Family-1933; Blue Sky Boys; Flatt & Scruggs & the Foggy Mountain Boys; Joan Baez; Kossoy Sisters; Hank Snow and Anita Carter. **OTHER NAMES**: I'll Never Marry (Country Gentlemen); **NOTES**: This ballad is also known as "Down by the Seashore" and "The Shells of the Ocean."

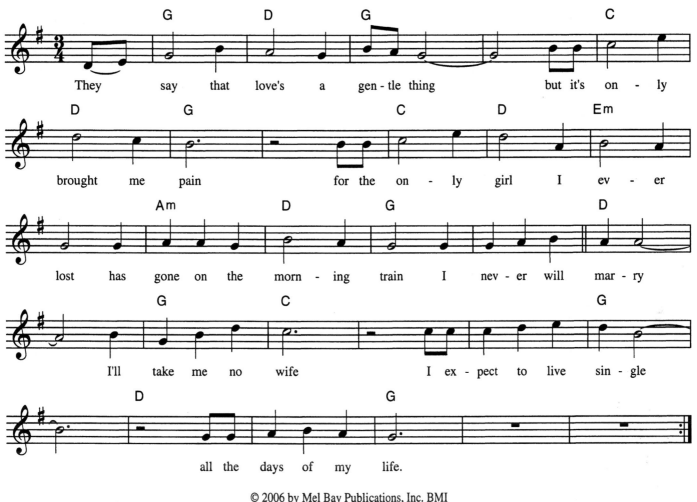

```
         G    D    G            C    D    G
They say that love's a gentle thing, But it's only brought me pain
         C    D    Em      Am        D    G
For the only girl I ever lost, Has gone on the morning train.
              D    G    C
I never will marry, I'll take me no wife
              G    D         G
I expect to live single,     All the days of my life.
```

The train pulled out and the whistle blew, With a long and a lonesome mourn
She's gone, she's gone like the morning dew, And left me all alone.

Well there's many a change in the winter wind, And a change in the clouds design
There's many a change in a young girl's heart, But never a change in mine.

I Shall Not Be Moved

Southern Gospel; Words and Music by Alfred H. Ackley; **DATE:** 1908; **CATEGORY:** Early Southern Gospel; **RECORDING INFO:** Bascam Lamar Lunsford; Gid Tanner; Mississippi John Hurt; Laurel River Band; **OTHER NAMES:** "We Shall Not Be Moved;" **NOTES:** "I Shall Not Be Moved" by Alfred H. Ackley is slightly different from the Southern Gospel version below.

G   C G D   G
Glory Hallelujah,   I shall not be moved, Anchored in Jehovah, I shall not be moved,
          C   G   D   G
Just like a tree that's planted by the water Lord, I shall not be moved.
      G   C G D   G
Chorus: I shall not be,   I shall not be moved, I shall not be, I shall not be moved,
          C   G   D   G
Just like a tree that's planted by the water, Lord I shall not be moved.

Though the tempest rages, I shall not be moved,
On the Rock of Ages, I shall not be moved,
Just like a tree that's planted by the water, I shall not be moved. *Chorus*

On my way to glory land, I shall not be moved
On this hallowed rock I stand, I shall not be moved
I'm like a tree that's planted by the water, I shall not be moved. *Chorus*

I Wish I Was A Mole in the Ground

Old-Time, Song and Breakdown; **DATE:** Early 1900's (1924 was Lunsford's recording); **CATEGORY:** Early Country and Bluegrass Songs; **RECORDING INFO:** Bascom Lamar Lunsford; Tommy Jarrell; Doc and Merle Watson; Hylo Brown; The Pine River Boys; **OTHER NAMES:** "Tempy;" "Mole in the Ground;" "Kimpy;" "My Doney, Where Have You Been So Long;" "Skipping Through the Frost and Snow;" "My Last Dollar;" "Girls, Quit Your Rowdy Ways;" "Alberta, Let Your Hair Hang (Stream) Down;" "Feeling Bad and Low;" "Sammie, Where (Have) You Been So Long;" "Kimble;" **RELATED TO:** "I Don't Like No Railroad Man" (floating lyrics); "My Last Gold Dollar" (floating lyrics); "New River Train" (tune, floating lyrics); "Black Dog Blues" (lyrics); "Hard Rocking Chair" (melody); **NOTES:** Bascom Lamar Lunsford reportedly learned one version in 1901, from Fred Moody of Haywood County, N.C.. How much Lunsford composed "Mole in the Ground" is unknown. The line "When I come back with a forty-dollar bill/ It's "Baby, where you been so long?"" is found in "Black Dog Blues," "My Doney, Where Have You Been So Long;" and Dock Boggs's "Sammie, Where (Have) You Been So Long?" "Kimpy/Kimble" is simply a mishearing of "Tempy," a common name for "Mole in the Ground."

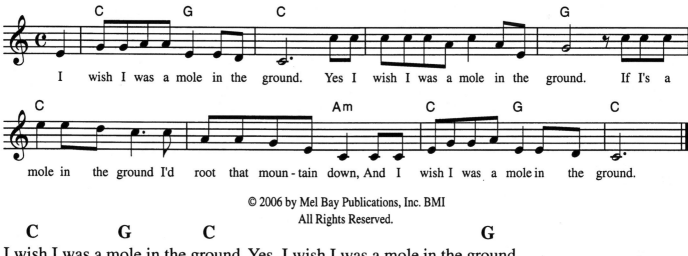

    C   **G**   **C**   **G**
I wish I was a mole in the ground. Yes, I wish I was a mole in the ground.
      C   **Am**
If I's a mole in the ground, I'd root that mountain down,
     C   **G**   **C**
And I wish I was a mole in the ground.

Oh, Tempy wants a nine-dollar shawl. Yes, Tempy wants a nine-dollar shawl;
When I come o'er the hill with a twenty-dollar bill,
It's "Baby, where you been so long?"

Oh, where have you been so long, Oh, where have you been so long,
I've been in the Bend with the rough and rowdy men,
It's baby where you been so long?

I don't like a railroad man. No, I don't like a railroad man;
A railroad man will kill you when he can,
And drink up your blood like wine.

I wish I was a lizard in the spring. Yes, I wish I was a lizard in the spring;
If I's a lizard in the spring, I could hear my darlin' sing,
I wish I was a lizard in the spring.

IDA RED

Traditional Old-Time, Breakdown; **DATE:** Late 1800's- early 1900's; Meade, Spottswood, Meade: Journal of American Folklore XXVIII, 1915. **CATEGORY:** Fiddle and Instrumental Tunes; **RECORDINGS:** Fiddlin' Powers & Family 1924; Riley Puckett 1926; Charlie Poole and the North Carolina Ramblers 1928; Bob Wills 1938; Gid Tanner and His Skillet Lickers; Tommy Jarrell; **OTHER NAMES:** "Idy Red;" "Shootin' Creek;" "Over the Road I'm Bound to Go;" **RELATED TO:** "Cripple Creek;" "Shootin' Creek" (Charlie Poole); "Feather Bed" (Cannon's Jug Stompers); "Over the Road I'm Bound To Go" (Uncle Dave Macon); "Down the Road" (Uncle Dave Macon & Flatt and Scruggs); **NOTES:** Ida Red was originally supposed to have been an African-American bad man (Lomax), but the gender of the character in most versions is feminine or androgynous. Riley Pucket's (north Georgia) version of the tune, released in 1926, became the second best-selling country music record for the year. There are two distinct branches of the Ida Red song: 1) The western branch includes Bob Wills's 1938 version which is based on "The Parlor is a Pleasant Place to Sit on Sunday Night," by Albert E. Porter 1886. 2) The southern branch features short clipped floating lyrics (Ida Red/Ida Green) similar to Cripple Creek. The Skillet Lickers and also Charlie Poole's versions are part of this line. Woody Guthrie, a popular radio entertainer in the 40's, sang "Ida Red", and its melody was used by rock and roll pioneer Chuck Berry for his 1955 classic "Mabelline." Some versions sing a verse then sing the chorus twice.

D
Verse: Ida Red, Ida Green
       A7 D
Prettiest gal I ever seen.
   D
Chorus: Ida Red, Ida Red
         A7 D
I'm just crazy 'bout Ida Red.

Ida Red lives in town
Weighs three hundred and forty pounds.

Ida red, Ida Red
I'm plum crazy about Ida Red.

Ida Red, Ida Blue
Ida bit a hoecake half in two.

Ida Red, Ida Red
Everybody's crazy 'bout Ida Red.

If I'd 'a listened to what Ida said
I'd 'a been sleepin' in Ida's bed.

If Ida said that she'd be mine
I'd be Ida's all the time.

If Ida said she'd be my wife
I'd be happy all my life.

If I Lose, I Don't Care

Traditional Old-Time and Bluegrass Song; **DATE:** Journal of American Folklore- 1911;**CATEGORY:** Early Country and Bluegrass Songs; **RECORDING INFO:** Charlie Poole and the North Carolina Ramblers-1927; J. E. Mainer's Mountaineers-1938; Stanley Brothers-1960; New Lost City Ramblers; Kirk Sutphin; Norman Blake; **OTHER NAMES:** "If I Lose, Let Me Lose;" "Let Me Lose;" **NOTES:** "If I Lose (Let Me Lose)" was first recorded by Eden, North Carolina native Charlie Poole and the North Carolina Ramblers in 1927. The melody is similar to the songs: "Bloody Wars," "Battleship of Maine" and "Whitehouse Blues." According to Kinney Rorrer, the song is of vaudeville origin. This is similar to Charlie Poole's version, which is different from standard bluegrass versions.

C   **C7**   **F**   **C**
I can't walk, neither can I talk, Just gettin' back from the state of old New York
     G7   **C**
One morning just before day.

             C   **G7**   **C**
Chorus: If I lose, let me lose, I don't care how much I lose
                 F
If I lose a hundred dollars while I'm tryin' to win a dime
    G7   **C**
For my baby, she needs money all the time.

Flossie, oh Flossie, now what is the matter? Walked all the way from old Cincinatta
One morning just before day   *Chorus*

The blood was a-runnin', and I was runnin' too give my feet some exercise, I had nothing else to do
One morning just before day   *Chorus*

See them girls sittin' at the tanks, Ready to catch a freight train they call old Nancy Hanks
One morning just before day   *Chorus*

I'LL FLY AWAY

Bluegrass Gospel Song by Albert E. Brumley; **DATE:** 1932; **CATEGORY:** Early Gospel Songs; **RECORDING INFO:** Kossoy Sisters; Chuck Wagon Gang; George Jones; Johnny Cash; Merle Haggard; Stanley Brothers; Osborne Bros., Bill Monroe; **NOTES:** Albert Edward Brumley (1905-1977) started working for Stamps Baxter Music Co. in 1943. Brumley appreciation day started in Spiro, OK, 1976 where he received a trophy for "I'll Fly Away" as recognition of the song being the most recorded gospel song in history. Brumley: "I was picking cotton on my father's farm and was humming the old ballad that went like this: 'If I had the wings of an angel, over these prison walls I would fly' and suddenly it dawned on me that I could use this plot for a gospel-type song. About three years later, I finally developed the plot, titled it 'I'll Fly Away,' and it was published in 1932 [in "Wonderful Message," Hartford Music Co.]. Those familiar with the song will note that I paraphrased one line of the old ballad to read 'Like a bird from prison bars have [has] flown.' When I wrote it, I had no idea that it would become so universally popular." Similar versions from the African-American tradition existed in the 30's and 40's.

© 1932 in "Wonderful Message" by Hartford Music Co.
Renewed 1960 by Albert E. Brumley & Sons/SESAC (admin. by ICG). All Rights Reserved. Used by Permission.

G   C   G

G   **C**   **G**
Some glad morning, when this life is over I'll fly away

                                   D   **G**
To a home on God's celestial shore I'll fly away.

        G
Chorus: I'll (fly away) fly away, Oh glory
C   **G**
I'll (fly away) fly away (in the morning)

When I die Hallelujah, by and by
         D   **G**
I'll (fly away) fly away (I'll fly away).

When the shadows of this life have grown I'll fly away
Like a bird from prison bars have flown I'll fly away   *Chorus*

Just a few more weary days and then I'll fly away
To a land where joys shall never end I'll fly away   *Chorus*

I'll Remember You, Love, in My Prayers

Old-Time and Bluegrass Gospel Song; Words and Music by Will S. Hays; **DATE:** 1869; **CATEGORY:** Fiddle and Instrumental Tunes; **RECORDING INFO:** Holland Puckett-1927; J. E. Mainer-1946; Carter Family; Wilma Lee Cooper; Bradley Kincaid; **OTHER NAMES:** "The Curtains of Night;" **NOTES:** A Bluegrass Gospel song by the great songwriter Will S. Hays, who also penned "Little Old Log Cabin in the Lane" as well as the original poem for the song "Life is like a Mountain Railroad."

G
When the curtains of night are pinned back by the stars
                                                      C
And the beautiful moon sweeps the sky
G   F   G   D   G
Dewdrops from heaven are kissing the rose, It's then that my memory flies.

Well, upon the wings of a beautiful dove
I'll hasten this message of cheer
And I'll bring you a kiss of affection and say
I'll remember you, love, in my prayers

Now the angels of Heaven are guarding the good
As God has ordained them to do
In answer to prayers that I offer to him
I know there's one waiting for you

Now go where you will upon land or on sea
And I'll share all your sorrows and cares
At night as I kneel by my bedside to pray
I'll remember you, love, in my prayers

Well, at night as I kneel by my bedside to pray
I'll remember you, love, in my prayers

I'm Bound To Ride

Traditional Bluegrass Song; **DATE:** Early 1900's; **CATEGORY:** Fiddle and Instrumental Tunes; **RECORDING INFO:** Fiddlin' Arthur Smith- 1937; Ralph Stanley; Legendary Stanley Brothers; Jim Mills; **OTHER NAMES:** "Bound to Ride;" "Honey Babe, I'm Bound to Ride;" **NOTES:** This piece comes from banjo king Oddie McWinders, who recorded with Clayton McMichen and Jimmie Rogers in 1932. Recorded by Flatt and Skaggs.

C   **G**
Coming down from Tennessee, riding on the line
G   **D**   **G**
Studying 'bout that gal of mine, couldn't keep from crying

            G
Chorus: Honey babe I'm bound to ride
D   **G**
Don't you want to go?

Going to Atlanta just to look around
Things don't suit me I'll hunt another town   *Chorus*

Riding on a streetcar, looking o'er the town
Eating salty crackers, ten cents a pound   *Chorus*

Working on a railroad saving all I can
Looking for that woman that ain't got no man   *Chorus*

If I die a railroad man, bury me under the ties
So I can see old number nine as she goes rolling by   *Chorus*

See that train a coming, coming round the bend
Goodbye, my little darling, I'm on my way again   *Chorus*

In the Garden

Gospel Song by C. Austin Miles; **DATE:** 1912; **CATEGORY:** Early Gospel Songs; **RECORDING INFO:** Lester Flatt & the Nashville Grass; Reno & Smiley; **NOTES:** A favorite Southern Gospel song first recorded by Williams and Williams in 1927.

   G   **C**   **G**
I come to the garden alone, While the dew is still on the roses
     D   **G**   **Am**   **D**
And the voice I hear falling on my ear , The Son of God discloses.
                    G   **D**
Chorus: And He walks with me, And He talks with me, And He tells me I am His
G   **D**   **C**   **G**   **D** **G**
own , And the joy we share as we tarry there, None other has ever known.

He speaks and the sound of His voice, Is so sweet the birds hush their singing
And the melody that He gave to me, Within my heart is ringing   *Chorus*

I'd stay in the garden with Him, 'Tho the night around me be falling
But He bids me go; through the voice of woe, His voice to me is calling   *Chorus*

IN THE PINES

Traditional Old-Time and Bluegrass Song; **DATE:** Early 1900's; **CATEGORY:** Early country and Bluegrass Songs; **RECORDING INFO:** Bascom Lamar Lunsford; Fiddlin' Arthur Smith and His Dixieliners; Bill Monroe & His Blue Grass Boys; Roscoe Holcomb; Blue Sky Boys; Louvin Brothers; Stanley Brothers; Doc Watson; **OTHER NAMES:** "To the Pines;" "Look Up Look Down that Lonesome Road;" "The Longest Train;" "Black Girl;" **NOTES:** First recorded by Doc Walsh in 1926, the song is closely related to "Long Lonesome Road" and "Longest Train" songs. This song became the basis of "Blue Diamond Mines" in the 1970's. "In The Pines/ Longest Train" has been traced to black convict coal miners. Sharp collected a version in Kentucky and it is found throughout the southern mountains. This version is similar to the classic Bill Monroe version with the tag after the chorus.

G		G7		C	G		

In the pines, in the pines, Where the sun never shines

           D   **G** **G** **G7 C**   **G**   **D**   **G**

And you shiver when the cold winds blow, Ooh,ooh,ooh,ooh,ooh,ooh, Ooh, ooh, ooh, ooh, ooh.

G   **G7**   **C** **G**   **D**   **G**

The longest train I ever saw, Went down that Georgia Line

G **G7**   **C**   **G**   **D** **G**

The engine passed at six o'clock, And the cab passed by at nine.   *Chorus*

Little girl, little girl, what have I done, That makes you treat me so
You've caused me to weep, you've caused me to mourn
You've caused me to leave my home.   *Chorus*

I asked my captain for the time of day, He said he throwed his watch away
It's a long steel rail and a short cross tie, I'm on my way back home.   *Chorus*

In The Sweet Bye and Bye

Gospel Standard by S. Filmore Bennett and J.P. Webster; **DATE:** 1868; **CATEGORY:** Early Gospel Songs; **RECORDING INFO:** Carter Family; Curly Ray Cline and His Lonesome Pine Fiddle; Elizabeth Cotton; Stanley Brothers; Mac Wiseman; Dolly Parton; **OTHER NAMES:** Sweet Bye and Bye; **NOTES:** One of my favorite hymn tunes.

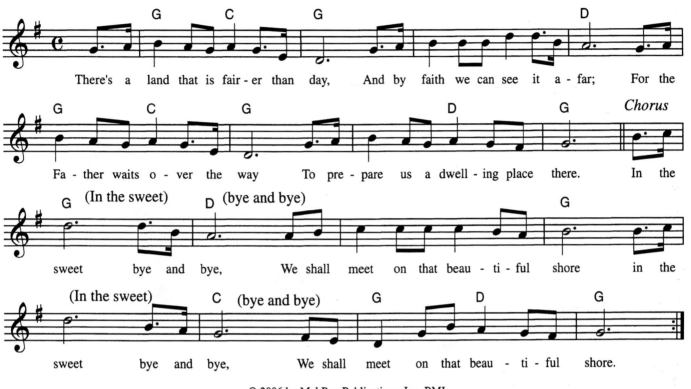

G		C	G		D	

There's a land that is fairer than day, And by faith we can see it afar;

G		C	G		D		G

For the Father waits over the way, To prepare us a dwelling place there.

G			D

Chorus: In the sweet (in the sweet) Bye and bye (bye and bye)

G

We shall meet on that beautiful shore; In the sweet (in the sweet)

C		G	D	G

Bye and bye (bye and bye) We shall meet on that beautiful shore.

We shall sing on that beautiful shore
The melodious songs of the blest,
And our spirits shall sorrow no more
Not a sigh for the blessing of rest.

To our bountiful father above
We will offer our tribute of praise;
For the glorious gift of His love
And the blessings that hallow our days.

THE JACKFISH

Old-Time, Breakdown; **DATE:** 1844; **CATEGORY:** Fiddle and Instrumental Tunes; Sung by Mr. Ebe Richards at St. Peter's School Calloway, Va., Aug. 18, 1918. From Cecil Sharp's EFSSA No. 251, pg. 361; **HOOK AND LINE SONGS:** The title for the large family of songs that have originated from the "Old Dad" minstrel song in 1844 which first appeared in printed form in a collection by Dan Emmett (composer of Dixie) called, Old Dan Emmett's Original Banjo Melodies, Second Series. The "hook and line" songs include "Shout Lula," "Shout Lou," "Shout Old Lulu," "The Shad," "Banjo Sam," "Mr. Catfish," "Shout Lulu," "Jackfish" "Seven and A Half," "Just From Tennessee," "Shout Oh Lulu," "Fish on a Hook," and "Buck Creek Gals." The "hook and line" songs can be split into two basic categories; the "hook and line" (Grab that catfish by its snout/ Turn that catfish wrong side out) songs that talk about fishing and the "Shout Lula" (Shout, Lulu, shout, Lulu, shout, shout/ What in the world you shoutin' 'bout?) songs. "Shout Lula" is a fast banjo version from the Appalachian region. **NOTES:** Jackfish is another name for a chain pickerel (common to the Appalachian region) and the song appears by that name from Sharp's English Folk Songs from the Southern Appalachians. It appears that the name originally was "catfish." Emmett did not claim the song as his own composition and, though the words may well be his, it is likely that the tune was already well-known, and may in fact be of British origin. A version of Hook and Line/Banjo Sam appears in the Journal of American Folklore in 1909 with the verse "the first fish bit was my old ad." Norm Cohen, who gives a transcription of Roscoe Holcomb's version of 'Hook & Line' in the marvelous booklet for 'Paramount Oldtime Tunes,' explains: Dan Emmett's composition titled 'Old Dad', published in 1844, leaves no doubt in my mind that "dad" is the original locution (of the 1909 JAF song), though whether it is indeed a fish, or a father, or some other stock minstrel figure is not clear to me. The fourth stanza of Emmett's "Old Dad" is related to one stanza of Wilmer Watts's "Banjo Sam."

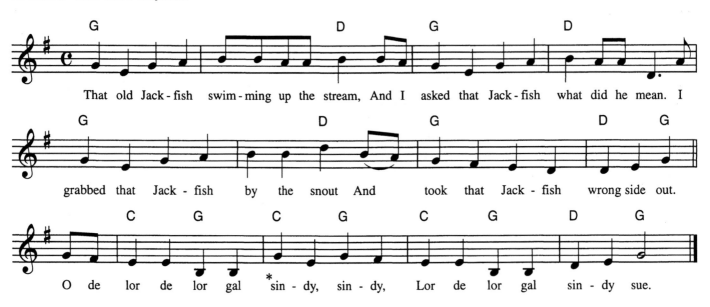

   G   **D**
That old Jackfish swimming up the stream,
      G   **D**
And I asked that Jackfish what did he mean.
   G   **D**
I grabbed that Jackfish by the snout,
      G   **D**   **G**
And took that Jackfish wrong side out.

     C   **G**   **C** **G**
O de lor de lor gal, *sindy, sindy,
C   **G**   **D**   **G**
Lor de lor gal, sindy, sue.

* Cindy, I've kept the original spelling.

JACK O' DIAMONDS

Old-Time, Texas Style; **DATE:** Early 1900's-First appears around 1910; **CATEGORY:** Fiddle and Instrumental Tunes. **RECORDING INFO:** Blue Sky Boys; Jules Allen; Curly Fox; Tommy Jarrell; Owen "Snake" Chapman; **OTHER NAMES:** "Drunken Hiccups/Hiccoughs;" "Rye Whiskey;" "Way Up On Clinch Mountain," "Clinch Mountain;" **NOTES:** The song, "Jack O' Diamonds" is an American branch of an old and large family of songs originating in the British Isles as "The Cuckoo." Both the "Jack O' Diamonds" and "Rye Whiskey" are well-known in America and as the fiddle tune "Drunken Hiccups." The "Jack O' Diamonds" is also a 1926 blues title by Blind Lemon Jefferson and the line "Jack O' diamonds is hard," appears in Big Joe Williams' "Baby Please Don't Go." The reference to the "Jack O' Diamonds" is that it's a bad (unlucky) card to hold. In the last 50 years (Randolph in 1954) and especially the last several decades, "Jack O' Diamonds" has been somewhat separated from "Rye Whiskey" although the titles are still interchanged.

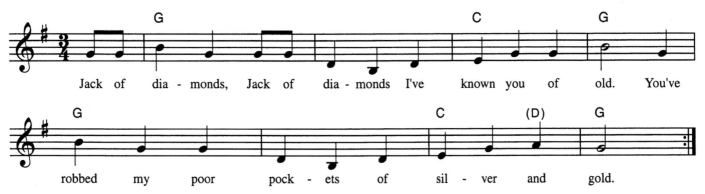

G
Jack O' Diamonds, Jack O' Diamonds,
    C   **G**
I know you of old
      G
You've robbed my poor pockets,
   C **(D) G**
Of silver and gold.

Whiskey you villain,
You've been my downfall
You've kicked me, you've cuffed me,
But I love you for all.

Her parents don't like me,
They say I'm too poor
They say I'm unworthy
To enter her door.

They say I drink whiskey,
But my money's my own
And them that don't like me
Can leave me alone.

O baby, O baby,
I've told you before
Do make me a pallet,
I'll lay on your floor.

I've no wife to quarrel,
No babies to bawl;
The best way of living,
Is no wife at all.

Way up on Clinch Mountain,
I wander alone,
I'm as drunk as the devil,
Oh, let me alone.

You may boast of your knowledge,
An' brag of your sense,
Twill all be forgotten,
A hundred years hence.

JACOB'S VISION

Traditional Bluegrass Gospel; **DATE:** Ca. 1871; **CATEGORY:** Early Gospel Songs; **RECORDING INFO:** Stanley Brothers; Ricky Skaggs with Kentucky Thunder; **OTHER NAMES:** Jacob's Ladder; **NOTES:** An early version with extra verses appears as "Jacob's Ladder" in Henry Ramsden Bramley and John Stainer, Christmas Carols New and Old printed in London: Novello, Ewer & Co., ca 1871. On Ricky Skaggs' Soldier of the Cross "Jacob's Vision" features guest vocals from Ralph Stanley and George Shuffler (two-thirds of the trio on the original Stanley Brothers record). The song is related to the Jacob's Ladder songs. Gary B. Reid's notes to *The Stanley Brothers: The Early Years 1958-1961* (Stardy/King KBSCD-7000): Of the song "Jacob's Vision," Ralph Stanley stated that we "learned (that) from Enoch Rose, he was a Free Will Baptist preacher from Caney Ridge, Virginia."

G
Hallelujah to Jesus who died on the tree
          D   **G**
To raise up this ladder of mercy for me

Press onward, climb upward, the top is in view
            D   **G**
There's a crown of bright glory awaiting for you

As Jacob was traveling, was weary one day
While at night on a stone for a pillow did lay
A vision appeared of a ladder so high
It stood on the earth while the top reached the sky   *Chorus*

This ladder is tall and yet so well made
Stood thousands of years and never decayed
High winds from the heavens they reel and they rock
But the angels they guard it from bottom to top   *Chorus*

JESSE JAMES (LAWS E1)

Old-Time Ballad and Bluegrass Song; **DATE:** Circa 1882; **CATEGORY:** Early Country and Bluegrass Songs; **RECORDINGS:** Bascom Lamar Lunsford 1924; Riley Puckett; Vernon Dalhart; Fiddlin' John Carson; Uncle Dave Macon; Bogtrotters; **NOTES:** Jesse James, living in St. Joseph, Missouri under his pseudonym "Thomas Howard" was shot by Robert Ford on April 4, 1882. Robert Ford was a member of Jesse's gang whom Jesse regarded as a friend. Ford shot Jesse in the back while Jesse was hanging a picture. According to Randolph the song became popular throughout the Midwest almost immediately after Jesse's death. Ford himself was shot in 1892 by another member of Jesse's gang.

   G   **C**   **G**   **D**
Jesse James was a lad who killed many a man, he robbed the Glendale train
   G   **C**   **G**   **D**   **G**
And the people they did say for many miles away, it was robbed by Frank and Jesse James
   C   **G**   **D**
Chorus: Jesse had a wife to mourn for his life, three children they were brave
   G   **C**   **G**   **D**   **G**
But that dirty little coward who shot Mr. Howard, has laid poor Jesse in his grave

It was on a Wednesday night, the moon was shining bright, they robbed the Glendale train
And the people they did say for many miles away, it was robbed by Frank and Jesse James *Chorus*

It was on a Saturday night when Jesse was at home, talking with his family brave
Robert Ford came along like a thief in the night and laid poor Jesse in his grave *Chorus*

Robert Ford, that dirty little coward, I wonder how he feels
For he ate of Jesse's bread and he slept in Jesse's bed and he laid poor Jesse in his grave *Chorus*

This song was made by Billy Gashade, as soon as the news did arrive
He said there was no man with the law in his hand, who could take Jesse James when alive. *Chorus*

JOHN HARDY [LAWS I2]

Traditional Old-Time Breakdown and Song; **DATE:** 1916 by Cecil Sharp. **CATEGORY:** Fiddle and Instrumental Tunes. **RECORDING INFO:** Carter Family-1928, Dock Boggs; Buell Kazee; Kingston Trio; Tony Rice; Country Gentlemen; **OTHER NAMES:** "John Hardy Was a Desperate Little Man." **NOTES:** John Hardy is popular not only as a song but also as an instrumental solo (banjo, fiddle, or guitar). John Hardy was a black man working in the tunnels of West Virginia. In fact, as Alan Lomax remarks, "the two songs ("John Henry" & "John Hardy") have sometimes been combined by folk singers, and the two characters confused by ballad collectors...." One payday, in a crap game at Shawnee Coal Company's camp (in what is today Eckman, WV), John Hardy killed a fellow worker. His white captors protected him from a lynch mob that came to take him out of jail and hang him. When the lynch fever subsided, Hardy was tried during the July term of the McDowell County Criminal Court, found guilty and sentenced to be hanged. While awaiting execution in jail, he is said to have composed this ballad, which he later sang on the scaffold. He also confessed his sins to a minister, became very religious, and advised all young men, as he stood beneath the gallows, to shun liquor, gambling and bad company. The order for his execution shows that he was hanged near the courthouse in McDowell County, January 19, 1894.

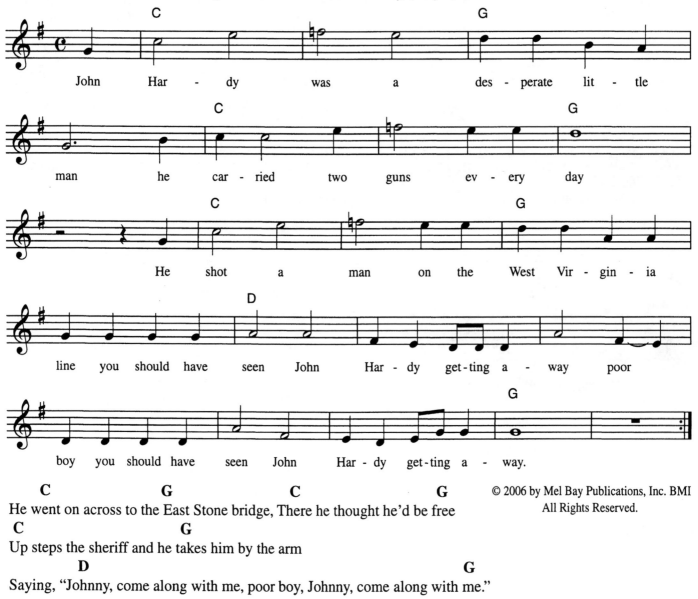

C   **G**   **C**   **G**
He went on across to the East Stone bridge, There he thought he'd be free
C   **G**
Up steps the sheriff and he takes him by the arm
      D   **G**
Saying, "Johnny, come along with me, poor boy, Johnny, come along with me."

He sent for his Mama and his Papa, too, To come and go his bail
But there weren't no bail on a murder charge
So they threw John Hardy back in jail, poor boy, Threw John Hardy back in jail.

John Hardy had a pretty little girl, The dress that she wore was blue
She came into the jailhouse hall
Saying, "Johnny, I'll be true to you, poor boy, Johnny, I'll be true to you."

I've been to the East and I've been to the West, Traveled this wide world around
Been to the river and I've been baptized
And now I'm on my hanging ground, Now I'm on my hanging ground.

John Henry [Laws I1]

Traditional Old-Time Breakdown and ballad; **DATE:** Ca. 1900; **CATEGORY:** Early Country and Bluegrass; **RECORDING INFO:** Kenny Baker and Josh Graves; Big Bill Broonzy; Tommy Jarrell; Lilly Brothers; Gid Tanner and the Skillet Lickers; Ralph Stanley; Flatt and Scruggs; **OTHER NAMES:** John Henry Blues; Death of John Henry; Steel Drivin' Man; **NOTES:** One of the earliest known versions of "John Henry" was printed as what is now known as the "Blankenship Broadside," "John Henry, the Steel Driving Man." There is no indication of date or place. Guy Johnson dated it based on information provided by the source of his copy of the broadside, a woman living in Rome, Georgia, as "ca 1900." One of the most popular of all American folksongs, the raging debate that started in the 1920's about the identity of the real John Henry goes on.

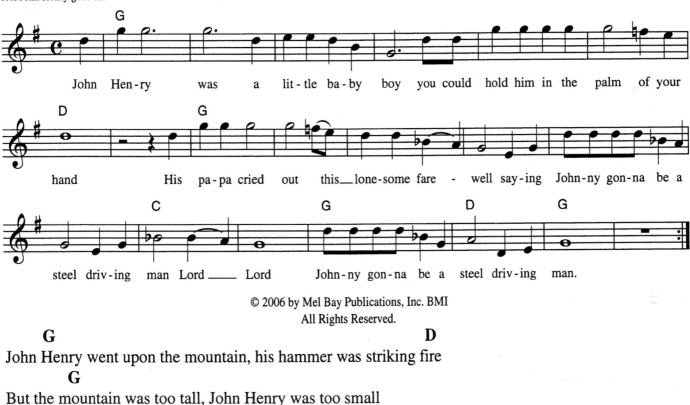

G   **D**
John Henry went upon the mountain, his hammer was striking fire
G
But the mountain was too tall, John Henry was too small
                                       C   **G**   **D**   **G**
So he laid down his hammer and he died. Lord, Lord, laid down his hammer and he died.

John Henry went into the tunnel, had his captain by his side
The last words that John Henry said,
"Bring a cool drink of water before I die. Lord, Lord, cool drink of water before I die."

Talk about John Henry as much as you please, say and do all that you can
There never was born in the United States
Never such a steel driving man, Lord, Lord, never such a steel driving man.

John Henry had a little woman and her name was Polly Ann
John Henry took sick and he had to go to bed
Polly drove steel like a man, Lord, Lord, Polly drove steel like a man.

John Henry told his captain, I want to go to bed
Lord, fix me a pallet, I want to lay down
Got a mighty roaring in my head, Lord, Lord, mighty roaring in my head.

Took John Henry to the graveyard and they buried him under the sand
Now every locomotive comes a roaring by
Says, "Yonder lies a steel driving man, Lord, Lord, yonder lies a steel driving man."

Johnny Booker

Traditional Old-Time Song and Breakdown; **DATE:** From Minstrel era (1840); Other documented versions appear in the early 1900's; **CATEGORY:** Fiddle and Instrumental Tunes; **RECORDING INFO:** Gus Cannon 1956; Jerry Jordan [pseud. for Walter Smith], "Old Johnny Booker Won't Do" (Supertone 9407B, 1929); Cousin Emmy [Cynthia May Carver], "Johnny Booker" (Decca 24214, 1947; on CrowTold01); New Lost City Ramblers; **OTHER NAMES:** "Mister Booger;" "Knock John Booker;" "John Booker;" "Old John Booker, You Call That Gone," "Johnny Bucca," "Johnny Bucka," "Do Me Johnny Boker;" "Do, Mr. Boker, Do;" "Old Johnny Pigger;" "Old Johnny Pucker;" "Old Johnny Bull" **NOTES:** The tune is known as a banjo/string band piece and comes from the minstrel era (J.W. Sweeny from 1840). The sea shanty versions tend to have names such as Johnny Booker/JohnnyBucca/Johnny Bucka/Dead Horse/Do Me Johnny Boker/Do, Mr. Boker, Do while the minstrel versions tend to have names like Old Johnny Booker/Poor Old Man/Johnny Booger/ Old Johnny Booger/Old Johnny Pigger/Old Johnny Pucker.

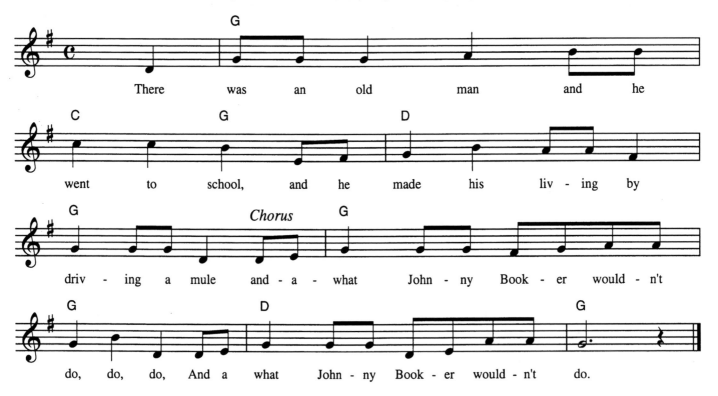

>   G   C   G
> There was an old man and he went to school
>   D   G
> And he made his living by drivin' a mule,
>
>
>   G   G
> **Chorus:** And a what, Johnny Booker, won't you do, do, do,
>   D   G
> And a what, Johnny Booker won't you do?

JOHNNY BOOKER

I drove him up to the foot of the hill
And I holler at the mule and the mule stopped still.   *Chorus*

I put my shoulder against the wheel,
And a-back in the mud I stuck my heel.   *Chorus*

I put my shoulder against the cart
And I hollered at the mule and the mule wouldn't start.   *Chorus*

I drove him up to the blacksmith shop,
I hollered at the mule and the mule didn't stop.   *Chorus*

I asked that farmer for to mend my yoke,
He hopped on the bellows and blowed out the smoke.   *Chorus*

He fixed my yoke and he mend my ring,
And he never charged me a nary thing.   *Chorus*

Then an old man came ridin' by,
And he says, "Young man, your mule's a gonna die."   *Chorus*

If he dies I'll tan his skin,
If he lives I'll ride 'em agin.   *Chorus*

I had an old mule and his name was Steve
He walked on his head as plain as his feet.   *Chorus*

I had an old mule and his name was Bill
I worked him on the holler and he died on the hill.   *Chorus*

I road him to the river and I couldn't get him in,
And I knocked him on the head with an old yard bin.   *Chorus*

I went to the river and I couldn't get across,
Hopped on a bull frog a big as a horse.   *Chorus*

JOHNSON BOYS

Traditional Old-Time, Song and Fiddle Tune; **DATE:** Tune older (mid 1800's); Words early 1900's; **CATEGORY:** Fiddle and Instrumental Tunes; **RECORDING INFO:** Al Hopkins & His Buckle Busters (1927); Grant Brothers (1928); New Lost City Ramblers; Flatt & Scruggs & the Foggy Mountain Boys; Freight Hoppers; Hillbillies; J. E. Mainer & the Mountaineers; Frank Proffitt; Wade Ward; The Tenneva Ramblers; **OTHER NAMES:** "Meet the Johnson Boys;" "Kentucky Boys; "Legend Of The Johnson Boys;" **RELATED TO:** "Aunt Sal's Song (The Man Who Didn't Know How to Court)" (theme); "Mister Booger;" "Doran's Ass/Dolan's Ass," "Spanish Ladies/The Spanish Lady;" "Billy Taylor/Willie Taylor," "Finnegan's Wake." **NOTES:** Banjoist Frank Proffitt (North Carolina), who learned the tune "from his father's picking and picked up verses from people on Beech Mountain, friends from Virginia, and others here and there" [Warner]. Paul Clayton identifies this as an old courting song, comic in nature. Warner (1984) says, "This is a dance tune for the fiddle and banjo - one of the oldest in the mountains. The words are incidental." Meade notes: "The tune is an adaptation of 'Doran's Ass' (see Laws Q19), dating from around 1860. It was also used with other Irish songs of the period." The earliest textual reference Meade gives for "Johnson Boys" is the Brown Collection vol III, #338, 394. In Ireland the tune is known as the comic song "Doran's Ass" and also is the tune for "Finnegan's Wake." Speculation about the Johnson Boys being a Civil War song has yet to be proven. The chorus is the last line of the verse repeated twice.

E   **B7**
Johnson boys, raised in ashes, Didn't know how to court a maid;
E   **B7**   **E**
Turned their backs and hid their faces, Sight of a pretty girl makes them afraid.
        E   **B7**   **E**
Chorus: Sight of a pretty girl makes them afraid.
        B7   **E**
Sight of a pretty girl makes them afraid.

I hear them Johnson boys a-coming, Singing and a-hollering and shooting off their guns;
All the other fellers scared as the devil, Johnson boys has got 'em on the run. *Chorus (Repeat last line)*

Johnson boys went to the mountain, They didn't reckon long to stay,
Met up with some high-borned ladies, Didn't get back till the break of day. *Chorus*

Johnson boys, they went a-courtin', Johnson boys, they didn't stay.
Reason why they went no further, Had no money fur to pay their way. *Chorus*

JORDAN

Bluegrass Song; **DATE**: 1954; **CATEGORY**: Bluegrass Gospel Song; **RECORDING INFO**: Stanley Brothers; Emmylou Harris; Grateful Dead; Kentucky Colonels; **OTHER NAMES**: Cold Jordan; **NOTES**: Gary B. Reid's notes to *The Stanley Brothers: The Early Years 1958-1961* (4-disc set; Stardy/King KBSCD-7000): "Jordan" is thought by many to be an older traditional song but it was written in 1954 by Fred Rich, a gospel songwriter from northern Georgia who conceived the chorus of the song at the Co-op where he worked in Blairsville, Georgia. The chorus features a solo voice with an echo by the group.

Oh lis-ten as you tread life's jour-ney take Je-sus as your dai-ly guide tho you may feel pure and safe-ly with out Him walk-ing by your side but when you come to make the cross-ing at the end-ing of your pil-grim's way if you ev-er will meet our Sav-ior you'll sure-ly meet Him on that day

Now look at that cold (cold Jor-dan) look at these deep (deep wa-ters) look at that wide (wide ri-ver) oh hear the migh-ty bill-ows roar you'd bet-ter take Je-(Je-sus with you) he's a true (true com-pan-ion) for I'm sure (sure with-out Him) that you ne-ver will make it o'er.

A
Oh listen as you take life's journey take Jesus as your guide
      B7   **E**
Though you may feel pure and safely without Him walking by your side
A
But when you come to make the crossing at the end of your pilgrim's way
      E   **A**
If you ever will meet our Savior you'll surely meet Him on that day.

Chorus: Now look at that cold Jordan, look at these deep waters, look at that wide river
Oh hear the mighty billows roar, You'd better take Jesus with you
He's a true companion, for I'm sure without Him that you never will make it o'er.

That awful Day of Judgement is coming in the bye and bye
We'll see our Lord descending in Glory from on high
So let us keep in touch with Jesus and in his grace the Love of God
That we may be ever called ready when He calls us over Jordan's Tide. *Chorus*

JUST A CLOSER WALK WITH THEE

Traditional Gospel Song; **DATE:** Late 1800's; **CATEGORY:** Early Gospel Songs; **RECORDING INFO:** Jethro Burns; Patsy Cline; John Jackson; Red Foley; Mahalia Jackson; **NOTES:** This gospel song has its roots in the African-American tradition. In the 1920's, Thomas Dorsey, a Georgia bluesman who later moved to Chicago, coined the term "Gospel" and was the acknowledged leader of the gospel movement. "Just a Closer Walk With Thee" is one of the popular Gospel numbers to come from this period, although there is some debate as to its origin.

C   **G7**   **C**
Just a closer walk with Thee, Grant it, Jesus, is my plea.
     C7   **F** **F♯dim**   **C**   **G**   **C**
Daily walking close to Thee,   Let it be, dear Lord, let it be.

C   **G7**   **C**
I am weak, but Thou art strong Jesus, keep me from all wrong.
     C7   **F** **F♯dim**   **C**   **G**   **C**
I'll be satisfied as long,   As I can walk, dear Lord, close to thee.

C   **G7**   **C**
In this world of toil and snares, If I falter, Lord, who cares?
     C7   **F** **F♯dim**   **C**   **G**   **C**
Who but Thee my burden shares?   None but Thee, oh Lord, none but Thee.

C   **G7**   **C**
When my weary life is o'er, Pain and suff'ring are no more.
     C7   **F** **F♯dim**   **C**   **G**   **C**
Who will lead me safely o'er,   Canaan's shore, that sweet Canaan's shore.

Just Over in Gloryland

Southern Gospel Song-Words by James W. Acuff; Music by Emmet S. Dean **DATE:** 1906; **CATEGORY:** Early Southern Gospel Songs; **RECORDING INFO**: J. E. Mainer's Mountaineers; Alex Campbell & Olabelle and the New River Boys; Red Rector; Mac Wiseman; **OTHER NAMES:** Over in Gloryland; **NOTES:** First recorded by the Carson family Quartet in 1926, Just Over in Gloryland is sung quartet style- in parts. The lead sing the first and third lines solo and all join in on the 2nd and 4th lines.

G   C   G   D
I've a home prepared where the saints abide, (Just over in Gloryland!)
G   C   G   D   G
And I long to be by my Savior's side. (Just over in Gloryland!)

             G   C   G
Chorus: Just over in the Gloryland, I'll join the happy angel band,
          D   G
Just over in the Gloryland! Just over in the Gloryland,
  C   G   D   G
There with the mighty host I'll stand, Just over in the Gloryland!

I am on my way to those mansions fair, (Just over in the Gloryland!)
There to sing God's praise and His glory share, (Just over in the Gloryland!)   *Chorus*

What a joyful thought that my Lord, I'll see, Just over in the Gloryland!
And with kindred saved, there forever be, Just over in the Gloryland!   *Chorus*

With the blood-washed throng, I will shout and sing, Just over in the Gloryland!
Glad hosannas to Christ, the Lord and King, Just over in the Gloryland!   *Chorus*

KATY CLINE

Old-Time Song and Breakdown- Originated from L. V. H. Crosby "Kitty Clyde" **DATE:** "Kitty Clyde" published in 1853; Recorded by Monroe Brothers in 1937.
CATEGORY: Early Country and Bluegrass Songs; **RECORDING INFO:** The Stoneman Family-1926; Greenbriar Boys; Monroe Brothers; Dillards; Red Fox Chasers The Stanley Brothers; **OTHER NAMES:** "Katie Klein," "Katie Cline," "Katy Kline," "Katy Klyne" **RELATED TO:** "Kitty Clyde," "Free Little Bird"
NOTES: "Katy Cline" is an adaptation of "Kitty Clyde," written and composed by L. V. H. Crosby and published in 1853; "Kitty Clyde" is the originator of both the "Free Little Bird" and "Katy Cline" songs. It was recorded by Monroe Brothers in 1937.

G   **D**
I love my darlin' Katy Cline, Who lives at the foot of the hill
  G   **C**   **G** **D** **G**
In a sly little nook by a babblin' brook, That turns her father's mill.

       G
Chorus: Tell me that you love me Katy Cline
               D
Tell me that your love's as true as mine
G   **C**
Tell me that you love your own turtle dove
D   **G**
Tell me that you love me Katy Cline.

It's way from my little cabin door
Oh it's way from my little cabin home
There's no one to weep and there's no one to mourn
And there's no one to see Katy Cline. *Chorus*

If I was a little bird
I'd never build my nest on the ground
I'd build my nest in some high yonder tree
Where them wild boys couldn't tear it down. *Chorus*

KEEP ON THE SUNNYSIDE

Southern Gospel Song- Words Ada Blenkhorn; Music J. Howard Entwisle; **DATE:** 1899; **NOTES:** Ada Blenkhorn's invalid cousin always insisted that she push his wheelchair down the "sunny side of the street." This inspired her to write "Keep on the Sunny Side of Life". It was recorded on a cylinder in 1910 but the Carter family made it famous and used it as their closing (trademark) song. They recorded it on May 9, 1928 and again on May 8, 1935 for the American Record Company.

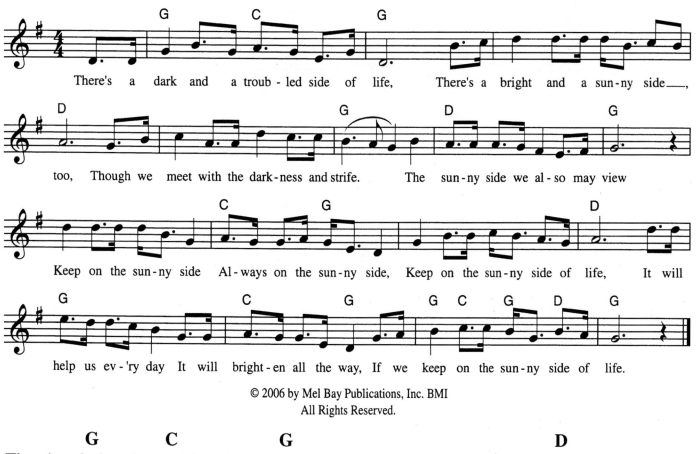

   G   **C**   **G**   **D**
There's a dark and a troubled side of life, There's a bright and a sunny side, too

                     G   **D**   **G**
Though we meet with the darkness and strife, The sunny side we also may view.

      G   **C**   **G**
Chorus: Keep on the sunny side, always on the sunny side

          D
Keep on the sunny side of life

   G   **C**   **G**
It will help us every day, it will brighten all the way

   G C **G**   **D** **G**
If we'll keep on the sunny side of life.

The storm and its fury broke today, Crushing hopes that we cherished so dear
Clouds and storm will in time pass away, The sun again will shine bright and clear.   *Chorus*

Let us greet with a song of hope each day, Though the moment be cloudy or fair
Let us trust in our Savior always, To keep us every one in his care.   *Chorus*

KNEEL AT THE CROSS

Southern Gospel Song- Charles E. Moody; **DATE:** Early 1900's; **CATEGORY:** Early Gospel Songs; **RECORDING INFO:** Georgia Yellow Hammers; Louvin Brothers; Stanley Brothers; **NOTES:** Born in Gordon Co. Georgia in 1891, Charles E. Moody traded a shotgun for his first fiddle. He also played guitar, banjo and harmonica with his band the Georgia Yellow Hammers. His other song in this collection is Drifting Too Far from the Shore.

G   **C**   **G**
Kneel at the cross, Christ will meet you there, Come while He waits for you
                                      A   **D**
Listen to His voice, leave with Him your cares, And begin life anew.
        G   **D**   **G**
Chorus: Kneel at the cross, (kneel at the cross) Leave every care, (leave every care)
            C   **G**   **D**   **G**
Kneel at the cross, (kneel at the cross) Jesus will meet you there (meet you there).

Kneel at the cross, there's room for all, Who will His glory share
Bliss there awaits, harm can nary fall, Those who are anchored there.   *Chorus*

Kneel at the cross, give your idols up, Look unto realms above
Turn not away, to life's sparkling cup, Trust only in His love.   *Chorus*

KNOCKIN' ON YOUR DOOR

Traditional Bluegrass Song; **DATE:** 1900's;**CATEGORY:** Early Country and Bluegrass Songs; **RECORDING INFO:** Old And In The Way; Jimmy King; Muleskinner; Peter Rowan; **NOTES:** David Grisman recorded a great version of Knockin' On Your Door with Jerry Garcia on banjo: "I first met Peter Rowan on the school grounds at Union Grove, North Carolina in 1963. The following year, Garcia and I crossed paths in the parking lot at Sunset Park in West Grove, Pa. Back then we were all on a quest, searching out that 'high lonesome sound' of Bill Monroe, Flatt and Scruggs, the Stanley Brothers, and other idols. The music on this disc, recorded live at a gig, embodies the spirit of that original Bluegrass quest, and a genuine affection for that superlative acoustic blend of banjo, guitar, fiddle, mandolin, string bass and voice(s)." It is also swing, "Knockin' At Your Door."

G   **C**   **D**   **G**
I'm knockin' on your door again my darlin', I'm knockin' on your door please answer me
                     C   **D**   **G**
Cause I've tried to make you realize my darlin', That no one else was ever meant for me.

I remember dear you said you'd always love me And you promised me your happiness so true
But now you gone away, dear, with another, And I wonder if you feel the way I do.

I'm knockin' on your door again my darlin', I'm knockin' on your door please answer me
Cause I've tried to make you realize my darlin', That no one else was ever meant for me.

I'm knockin' on your door again my darlin', I'm knockin' on your door please answer me
I never read the letter that you wrote my little darlin', I'm sailing far across the deep blue sea.

I'm knockin' on your door again my darlin', To return the letters that you wrote to me.
I'm knockin' on your door again my darlin', This time honey, I'm sure things gonna be.

So good-bye dear, I know you'll soon forget me, And I hope that you find happiness so true
But whenever you make love, sweetheart, remember There will never always be the same for you.

Life Is Like a Mountain Railway

Gospel Song by M.E. Abbey and C.D. Tillman; Based on a 1886 poem by Will S. Hays "The Faithful Engineer." **DATE:** 1890; **CATEGORY:** Early Gospel Songs; **RECORDING INFO:** Greenbriar Boys; Bradley Kincaid; Bill Monroe; **OTHER NAMES:** Life's Railway to Heaven; **NOTES:** "Life's Railway to Heaven" is related to "The Girl I Left in Sunny Tennessee;" "Old True Love/Lover." It is the melody for "Miner's Lifeguard;" "Weaver's Life;" "Ballad of the Braswell Boys;" "Wreck of the Happy Valley."

    G   **C**   **G**
Life is like a mountain railway with an engineer that's brave
                      A7   **D**
We must make the run successful from the cradle to the grave
    G   **C**   **G**
Watch the hills, the curves, and tunnels never falter, never fail
                   D   **G**
Keep your hands upon the throttle and your eyes upon the rail
    C   **G**   **D**
Oh blessed saviour thou wilt guide us, til we reach that blissful shore
    G   **C**   **G D** **G**
Where the angels come to join us, in God's grace forever more.

As you roll across the trestle spanning Jordan's swelling tide
You behold the Union depot into which your train will glide
There you'll meet the superintendent God the Father, God the Son
With a hearty, joyous plaudit weary pilgrim welcome home.

L'IL LIZA JANE

Old-Time, Bluegrass, Western Swing-Composed by Countess Ada de Lachau; **DATE:** Published in 1916; **CATEGORY:** Fiddle and Instrumental Tunes; **OTHER NAMES:** "Little Liza Jane" "Sweet Little Liza Jane" Used for other "Liza Jane" songs. **RECORDING INFO:** First recorded "L'il Liza Jane" by Harry C. Brown in 1918, Co A2622; Bob Wills and his Texas Playboys 1941 on OK 06371; Charlie Monroe and the Kentucky Pardners; **NOTES:** Composed by Countess Ada de Lachau in 1916, "L'il Liza Jane" was a take off on the earlier minstrel songs and was written in minstrel dialect. It is similar to "Camptown Races" by Stephen Foster with "L'il Liza Jane" substituted for "Oh doo-day day." The "L'il Liza Jane" song ("I's got a gal and you've got none, L'il Liza Jane") is an entirely different song than "Liza Jane." The tag (Chorus) was added making it a unique adaptation: "Oh Liza, L'il Liza Jane; Oh Liza, L'il Liza Jane."

A
I've got a gal and you've got none, L'il Liza Jane
       E7 **A**
I've got a gal that calls me hon', L'il Liza Jane
   A **D A**   **D A E7** **A**
Chorus: Oh Eliza, L'il Liza Jane; Oh Eliza, L'il Liza Jane.

Come my love and live with me; L'il Liza Jane
I will take good care of thee; L'il Liza Jane.

Jimmy John is layin' low, L'il Liza Jane
Come and take me for you beau, L'il Liza Jane. *Chorus*

Gonna throw the dice away, L'il Liza Jane
When you name that happy day, L'il Liza Jane. *Chorus*

Liza Jane done come to me; L'il Liza Jane
Both as happy as can be; L'il Liza Jane. *Chorus*

Ev'ry mornin' when I wakes, L'il Liza Jane
Smell the ham an' buck-wheat cakes, L'il Liza Jane. *Chorus*

House an' lot in Baltimo', L'il Liza Jane
Lots of children roun' the door, L'il Liza Jane. *Chorus*

Never more from you I'll roam; L'il Liza Jane.
Best place is home sweet home; L'il Liza Jane. *Chorus*

LITTLE BESSIE

Old-Time and Bluegrass Song- R.S. Crandall- words; arranged by W.T. Porter; **DATE**: ca. 1870; **CATEGORY**: Early Country and Bluegrass Songs; **RECORDING INFO**: Blue Sky Boys; Ricky Skaggs 'Ancient Tones' Skaggs Family Records; Roscoe Holcomb; Walter Smith & Friends; Stanley Brothers; **NOTES**: Most versions come from the classic Blue Sky Boys 1938 recording. Ricky Skaggs's note to the song reads: "Here is another song that I first heard from the Stanley Brothers. I loved their version very much. Then, one day, I found an old songbook that had many more verses to it than what they had recorded. I asked my dad if he knew anyone who could sing the old mountain style version of 'Little Bessie.' He said he thought he did. So we went down the road to a neighbor's house. Their names were Alvie and Vernie Fyffe. Vernie knew the old way of singing that song. So I learned it from her."

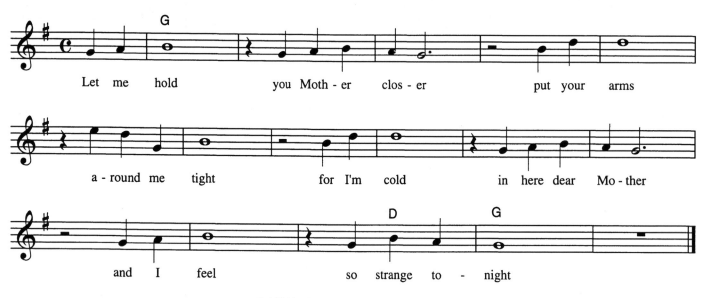

G
Let me hold you Mother closer put your arms around me tight

         D   **G**
For I'm cold in here dear Mother and I feel so strange tonight.

Something hurts me oh dear Mother like a stone upon my breast
Can I wonder, Mother, wonder why it is I cannot rest.

On the day while you were working as I lay upon my bed
I was trying to be patient and remember what you said.

Just before the lamps were lighted, just before the children came
While the moon was very quiet, I heard someone call my name.

Come up here, my little Bessie, come up here and live with me
Where little children never suffer through the long eternity.

In the silent hour of midnight, in the silence, calm and deep
Lying in her Mother's bosom, Little Bessie fell asleep.

Now up yonder past the portals that are shining very far
Little Bessie now is tended by her Saviour's love and care.

LITTLE BIRDIE

Traditional Bluegrass Song; **DATE**: early 1900's; **CATEGORY:** early Country and Bluegrass Songs; **RECORDING INFO**: Vernon Dalhart-1925; Coon Creek Girls; Greenbriar Boys; Wade Mainer; Roscoe Holcomb; Frank Proffitt; Stanley Brothers-1952; Bray Brothers; **NOTES:** From the notes on Frank Proffitt's second Folk-Legacy solo recording (C-36): This banjo song, now well-known through the performances of Ralph Stanley and Roscoe Holcomb, can be heard almost anywhere in the Appalachians.

    C   G   C
Little Birdie, little birdie, What makes you fly so high?
        G   C
It's because I'm a true little bird, And I do not fear to die.

        C   G   C
Chorus: Little Birdie, little birdie, Come and sing me a song
        G   C
Got a short time to be here, Got a long time to be gone.

I'm a long way from old Dixie, And my old Kentucky home
Now my parents are both dead and gone, Have no place to call my home.

Little birdie, little birdie, What makes you act so queer
You've got no cause to worry, And don't need no clothes to wear.

LITTLE MAGGIE

Old-Time, Bluegrass; Breakdown and Song. **DATE:** Late 1800's; **CATEGORY:** Fiddle and Instrumental Tunes; **RECORDING INFO:** "Little Maggie With a Dram Glass In Her Hand" was first recorded by Grayson and Whittier in 1928; The Stanley Brothers; Fred Cockerham; Kingston Trio; Ricky Skaggs; **NOTES:** "Little Maggie" is part of the "Darling Cory/Corey" family of "white blues" songs that include "Country Blues/Hustling Gamblers" which were found in the Appalachian region in the late 1800's. Barry O'Connell suggests that this "lyric and tune family has been around in the southern mountains for over a century. The family of tunes probably originates late in the 19th century and belongs to the then developing tradition of white blues ballads." "Little Maggie" was recorded by the Stanley Brothers in 1946, when their music was more old-time than bluegrass in style. Mt. Airy, North Carolina fiddler Tommy Jarrell remembered the tune "going around" the Round Peak area (where he grew up) around 1915 or 1916, and it became quite popular with the younger folk.

G   **F**   **G**   **D**   **G**
Yonder stands little Maggie with a dram glass in her hand
                     F   **G**   **D**   **G**
She's passing away her troubles by courting another man.

Oh how can I ever stand it just to see them two blue eyes
A-shining in the moonlight like two diamonds in the skies.

Pretty flowers were made for blooming, pretty stars were made to shine
Pretty women were made for loving, Little Maggie was made for mine.

Last time I saw little Maggie she was setting on the banks of the sea
With a forty-four around her and a banjo on her knee.

Lay down you last gold dollar, lay down you gold watch and chain
Little Maggie's gonna dance for Daddy, listen to this old banjo ring.

I'm going down to the station with my suitcase in my hand
I'm going away for to leave you, I'm going to some far distant land.

Go away, go away little Maggie, go and do the best you can
I'll get me another woman, you can get you another man.

LITTLE OLD LOG CABIN IN THE LANE

Old-Time, Song Tune. Words & Music by William S. Hays; **DATE:** 1871; **CATEGORY:** Fiddle and Instrumental Tunes; **RECORDING INFO:** Fiddlin' John Carson; Wade Mainer; Tennessee River Boys; Mac Wiseman; **OTHER NAMES:** "Little Old Log Cabin Down the Lane;" "Hungry Hash House (Blues);" "Fiddle and Bow;" "Little Joe, the Wrangler," "Lily of the Valley;" "Little Old Sod Shanty (on the Claim);" "Little Red Caboose Behind the Train," "Another Fall of Rain" "Little Joe the Wrangler," "Beans, Gravy and Bacon." **NOTES:** The song was written and published in 1871 by a Kentucky riverman turned vaudeville songwriter, Will Hayes. The southern gospel hymn, "Lily of the Valley," with words by Charles W. Fry (1881) was adapted from Hays' "Little Old Log Cabin." The piece was first released in 1923 when Fiddlin' John Carson's (north Georgia) version became the second best-selling country music record for that year. Yet another performance, Ernest Stoneman's, made the charts that decade, in 1926 when his version became the fifth best-selling country music record. Some bluegrass versions are played in the Key of F but immediately change to the Key of G for the solos.

    G   **C**   **G**
Oh, the paths have all growed up that led around the hill
        D
The fences have all gone to decay
    G   **C**   **G**
And the streams they have all dried up where we used to go to mill
        D   **G**
Ev'ry thing has changed its course another way.

    C   **G**
Chorus: Oh, the chimney's falling down and the roof is all tumblin' in
       D
Letting in the sunshine and the rain
    G   **G**
And the only friend I've got now is that good old dog of mine
      D   **G**
And that little old log cabin in the lane.

Oh, I ain't got long to stay here, what little time I got, I want to rest content while I remain
Till death shall call this dog and me to find a better home
And that little old log cabin in the lane. *Chorus*

LITTLE SADIE (LAWS I8)

Old-time Appalachian Blues; **CATEGORY:** Early Country and Bluegrass Songs; **DATE:** Early 1900's (1922); **RECORDING INFO:** Clarence Ashley -1930; Freight Hoppers; Tommy Jarrell; Doc Watson; Hedy West; **OTHER NAMES:** "Bad Man's Blunder," "Bad(Man) Lee Brown;" "Penitentiary Blues;" "Bad Man Ballad;" "Cocaine Blues;" "Chain Gang Blues;" **NOTES:** "Little Sadie" originated in the Appalachian region but has been found as far west as Arkansas as early as 1939. "Bad Man's Blunder," by Hays and Cisco Houston is a variant of "Little Sadie" that was a hit for the Kingston Trio. "Penitentiary Blues/Cocaine Blues," was released by Johnny Cash in 1960 and redone by George Thorogood many years later. In the song lyrics the reference to Thomasville (North Carolina) and Jericho (South Carolina) could possibly represent a local North Carolina murder ballad.

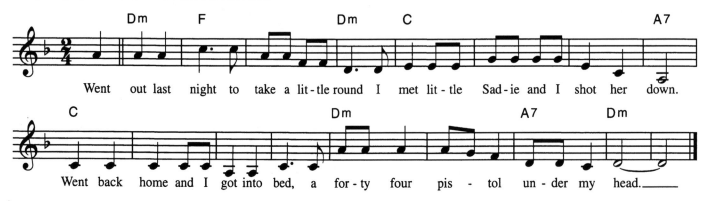

Dm   F   Dm   C   A 7
Went out one night to make a little round, I met little Sadie and I shot her down.
C   Dm   A7   Dm
Went back home, and I got into bed, Forty-four pistol under my head.

Wake up the next morning about half past nine, The hacks and the buggies all standing in line.
Gents and the gamblers all standin' around, Taking Little Sadie to her buryin' ground.

Then I begun to think of what a deed I'd done, I grabbed my hat and away I run.
I made a good run but a little too slow, They overtook me in Jericho.

I was standin' on the corner a readin' the bill, When up stepped the sheriff from Thomasville.
He said young man ain't your name Brown, Remember the night you shot Sadie down.

Well I says, "Yes sir, my name is Lee, And I shot little Sadie in the first degree.
First degree, second degree, If you got any papers won't you read them to me."

They took me down town, dressed me in black, And they put me on a train and started me back.
All the way back to that Thomasville jail, And I had no money for to go my bail.

That judge and the jury took their stand, The judge had the papers in his right hand.
Forty-one days, and forty-one nights, Forty-one years to wear the ball and stripes.

LITTLE WHITE CHURCH

Traditional Bluegrass Gospel; **DATE**: Late 1800's; **CATEGORY:** Fiddle and Instrumental Tunes; **RECORDING INFO:** Mac Wiseman and Bobby Osborne; Jimmy Martin; Jim and Jesse; Country Gentlemen; **NOTES:** Mac Wiseman sings the "Little White Church" on Jim and Jesse's "Music Among Friends" CD as well as with the Osborne Brothers.

    G   **C**   **G**

There's a little white church in the valley, That stands in my memory each day

                        A   **D**

And it seems I can hear the bells now ringing, Though I am many miles away

   G   **C**   **G**

And many times in church on Sunday morning, That whole countryside would gather there

                     D   **G**

They would all kneel down by the altar, As they lifted up their voices in prayer

                 C   **G**   **D**

Chorus: Oh, the church in the valley, oh, that little white church, Is the place I love so well

   G   **C**   **G** **D** **G**

Now I'm sad and lonely, yes I'm sad and lonely for that little white church in the dell

They would sing the old song Rock of Ages, Oh Christ, let me hide myself in thee
And I know some of them are now waiting, Just o'er the dark and stormy sea.
I know that troubles all are ended, And happy forever they will be.
They are waiting and watching up yonder, And happy forever they will be.

153

LIZA JANE

Old-Time; Bluegrass; Western Swing; Breakdown; **DATE:** Late 1800's **OTHER NAMES:** "Lasses Cane," "It's Goodbye Liza Jane," "Tumblin' Creek Liza Jane," "Liza Jane," "Susan Jane," "Saro Jane" (Should not be confused with "Rock About My Saro Jane," or "L'il Liza Jane"-different songs); "Goodbye Liza Jane;" "Little Saro Jane" "My Little Dony;" "I Lost My Liza Jane." **RECORDING INFO:** The first influential recording was by the East Tennessee string band, The Hill Billies, who released it under the title "Mountaineer's Love Song" and the second was by another band from the same area, the Tenneva Ramblers, as "Miss Liza, Poor Gal." Bob Wills (Texas), the father of western swing, said this was the first tune he learned (as "Goodbye, Miss Liza Jane") to fiddle. **NOTES:** "Liza Jane/Goodbye Liza Jane" is part of the large family of songs cross referenced to other tunes including "Molly and Tenbrooks," and "Pig in a Pen." The "Liza Jane" lyrics are also sung to different tunes such as "Git Along Home Cindy." The name and lyrics appear in a variety of other songs including "Run Mollie Run" (lyrics) "Push Boat" (lyrics) "Cindy" (floating lyrics) "Old Joe Clark" (lyrics). The "Little Liza Jane" or "L'il Liza Jane" songs composed by Countess Ada de Lachau in 1916 are not part of the "Liza Jane" song family and are frequently confused with "Liza Jane" songs. From the Library of Congress: "In short, the tune is cut of a cloth so common in the Upper South, and in musical domains touched by the influence of the Upper South, that it could be described as a paradigmatic Southern tune, appearing in so many related versions, allied forms and modified guises that it almost defies genetic tracing." Eddie Cox, a minstrel show performer, published "Good-bye, Liza Jane" in the 1880's. He didn't claim any credit for writing it, just arranging it. In 1903 the Tin Pan Alley composer, Harry von Tilzer, published "Good-Bye, Eliza Jane" which was a different song altogether. Charlie Poole did a cover of the Tilzer version leading some to assume that it was a folk version. In 1917 Cecil Sharp collected "Liza Anne" in Kentucky that also seems to blend "Liza Jane" and the "Possum Up a Gum Stump."

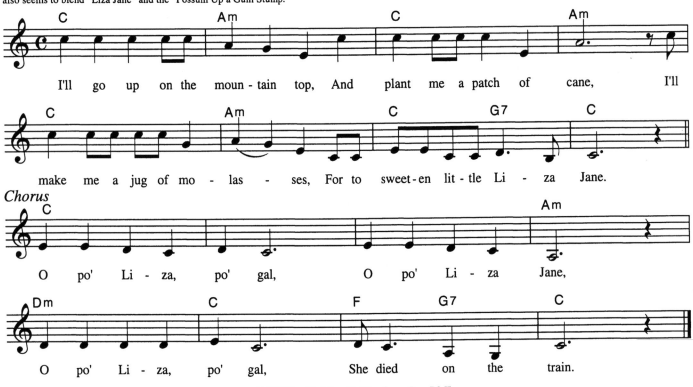

C   **Am**
I'm goin' up on the mountain top,
    C   **Am**
To plant me a patch of cane,
    C   **Am**
I'll make me a jug of molasses,
    C   **G7 Am**
For to sweeten little Liza Jane.
    C
Chorus: O po' Liza, po' gal,
    Am
O po' Liza Jane,
Dm   **C**
O po' Liza, po' gal,
F   **G**   **C**
She died on the train.

When I go a-courtin',
I'll go on the train.
When I go to marry,
I'll marry Liza Jane.

The hardest work I ever did,
Was a-brakin' on a train;
The easiest work I ever did,
Was a-huggin' Liza Jane.

When I went to see her,
She wrung her hands and cried;
She swore I was the ugliest thing,

That ever lived or died.
I ask little Liza to marry me-
What do you reckon she said?
Said she would not marry me,
If everybody else was dead.

Old corn likker's done made,
Still's tore out an' gone.
What will pore little Liza do,
When I'm took off an' gone?

Don't you weep, my darling,
Don't you weep nor cry;
I'll be back to see you
In the long old by-and-by.

Lonesome Valley

Traditional Bluegrass Gospel; **DATE:** 1800's; **CATEGORY:** Early Country and Bluegrass Songs; **RECORDING INFO:** Bluegrass Messengers on "Farther Along;" Carter Family- 1935; Erik Darling; Joan Baez; Roy Acuff; Mainer's Mountaineers; Monroe Brothers; **OTHER NAMES:** You Got To Walk That Lonesome Valley; That Lonesome Valley; Jesus Walked That Lonesome Valley; **NOTES:** This American spiritual has become a favorite bluegrass song. It was a country hit as "John the Baptist" by Vernon Dalhart in 1925 and was popularized by the Carter Family in the 1930's. Below are the lyrics from Bluegrass Messengers on "Farther Along:"

```
              G   C        G
Chorus: You got to walk  that lonesome valley
              D  C      G
You got to walk it by yourself;
                 C         G   E7
Ain't nobody else, can walk it for you.
          A7              D        G
You got to walk that lonesome valley by yourself.
```

Some say John, he was a Baptist
Some say John he was a Jew
I say John, just like the bible,
I say John, John, John, he was a preacher man too.

You got to walk that lonesome valley
You got to walk it by yourself;
Ain't nobody else, can walk it for you.
You got to walk that lonesome valley for yourself.

There is a road, that leads to glory,
Through a valley so far away,
Ain't nobody else, can walk it for you,
All they can do, is point the way. *Chorus*

LONG JOURNEY HOME

Traditional Bluegrass Song, **DATE:** 1890's; **CATEGORY:** Early Country and Bluegrass Songs; **RECORDING INFO:** Wilma Lee Cooper; Jim Eanes and the Shenandoah Valley Boys; Lilly Brothers; Wade Mainer; Monroe Brothers; Don Reno and Bill Harrell with the Tennesse Cutups; Doc Watson; **OTHER NAMES:** My Long Journey Home; Two Dollar Bill; Lost All My Money But a Two Dollar Bill; **NOTES:** Categorized by Meade as "Yonder Come the High Sherriff" it was recorded by the Monroes in 1936. Delmore Brothers called it, "Big Ball in Texas." It is commonly known in most bluegrass circles as "Two Dollar Bill."

G
Lost all my money but a two dollar bill
              C   **G**
Two dollar bill, boys, two dollar bill

Lost all my money but a two dollar bill
        D   **G**
I'm on my long journey home.

Cloudy in the West and it looks like rain
Looks like rain, boys, looks like rain
Cloudy in the west and it looks like rain
I'm on my long journey home. *Chorus*

Black smoke a rising and it surely is a train
Surely is a train, boys, surely is a train
Black smoke arising and it surely is a train
I'm on my long journey home. *Chorus*

Starting into raining and I've got to go home
Got to go home, boys, got to go home
Starting into raining and I've got to go home
I'm on my long journey home. *Chorus*

Lord, I'm Coming Home

Southern Gospel Song by William Kirkpatrick; **DATE**: 1892; **CATEGORY**: Early Country and Bluegrass Songs; **RECORDING INFO**: Country Gentlemen; Jimmy Martin; **OTHER NAMES**: "A Sermon To Men;" **NOTES**: First recorded by Hugh Gibbs String Band in 1927. The usual bluegrass arrangement as recorded by Jimmy Martin is for the lead to sing the first and third lines and other singers join on the second and fourth lines of the verse.

G   C   G   D
I wandered far away from God now I'm coming home
    G   C   G   D   G
The path of sin too long I've trod, Lord, I'm coming home.

          G   C   G   D
Chorus: Coming home, coming home, never more to roam
   G   C   G   D   G
Open wide thine arms of love, Lord, I'm coming home.

I've wasted many precious years, now I'm coming home
I now repent with bitter tears, Lord, I'm coining home. *Chorus*

I'm tired of sin and straying, Lord, now I'm coming home
I'll trust Thy love, believe Thy word, Lord, I'm coming home. *Chorus*

My soul is sick, my heart is sore, now I'm coming home
My strength renew, my hope restore, Lord, I'm coming home. *Chorus*

My only hope, my only plea, now I'm coining home
That Jesus died and died for me, Lord, I'm coming home. *Chorus*

I need His cleansing blood I know, now I'm coming home
Oh wash me whiter than the snow, Lord, I'm coming home. *Chorus*

LOST AND I'LL NEVER FIND THE WAY

Traditional Old-Time and Bluegrass Song; **DATE:**1900's; **CATEGORY:** Early Country and Bluegrass Songs; **RECORDING INFO:** Stanley Brothers; Ricky Skaggs; Cedar Hill; **OTHER NAMES:** "I'm Lost, I'll Never Find the Way;" **NOTES:** The classic version of this song is The Stanley Brothers & The Clinch Mountain Boys available on Bear Family BCD 15681 BH.

      G   **C**   **G**   **D**
Chorus: Lonesome, lonesome pining away
      G   **C**
Now you said it's best we part even though it breaks my heart
  G   **D**   **G**
I'm lost and I'll never find the way.

Since you said we must part, darling you broke my heart
I'm drifting like a ship lost at sea
In a world of despair it is so lonesome there
Dear, why don't you come back to me.   *Chorus*

Now you said you'd be true, no one else would ever do
I believed in you with all my heart and soul
But you broke every vow and it's all over now
I'm left in this world alone and cold.

LOVE SOMEBODY, YES I DO

Traditional Old-Time and Bluegrass Song; **DATE:** 1839 as Richmond Blues; **CATEGORY:** Fiddle and Instrumental Tunes; **RECORDING INFO:** Uncle Dave Macon; North Carolina Ramblers; Clark Kessinger; **OTHER NAMES:** I Love Somebody; Too Young to Marry; My Love Is But A Lassie Yet; **NOTES:** This fiddle tune melody has a large number of names and is traced to My Love Is But A Lassie Yet. Sharp recorded it from Mrs. Stella Reynolds along the Blue Ridge in Meadows of Dan, Virginia, as "I'm Seventeen Come Sunday" (*English Folk Songs from the Southern Appalachians*, vol. 2, 158, #127-D).

G		D	G		D

Love somebody, yes I do, Love somebody, yes I do,

G		C	G	D7	G

Love somebody, yes I do, Love somebody, but I won't tell who.

G				D	

Love somebody, yes I do, Love somebody, yes I do,

G			D		G

Love somebody, yes I do, And I hope somebody loves me too.

Love somebody, can't guess who, Love somebody, can't guess who,
Love somebody, can't guess who, Love somebody, but I won't tell who.

Love somebody, yes I do, Love somebody, yes I do,
Love somebody, yes I do, 'tween sixteen and twenty-two.

LULA WALLS

Traditional Old-Time and Bluegrass Song; **DATE**: 1888; **CATEGORY**: Early Country and Bluegrass Songs; **RECORDING INFO**: Bascom Lamar Lunsford-1927; Carter Family- 1929;Aunt Idy Harper & Coon Creek Girls 1938; **OTHER NAMES**: Lulu Wall; **NOTES**: The Carter Family popularized this old-time love song. It first appears in Wehman's Collection of Songs Jan. of 1888, issue number #17. The lyrics resemble Lunsford but I've used the Carter family chords.

She's a maid-en bright and fair. She has love-ly gold-en hair. She's as love-ly as an an-gel from on high. She has stole my heart a-way. Has left me in sad dis-may. She's that ag-gra-va-tin' beaut-y, Lu-la Walls. And ev-'ry lit-tle while she greets me with a smile. She'll ask me to her hap-py home to call. If she'd on-ly be my wife, I'd be hap-py all my life with that ag-gra-va-tin' beaut-y, Lu-la Walls.

G   **C**   **G**
One evening after dark, I met her in the park
                           D
I knew my time to fall in love had come
G   **C**   **G**
I lifted up my hat and we began to chat
            D7   **G**
She said that I could see her at her home. *Chorus*

One evening it was late and I met her at the gate
She said that she would wed me in the Fall
but no answer would she say and only turned away
She's that aggravating beauty Lula Walls.   *Chorus*

Oh if she were only mine I'd build a mansion fine
And around it I'd build a fence so tall
And I would so jealous be if any one but me
Could gaze upon the beauty of Lula Walls. *Chorus*

                                    C   **G**
Chorus: And ev'ry little while she greets me with a smile.
                                    D
She'll ask me to her happy home to call.
          G   **C**   **G**
If she'd only be my wife, I'd be happy all my life
                              D   **G**
with that aggravatin' beauty, Lula Walls.

MAMA DON'T 'LOW

Traditional Old-Time and Bluegrass Song; **DATE**: Early 1900's; **CATEGORY**: Early Country and Bluegrass Songs; **RECORDING INFO**: Riley Puckett-1928 Roots RL-701, LP (1971), cut# 10; Allen Brothers; Shelton Brothers; J. E. Mainer's Mountaineers; Cow Cow Davenport; **OTHER NAMES**: No Low Down Hangin' Around; Mama Won't Allow No Low Down Hangin' Around; Mama Don't Allow; **NOTES**: First recorded by Riley Puckett as *Mama Won't Allow No Low Down Hangin' Around* in 1928, the exact source of this skiffle song is unknown. The melody is quite popular and has been used in a variety of songs from both black and white sources including "Mama Don't 'low no Easy Riders Here," "The Crawdad Song," versions of "Frog Went a Courtin'," Woody Guthrie & the Almanacs "Pittsburgh Town," and Mississippi Fred McDowell's "My Babe." Alan Lomax collected a version entitled "Cap'n Don't 'Low no Truckin'" in his 1939 field recording trip.

G
Mama don't 'low no banjo playing round here
                                                        D
Mama don't 'low no banjo playing round here
G   **C**
We don't care what mama don't 'low. Gonna pick my banjo anyhow,
G   **D**   **G**
Mama don't 'low no banjo playing round here.

Mama don't 'low no guitar playing round here
Mama don't 'low no guitar playing round here
I don't care what mama don t 'low. Gonna play my guitar anyhow,
Mama don't 'low no guitar playing round here.

Mama don't 'low no talking round here
Mama don't 'low no talking round here
I don't care what mama don't 'low. Gonna shoot my mouth off anyhow,
Mama don't 'low no talking round here.

Mama don't 'low no singing round here
Mama don't 'low no singing round here
I don't care what mama don't 'low. Gonna sing my head off-anyhow,
Mama don't 'low no singing round here.

MAN OF CONSTANT SORROW

Traditional Song and White "Blues;" **DATE:** 1913 Burnett; 1917 Sharp. Earlier through the "Drowsy Sleeper" branch (1812). **CATEGORY:** Early Country and Bluegrass Songs; **RECORDING INFO:** The best-known period version of "I Am A Man Of Constant Sorrow" was Emry Arthur's 1928 recording (Vo 5208). The Stanley Brothers; Roscoe Holcomb; Frank Proffitt; **OTHER NAMES:** "Farewell Song;" "I Am a Man of Constant Sorrow;" **NOTES:** The first published versions of "Man Of Constant Sorrow" are the "Farewell Song" from a 1913 songbook printed by Richard Burnett of Monticello, Ky. and "In Old Virginny" from Sharp's English Folk Songs from the Southern Appalachians. Both "The Farewell Song" and Sharp's "In Old Virginny" Version C are early versions of "The Man of Constant Sorrow," which is a branch of "East Virginia Blues." Richard Burnett was born in 1883, married in 1905, and blinded in 1907. The second stanza of "Farewell Song" mentions the singer has been blind six years, which would date it at 1913. In later years, Richard Burnett was asked about the song. He himself could not remember, at that time, if he had composed it, or copied it, or — perhaps most likely — adapted it from something traditional. With the "O Brother Where Art Thou?" phenomena "The Man of Constant Sorrow" has become a crossover pop hit.

A7	**D**
(In constant sorrow through all his days)	

D	**G**
I am a man of constant sorrow	

A	**D**
I've seen trouble all my days	

	G
I bid farewell to old Kentucky	

A	**D**
The place where I was borned and raised	
(The place where he was borned and raised)	

For six long years I've been in trouble
No pleasure here on earth I find
For in this world I'm bound to ramble
I have no friends to help me now
(He has no friends to help him now)

It's fare thee well my own true lover
I never expect to see you again
For I'm bound to ride that northern railroad
Perhaps I'll die upon this train
(Perhaps he'll die upon this train)

You can bury me in some deep valley
For many years where I may lay
Then you may learn to love another
While I am sleeping in my grave
(While he is sleeping in his grave)

Maybe your friends think I'm just a stranger
My face you'll never see no more
But there is one promise that is given
I'll meet you on God's golden shore
(He 'll meet you on God's golden shore)

162

METHODIST PIE

Traditional Old-Time and Bluegrass Gospel Song; **DATE:** 1881; **CATEGORY:** Early Country and Bluegrass Songs; **RECORDING INFO:** Bradley Kincaid- 1928; Greenbriar Boys- Ragged But Right; Gene Autry; Cedar Hill; Grandpa Jones. **NOTES:** Methodist Pie was first printed in Medley of Jubilee Hymns p. 30-1881.

Now they all go there to have some fun and eat their grub so fine
Have apple sauce better & sugar in the gourd & a great big Methodist pie
You aughta hear 'em ringing when they all get to singing that good old Bye & Bye
Brother Jimmy McGee in the top of a tree hollered Lord I was born to die   *Chorus*

Now they all join hands, dancing round a ring, keep singing all the while
You'd think it was cyclone coming through the air you can hear 'em shout half a mile
Then the bell rings loud & the great big crowd breaks ranks & up they fly
While I pour on the sugar in the gourd and clean up the Methodist pie   *Chorus*

MIDNIGHT ON THE STORMY DEEP (LAWS M1)

Traditional Old-Time and Bluegrass Song; **DATE:** Early 1900's; **CATEGORY:** Early Country and Bluegrass Songs; **RECORDING INFO:** Earnest Stoneman; Blue Sky Boys; The Tony Rice Unit, on "Manzanita," Rounder 0092; "Hills of Home," Rounder; Bill Monroe and Doc Watson. **OTHER NAMES:** Early, Early in the Morning; Midnight on the Stormy Sea; **NOTES:** Categorized as "Early, Early in the Spring" by Meade, with words by Wilhelm Hauff- music is traditional German song; Recorded by Earnest Stoneman in 1927.

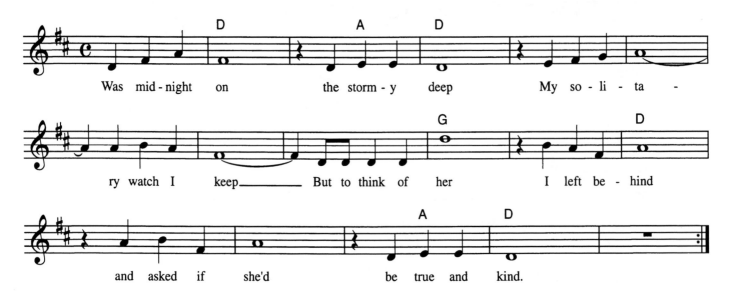

    D   **A**   **D**
Was midnight on the stormy deep, My solitary watch I keep
        G   **D**   **A**   **D**
But to think of her I left behind, And asked if she'd be true and kind.

    D   **A**   **D**
I never shall forget the day, that I was forced to go away
        G   **D**   **A**   **D**
In silence there my head she'd rest and hold me to her loving breast

Oh Willie, don't go back to sea, there's other girls as good as me
But none can love you true as I, pray don't go where the bullets fly

The deep, deep sea may us divide and I may be some other's bride
But still my thoughts will sometimes stray to thee when thou art far away

I never have proved false to thee, the heart I gave was true as thine
But you have proved untrue to me, I can no longer call thee mine

Then fare thee well, I'd rather make my home upon some icy lake
Where the southern sun refuse to shine, than to trust a love so false as thine

MIDNIGHT SPECIAL

Traditional Old-Time and Bluegrass Song; **DATE**: Early 1900's; **CATEGORY**: Early Country and Bluegrass Songs; **RECORDING INFO**: Hoyt Axton; Blue Sky Boys; Leadbelly; Brownie McGhee and Sonny Terry; Mac Wiseman; **NOTES**: Leadbelly's arrangement of the Midnight Special has become the most popular arrangement for this song. A character from the song "Midnight Special": "Sheriff Benson will arrest you..." if you go to Houston, the song warns. The sheriff in the song may have a historical basis in an actual sheriff, T.A. Binford, county sheriff of Harris County, Texas, from Dec. 1918 to Jan. 1, 1937. Indeed, Leadbelly sang "Binford," not "Benson" in his version of "Midnight Special."

(G)   **C**   **G**
Yonder come Miss Rosie, How in the world do you know?
       D7   **G**
I can tell her by her apron, And the dress she wore
       C   **G**
Umbrella on her shoulder, Piece of paper in her hand
       D7   **G**
Goes a marchin' to the Captain, Says I want my man.   *Chorus*

Now here comes jumpin' Judy, I'll tell you how I know
You know, Judy brought jumpin', To the whole wide world
She brought it in the morning, Just about the break of day
You know, if I ever get to jumpin', Oh Lord, I'll up and jump away.   *Chorus*

165

MIDNIGHT TRAIN

Traditional Old-Time and Bluegrass Song; **DATE**: Early 1900's; **CATEGORY**: Early Country and Bluegrass Songs; **RECORDING INFO**: Maddox Brothers and Rose; Delmore Brothers; Dub Crouch/Norman Ford & the Bluegrass Rounders; Don Reno; Stanley Brothers; Doc Watson. **OTHER NAMES**: Ridin' That/The Midnight Train; Riding on that Midnight Train; **NOTES**: This song is similar to "Lonesome Road Blues" songs. The Delmore Brothers version is different. The Stanley Brothers, Roy Cobb and Don Reno all have similar versions.

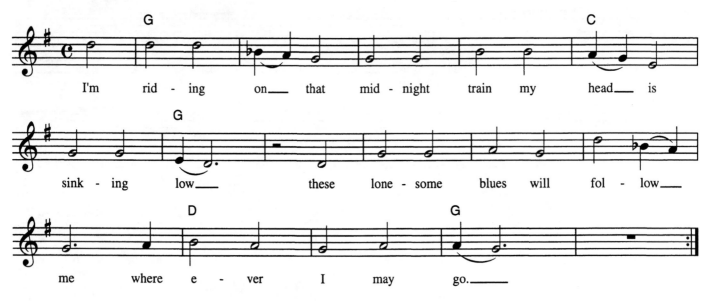

        G
Chorus: I'm riding on that midnight train
   C   **G**
My head is sinking low

These lonesome blues will follow me
    D   **G**
Where ever I may go.

No matter what I say or do
You're never satisfied
I tried and tried so many times
I'm leaving you now goodbye.   *Chorus*

Oh, why on Earth was I ever born
I'll never understand
To fall in love with a woman like you
In love with another man.   *Chorus*

Model Church

Gospel Song by John Yates and E.O. Excell; **DATE:** 1884; **CATEGORY:** Early Gospel Songs; **RECORDING INFO:** Asa Martin- 1929; J.D. Crowe 'The Model Church' Sundown SDLP 038; Tony Rice, Doyle Lawson, Bobby Hicks, Todd Phillips; **NOTES:** J. D. Crowe's excellent version was on Lemco 611, it is available on CD, Rebel 1585.

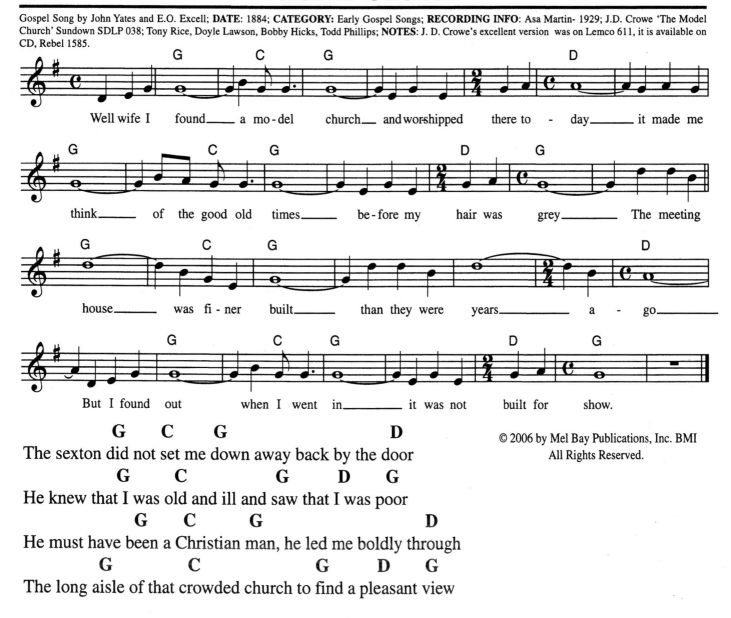

Well wife I found a mo-del church and worshipped there to-day it made me think of the good old times be-fore my hair was grey The meeting house was fi-ner built than they were years a-go But I found out when I went in it was not built for show.

```
         G     C    G                 D
The sexton did not set me down away back by the door
         G       C          G       D    G
He knew that I was old and ill and saw that I was poor
           G        C        G              D
He must have been a Christian man, he led me boldly through
        G        C         G      D    G
The long aisle of that crowded church to find a pleasant view
```

I wish you'd heard the singing choir, it had the old time ring
The preacher said with trumpet voice, "Let all the people sing".
Old Correlation was the tune, the music upward rose
I thought I heard the angel choir strike on their harps of gold

I tell you wife it did me good to sing those hymns once more
I felt just like some wrecked Marine who gets a glimpse of shore
It made me want to lay aside this weather beaten boat
And anchor in that blessed port, forever from the storm

Dear wife the toil will soon be o'er, the Victory soon be won
But a shining strand is just ahead, our race is nearly run
We're nearing Canaan's happy shore, our hopes are bright and fair
Thank God we'll never sin again, there'll be no sorrow there
There'll be no sorrow there, In heaven above where all in love, There'll be no sorrow there.

MOLLY AND TENBROOKS

Traditional Old-Time and Bluegrass Song; **DATE:** Late 1878; **CATEGORY:** Early Country and Bluegrass Songs; **RECORDING INFO:** "Tim Brook" was recorded by The Carver Boys in 1929; Henry Thomas- Run, Mollie Run- 1927; Bill Monroe & His Blue Grass Boys; Warde Ford; The Stanley Brothers; **OTHER NAMES:** Run Mollie Run; Tim Brook; **NOTES:** Originally called "an old Kentucky folk song," about the horse race of Kentucky thoroughbred Ten Broeck and mare Miss Mollie McCarthy, the song has been identified with several versions by Bill Monroe (1948) and the Stanley Brothers. The race on July 4, 1878 between between Ten Broeck and Miss Mollie McCarthy was won by Ten Broeck.

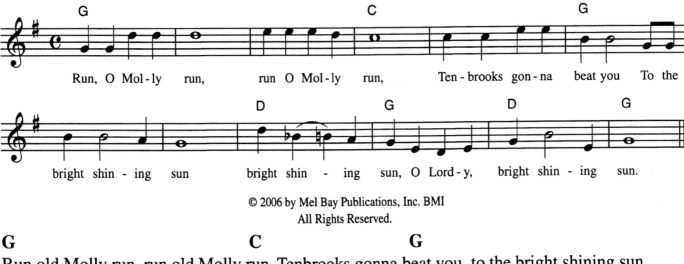

G   **C**   **G**
Run old Molly run, run old Molly run, Tenbrooks gonna beat you, to the bright shining sun.
    D   **G**   **D**   **G**
To the bright shining sun, Lord, to the bright shining sun.

Tenbrooks was a big bay horse, wore a shaggy mane.
He ran all 'round the Midwest, and beat the Memphis train.
Beat the Memphis train, Lord, beat the Memphis train.

Out in Californy, where Molly did as she pleased.
Come back to old Kentucky, got beat with all ease.
Beat with all ease, Lord, beat with all ease.

See old Molly coming, she's coming around the curve.
See old Tenbrooks running, straining every nerve.
Straining every nerve, Lord, straining every nerve.

Kyper, Kyper, you're not riding right. Molly's a-beating old Tenbrooks, clear 'round the side.
Clear 'round the side, Lord, clear 'round the side.

Kyper, Kyper, Kyper my son. Give old Tenbrooks the bridle, and let old Tenbrooks run.
Let old Tenbrooks run, Lord, let old Tenbrooks run.

Women's all a-laughing, children's all a-crying, Men folks all a-hollin', old Tenbrooks a-flying.
Old Tenbrooks a-flying, Lord, old Tenbrooks a-flying.

Go a-catch old Tenbrooks, said hitch him in the shade.
We're gonna bury old Molly, in a coffin ready made.
Coffin ready made, Lord, a coffin ready made.

MORE PRETTY GIRLS THAN ONE

Traditional Old-Time and Bluegrass Song; **DATE**: Early 1900's; **CATEGORY**: Early Country and Bluegrass Songs; **RECORDING INFO**: First recorded in 1927 by Jesse James and J.D. Foster; Arthur Smith Trio; Lester Flatt and Earl Scruggs; Highwoods Stringband; More Pretty Girls Than One; New Lost City Ramblers; Mac Wiseman; **OTHER NAMES**: There's More Pretty Girls Than One; **NOTES**: More Pretty Girls has a close relationship with *Lonesome Road* and *Goodbye, Little Bonnie Blue Eyes*. It's also related to *Lost Love Blues* and *You May Forsake Me*.

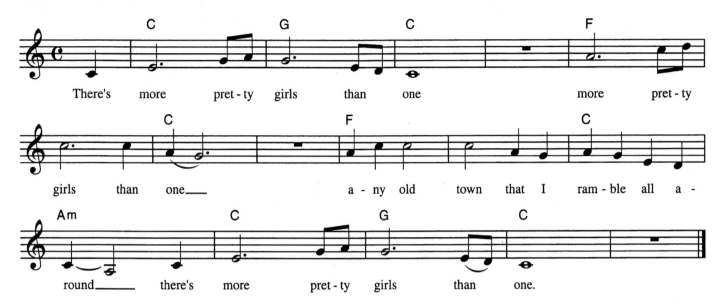

```
     C       G     C    F           C
There's more pretty girls than one, More pretty girls than one
F           C     Am        C      G        C
Any old town that I ramble all around, There's more pretty girls than one.
```

Mama talked to me last night, She gave to me some good advice
She said, "Son, you oughta quit this old rambling around
And marry you a sweet loving wife."   *Chorus*

Honey, look down that old lonesome road, Hang down your pretty head and cry
Cause I'm thinking all about them pretty little gals
And hoping that I'll never die.   *Chorus*

MOUNTAIN DEW

Old-Time and Bluegrass Song; **DATE:** 1920; **CATEGORY:** Early Country and Bluegrass Songs; **RECORDING INFO:** Bascam Lamar Lunsford- 1928; Delmore Brothers- 1940; Brickman, Weissberg & Company; Curly Fox; Lula Belle & Scotty; Uncle Dave Macon; Doc Watson; **OTHER NAMES:** Old Mountain Dew; Good Ol' Mountain Dew; Real Old Mountain Dew. **NOTES:** The original "Mountain Dew" was created by banjoist Bascom Lunsford, who has directed a mountain folk festival in Asheville, North Carolina, for almost 30 years. About 1920 I composed the words and the tune to this song, and I put it on a Brunswick record about 1928. Of course, it was somewhat stilted, but it did very well as a record. But following that, the eminent singer 'Scotty,' Scott Wiseman of Lulu Belle and Scotty fame, added some more modernized stanzas, sang it, put it on a record, and it was re-popularized. Now we hear it on every hand by the folk singers and entertainers there with their own words, and the tune has stayed very much the same way, but it's well to know the growth of the thing. So I will give just as I composed it in 1920."

There's an ol' holl-er tree down the road here from me Where you lay down a dol-lar or two.___ You go 'round the bend and when you come back a-gain There's a pint of that good ol' moun-tain dew.___

Chorus: Oh they call it that good ol' mountain dew, And them that refuse it are few.

I'll hush up my mug if you'll fill up my jug, With that good ol' mountain dew.

There's an old hollow tree down the road here from me
Where you can lay down a dollar or two.
You go 'round the bend and when you come back again
There's a pint of that good old mountain dew. *Chorus*

My uncle Bill has a still on the hill, Where he runs off a gallon or two
The buzzards in the sky get so high that they can't fly
From sniffin' that good old mountain dew. *Chorus*

Now my old cousin Mort he's sawed off and short, He stands about four foot two.
But he feels just like a giant when you give him a pint
Of that good old mountain dew. *Chorus*

My old aunt June got some brand new parfume, It had such a sweet smellin' pew
When we had it analyzed much to our surprise
It was nothin' but that good ol' mountain dew. *Chorus*

MY HOME'S ACROSS THE SMOKY MOUNTAINS

Traditional Old-Time and Bluegrass Song; **DATE:** 1909; **CATEGORY:** Early Country and Bluegrass Songs; **RECORDING INFO:** Kelly Harrell- 1925; Carolina Tar Heels; Carter Family- 1937; Arthur Smith Trio; Delmore Brothers; Doc Watson; **OTHER NAMES:** My Home's Across the Blue Ridge Mountains; **NOTES:** First appears in the Journal of American Folklore, No. 222 in 1909. The melody to *Aunt Rhody* and *Go Tell It on the Mountain* have very much in common. A.P.Carter (of the Carter Family) and Thomas Ashley (of The Carolina Tar Heels- Doc Walsh (1901-1967), Clarence Ashley (1895-1967) and Garley Foster (1905-1968)) who recorded for Victor between 1927 and 1929) have recorded two essential versions.

G   **D**   **G**
My home's across the Smoky Mountains, My home's across the Smoky Mountains
                                                D   **G**
My home's across the Smoky Mountains, And I never get to see you any more.

Goodbye my little Sugar Darling, Goodbye my little Sugar Darling
Goodbye my little Sugar Darling, And I never get to see you any more.

Rock my baby, feed it candy, Rock my baby, feed it candy
Rock my baby, feed it candy, And I never get to see you any more.

My home's across the Smoky Mountains, My home's across the Smoky Mountains
My home's across the Smoky Mountains, And I never get to see you any more.

NEW RIVER TRAIN

Traditional Old-Time, Breakdown & Song; **DATE:** Late 1800's; **CATEGORY:** Fiddle and Instrumental Tunes **RECORDING INFO:** Kelly Harrell, "New River Train" (Victor 19596, 1925; on KHarrell01) Tommy Jarrell; Doc Watson, Fred Price & Clint Howard; Monroe Brothers – Feast Here Tonight/RCA; Charlie Poole and the Highlanders; Roscoe Holcomb and Wade Ward; **OTHER NAMES:** "Darlin' You Can't Have One;" "A Trip to New York On the Train (Instrumental)." **NOTES:** The Chesapeake & Ohio Railroad through the beautiful New River Gorge in southern West Virginia was completed in early 1873. The "New River Train" was probably written shortly after the railroad was completed. Fields Ward of the Ward Family, of Galax, VA, says he learned the song circa 1895. The version quoted from Bill Monroe is Harrell's. Later, Vance Randolph collected a version that went up to ten. The melody has been described as a "Blue Ridge Mountain standard." The tune and lyrics are similar to "Mole in the Ground" and "My Last Gold Dollar." There is also a resemblance to "Crawdad".

G
I'm riding on that new river train
               D
Riding on that new river train
G   **C**
Same old train that brought me here
      G   **D**   **G**
Gonna take me away again.

Darling, you can't love one,
Darling, you can't love one
You can't love one and have any fun,
Darling, you can't love one. *Chorus*

(Verse Two) You can't love two and still be true
(Verse Three) You can't love three and still love me
(Verse Four) You can't love four and love any more
(Verse Five) You can't love five and get money from my hive
(Verse Six) You can't love six, for that kind of love don't mix

NINE POUND HAMMER

Old-time Song; **DATE:** Late 1800's- Early 1900's; **CATEGORY:** Early Country and Bluegrass Songs; **RECORDING INFO:** Al Hopkins & his Buckle Busters (Brunswick 177, 1927); Frank Blevins & his Tar Heel Rattlers; Grayson and Whitter-1928; Flatt & Scruggs & the Foggy Mountain Boys; Greenbriar Boys; Jim & Jesse and the Virginia Boys; Monroe Brothers; Don Reno and Bill Harrell with the Tennesse Cutups; Merle Travis; **OTHER NAMES:** "Spikedriver Blues;" "Roll On, John;" "Roll On Buddy, Roll On" "Take This Hammer." **NOTES:** "Nine Pound Hammer" is one of the few work songs to ever enjoy popularity. Early string bands such as Frank Blevins' Tar Heel Rattlers and Al Hopkins Bucklebusters were the first to introduce it as a performance piece. Bluegrass pioneers Bill and Charlie Monroe and fingerpicker Merle Travis brought it to a wider audience and are largely responsible for its continuing popularity. Some versions use a second part that echos the melody.

    G   **C**   **G D**   **G**
This nine pound hammer is a little too heavy, For my size, buddy for my size
            C   **G D**   **G**
Roll on buddy, don't you roll too slow, How can I roll when the wheels won't go.

It's a long way to Harlan, it's a long way to Hazard
Just to get a little booze just to get a little booze
Oh, the nine pound hammer killed John Henry
Ain't gonna kill me, ain't gonna kill me.

There ain't one hammer down in this tunnel
That can ring like mine, that can ring like mine
Rings like silver, shines like gold,
Rings like silver, shines like gold.

Buddy when I'm long gone, won't you make my tombstone
Out of number nine coal, out of number nine coal
I'm going on the mountain, just to see my baby
And I ain't coming back, no I ain't coming back.

OH DEATH

Traditional Old-Time and Bluegrass Song; **DATE**: Early 1900's; **CATEGORY:** Early Country and Bluegrass Songs; **RECORDING INFO**: Carter Family; (Charlie) Monroe's Boys; Dock Boggs; Sarah Ogan Gunning; Ralph Stanley; New Lost City Ramblers; **OTHER NAMES**: Money Cannot Buy Your Soul; Death Have Mercy on my Age/Soul; Conversation With Death; Death Is Awful; Awful Death; **NOTES**: A gripping version of "O Death" is sung by Ralph Stanley on the soundtrack of the movie "O Brother, Where art Thou?" Oh Death is found in both the white and black tradition from Texas to the Georgia Sea Islands and is available today in widely contrasting settings: unaccompanied vocal solo, hillbilly duet (with guitars), and bluegrass band. A similar dialogue with Death turns up in the traditional English song "Death and the Lady" published by J. Deacon between 1683 and 1700.

D
Well what is this that I can't see, With ice cold hands taking hold of me?
                                              C   **D**
"Well I am death, none can excel, I'll open the door to heaven or hell."
D   **C**   **D**
Chorus: Oh, death- Oh death- Won't you spare me over til another year?

Whoa, death, someone would pray. Could you wait to call me til another day?
The children pray, the preacher preached; Time and mercy is out of your reach.

"I'll fix your feet til you can't walk, I'll lock your jaw til you can't talk,
I'll close your eyes so you can't see- This very hour come and go with me."

"In death I come to take the soul, Leave the body and leave it cold;
To drop the flesh off of the frame; The earth and worms both have a claim."

My mother came to my bed, Placed a cold towel upon my head,
My head is warm, my feet are cold, Death is a-movin' upon my soul.

Oh death, how you're treatin' me, You close my eyes so I can't see.
Well, you're hurtin' my body, you make me cold, You run my life right out of my soul.

Oh, death, please consider my age. Please don't take me at this stage.
My wealth is all at your command, If you'll remove your icy hands.

"Oh the young, the rich or poor , All alike to me you know.
No wealth, no land, no silver or gold, nothin' satisfies me but your soul."

OLD BLUE

Traditional Old-Time and Bluegrass Song; **DATE:** Early 1900's; **CATEGORY:** Early Country and Bluegrass Songs; **RECORDING INFO:** Jim Jackson- 1928; Mike Seeger and Alice Gerrard; Dillards; **OTHER NAMES:** Dog Blue; **NOTES:** Hill people and back country folk used to live off hunting, and a good hound dog was worth his weight in gold. Old Blue has been sung by African-American construction gangs, 1915-1916 and Perrow collected a version in 1909.

    D   **A7**   **D**
I had an old dog and his name was Blue, Betcha five dollars he's a good dog too.
    D   **A7**   **D**
Every night just about good dark, Blue goes out and begins to bark
    A7   **D**   **A7**   **D**
Come old Blue, you good dog you. Come old Blue, you good dog you.

Blue chased a possum up a 'simmon tree, Barked at the possum and grinned at me.
Chased that possum way out on a limb, Blue sat down and he talked to him
Come old Blue, you good dog you. Come old Blue, you good dog you.

Blue got sick, he got mighty sick, Called for the doctor to come right quick.
The doctor come and he come in a run, But he said old Blue your huntin's done.
Come old Blue, you good dog you. Come old Blue, you good dog you.

Old Blue died and he died so hard, He shook the ground in my back yard.
I dug his grave with a silver spade, And lowered him down with a length of chain.
Come old Blue, you good dog you. Come old Blue, you good dog you.

There's just one thing that troubles my mind, Blue went to heaven and left me behind.
When I get to heaven, first thing I'll do, Is get my horn and call for Blue.
Come old Blue, you good dog you. Come old Blue, you good dog you

OLD DAN TUCKER

Old-Time and Bluegrass Song- Daniel Decatur Emmett; **DATE**: 1841; Published in 1843; **CATEGORY:** Early Country and Bluegrass Songs; **RECORDING INFO**: Fiddlin' John Carson- 1924; Uncle Dave Macon- 1925; Homer and the Barnstormers; **OTHER NAMES**: Dan Tucker; **NOTES**: In Richard Walser's *'North Carolina Legends'*, 1980, is the legend of *'Old Dan Tucker'*, where it is said that he was born in London in 1714, and moved with his parents to Bath Town, North Carolina six years later. He is said to have married Margaret DeVane in 1740 and moved to what is now Randolph County and built a cabin there. Daniel Decatur Emmett wrote the song from black sources and published it in 1843. The *Dan Tucker* melody used was by Bob Wills in "Stay All Night" and is similar to the *Johnny Booker* songs.

G   **D**
Old Dan Tucker's a fine old man, Washed his face in a frying pan,
G   **D**   **G**
Combed his hair with a wagon wheel, Died of toothache in his heel.
                    G   **C**   **D**   **G**
Chorus: Get out the way old Dan Tucker, You're too late to get your supper,
                                    C   **D**   **G**
Supper's gone and dinner's a-cookin', Old Dan Tucker's just stands there lookin'.

Old Dan Tucker he come to town, Riding on a billygoat, leading a hound,
Hound dog bark and the billygoat jump, Throwed Dan Tucker on top of a stump.

Old Dan Tucker, he got drunk, Fell in the fire and he kicked up a chunk,
Red hot coal got in his shoe, Oh my Lawdy how the ashes flew.

Old Dan Tucker, he come to town, Swinging the ladies round and round,
First to the right and then to the left, And then to the gal that he loved best.

And now old Dan is a dead gone sucker, And never will go home to his supper,
Old Dan he has had his last ride, And the banjo's buried by his side.

OLD GOSPEL SHIP

Traditional Southern Gospel Song; **DATE**: Early 1900's; **CATEGORY**: Early Southern Gospel Songs; **RECORDING INFO**: Carter Family-1935; Monroe Brothers-1937; Red Smiley and the Bluegrass Cut-Ups; Joan Baez; New Lost City Ramblers; **OTHER NAMES**: Gospel Ship; **NOTES**: This popular Southern gospel song shares the melody with "Have a Feast Here Tonight." A.P. Carter and the Carter Family have an excellent version. Alan Lomax collected a version from Ruby Bass on Southern Journeys- Vol. 4, Brethren, We Meet Again: Southern White Spirituals. The melody for the chorus is almost identical to the verse.

C   F   C
I have good new to bring and that is why I sing,
          G7
All my joys with you I will share
    C   F   C
I'm gonna take a trip on that old gospel ship,
      G7   C
And go sailing through the air.
      C   F   C
Chorus: I'm gonna take a trip on that old gospel ship
       G7
I'm going far beyond the sky
 C   F   C
I'm gonna shout and sing, until the bells do ring
         G   C
When I'm bidding this world good-bye.

If you are ashamed of me, you ought not to be
And you better have a care
If too much fault you find, you'll sure be left behind
When I'm sailing through the air.

I can hardly wait, I know I won't be late
I'll spend all my time in prayer
And when my ship comes in, I'll leave this world of sin
And go sailing through the air.

OLD JOE CLARK

Traditional Old-Time and Bluegrass Song; **DATE**: Late 1800's, Journal of American Folklore 1912; **CATEGORY**: Early Country and Bluegrass Songs; **RECORD-ING INFO**: Fiddlin' John Carson 1923; Carter Family; Dillards; Kentucky Colonels; Clark Kessinger; Kingston Trio; **NOTES**: Bayard thinks it was originally a song tune that later became a fiddle standard and play party tune. Mike Seeger relates the local story of the origins of the tune where he lives in Rockbridge County, Va.: Joe Clark's father settled around Irish Creek, near South River, in the early 1800's. Joe Clark had a daughter, and a jilted beau is said to have written the song, out of jealousy, in the late 1800's. The Clarks have been family-style string musicians right down through the years. Another investigation determined the source of the tune to be the murder in Maryland of a traveling salesman named Herbert Brown by Joe Clark and Brown's wife Betsy sometime after the Civil War. Joe and Betsy attempted to cover up the crime by asserting that Brown was on a trip up North. This perhaps explains the verse: Old Joe Clark killed a man/Layed him in the sand" and the chorus which includes "goodbye Betsy Brown." Virginia family band "Fiddlin'" Cowan Powers and Family's recording of the piece was the third best-selling country music record of 1924, while the Skillet Lickers (north Georgia) 1926 recording was the fourth best-selling for that year. Typically it is played A A B B form.

G   **F**
Old Joe Clark was a good old man, Never did no harm
G   **D**   **G**
Said he would not hoe my corn, Might hurt his fiddling arm.

I went down to Old Joe's house, Never been there before
He slept on a feather bed, And I slept on the floor.

                G   **F**
Chorus: Fare thee well Old Joe Clark, Fare thee well I say
G   **D**   **G**
Fare thee well Old Joe Clark, I am going away

I went down to Old Joe's house, Old Joe wasn't home
Ate up all of Old Joe's meat, And left Old Joe the bone.

I went down to Old Joe's house, He invited me to supper
Stumped my toe on a table leg, And stuck my nose in the butter.   *Chorus*

OLD RATTLER

Traditional Old-Time and Bluegrass Song; **DATE**: Early 1900's; **CATEGORY**: Early Country and Bluegrass Songs; **RECORDING INFO**: George Reneau- 1924; Elizabeth Cotton; Grandpa Jones-1947; John Snipes; **OTHER NAMES**: Here Rattler Here; **NOTES**: Listed as *Here Rattler Here* by Meade from George Reneau's 1924 recording, Old Rattler closely resembles the song, Fox Chase. The classic recording of this song is Grandpa Jones recording on King 668 in 1947.

C   **G7**
Old Rattler was a good old dog; As blind as he could be
              C
Ev'ry night at supper time; I believe that dog could see.
             G7
Chorus: Here! Rattler, (Help! Help!) Here! Rattler! (Help!)
          C
Call old Rattler from the barn; Here! Rattler! Here!

Old Rattler tree'd the other night; And I tho't he'd tree'd a 'coon
When I come to find out; He was barkin' at the moon.
Well, grandma had a yeller hen; We set her as you know
We set her on three buzzard eggs; And hatched out one old crow.

Grandpa had a muley cow; She was muley when she's born
It took a jaybird forty year; To fly from horn to horn.
Now if I had a needle and thread; As fine as I could sew
I'd sew my sweetheart to my back; And down the road I'd go

Old Rattler was a smart old dog; Even tho' he was blind
He wouldn't hurt one single thing; Tho' he was very fine.
One night I saw a big fat 'coon; Climb up in a tree
I called old Rattler right away; To get 'im down fer me.

But Rattler wouldn't do it; Because he liked that 'coon
I saw them walkin' paw in paw; Later by the light of the moon.
Now old Rattler's dead and gone; Like all good dogs do
You better not act a dog yourself; Or you'll be goin' there too.

OLD SOLDIER (RED HAIRED BOY)

Traditional Irish and American Reel or Breakdown; **DATE:** Bunting's 1840: A Collection of the Ancient Music of Ireland; **CATEGORY:** Fiddle and Instrumental Tunes; **RECORDING INFO- REDHAIRED BOY:** Doc Watson; Tony Rice; Norman Blake; **OTHER NAMES:** Red Haired Boy; "The Duck Chews Tobacco," "The First of May", "Gilderoy" "Johnny Dhu," "The Little Beggarman" "The Old Soldier with a Wooden Leg" **NOTES:** "Old Soldier with a Wooden Leg" from the Civil War period, is a US version of the "Red Haired Boy" tune popular at bluegrass and fiddle conventions. The song is quite common as "The Little Beggarman" throughout the British Isles.

       C   **F**
Oh, there was an old soldier and he had a wooden leg.
     C   **B♭**   **C**   **F**
He had no tobacco but tobacco he could beg. Another old soldier, as sly as a fox,
     C   **G**   **C**
He always kept tobacco in his old tobacco box.

Said one old soldier, "Won't you give me a chew?"
Said the other old soldier, "I'll be hanged if I do,
Just save up your money and put away your rocks,
And you'll always have tobacco in your old tobacco box."

Well, the one old soldier, he was feeling mighty bad,
He said, "I'll get even, I will begad!"
He goes to a corner, take a rifle from the peg,
And stabs the other soldier with a splinter from his leg.

Now there was an old hen and she had a wooden foot,
And she made her nest by the mulberry root,
She laid more eggs that any hen on the farm,
And another wooden leg wouldn't do her any harm.

OLD TIME RELIGION

Traditional Old-Time and Bluegrass Song; **DATE:** 1880; **CATEGORY:** Early Country and Bluegrass Songs; **RECORDING INFO:** Red Ellis and the Huron Valley Boys; Jim and Jesse; E. C. and Orna Ball; Clyde Moody; Johnson Family Singers; **OTHER NAMES:** Give Me That Old Time Religion; Give Me Old Time Music; **NOTES:** This piece was copyrighted in 1891 by Charlie D. Tillman but given that the text sung by the Fisk Jubilee Singers was printed in 1880, the claim is in error. First recorded by Homer Rodenheaver in 1923 on Co A3856, this spiritual has been popular among black and white performers. "Give Me Old Time Music" was recorded by Arthur Smith & His Dixie Liners on October 1, 1938, which is a parody of "That Old-Time Religion."

           G   **D**   **G**

Chorus: Gimme that old time religion, Gimme that old time religion

            C   **G**   **D**   **G**

Gimme that old time religion, It's good enough for me.

It was good for the Hebrew children
It was good for the Hebrew children
It was good for the Hebrew children
It's good enough for me.

It will do when the world's on fire
It will do when the world's on fire
It will do when the world's on fire
It's good enough for me.

It was good for Paul and Silas
It was good for Paul and Silas
It was good for Paul and Silas
That's good enough for me

It makes me love everybody
It makes me love everybody
It makes me love everybody
It's good enough for me.

OMIE WISE (LAWS F4)

Traditional Old-Time and Bluegrass Song; **DATE:** 1874; **CATEGORY:** Early Country and Bluegrass Songs; **RECORDING INFO:** Grayson & Whitter-Victor 21625, 1927; Clarence Tom Ashley-1929; Doug Wallin; Dock Boggs; Roscoe Holcomb; Doc Watson; **OTHER NAMES:** Naomi Wise; **NOTES:** Nineteen year old Naomi Wise was murdered in the summer of 1808, in Deep River near Asheboro NC. Her husband Jonathon Lewis was arrested for the crime, escaped, and not recaptured until 1815 at which time he was acquitted.

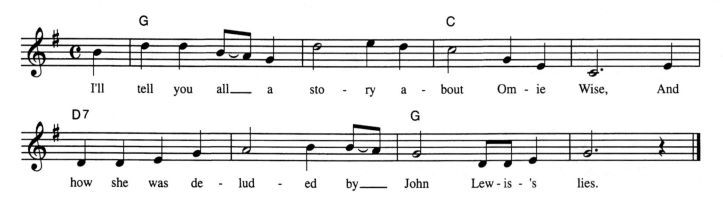

    G   **C**   **D7**   **G**
I'll tell you all a story about Omie Wise, How she was deluded by John Lewis's lies
    G   **C**
He told her to meet him at Adams's spring
    D7   **G**
He'd bring her some money and some other fine things.

He brought her no money nor other fine things
But get up behind me, Omie, to Squire Ellet's we'll go
She got up behind him, so caref'ly we'll go
They rode 'til they came where deep waters did flow.

John Lewis he concluded to tell her his mind
John Lewis he concluded to leave her behind
She threw her arms around him "John spare me my life
And I'll go distracted and never be your wife."

He threw her arms from 'round him and into the water she plunged
John Lewis he turned 'round and went back to Adams's hall
He went inquiring for Omie but Omie she is not here
She's gone to some neighbor's house and won't be gone very long.

John Lewis was took a pris'ner and locked up in the jail
Was locked up in the jail around, was there to remain a while
John Lewis he stayed there for six months or maybe more
Until he broke jail, into the army he did go.

PALLET ON THE FLOOR (ATLANTA BLUES)

Old-Time, Blues Tune; **CATEGORY:** Early Country and Bluegrass Songs; **DATE:** Early 1900's; 1923 by W.C. Handy; **RECORDING INFO:** Leake County Revelers in 1928 on Columbia 15264-D; Bogtrotters; Original Bogtrotters; Mississippi John Hurt; Mike Seeger and Paul Brown; Doc Watson; **RELATED TO:** "Ain't No Tellin';" **OTHER NAMES:** "Make Me a Pallet on Your Floor;" "Atlanta Blues;" "Make Me a Bed on Your Floor;" **NOTES:** The title was recorded for the Library of Congress by musicologist/folklorist Vance Randolph from Ozark Mountain fiddlers in the early 1940's. The first printed version by W. C. Handy is under the title, "Atlanta Blues" in 1923 with lyrics by Dave Elman. The song is referenced in the Journal of American Folklore XXIV 278 in 1911. A favorite amongst blues players, it was remembered as one of the Bolden Band's specialties. W. C. Handy used it as a strain in his 1917 recording "Sweet Child."

       C   **G**
Chorus: Make me down a pallet on your floor
C   **D**
Make me a pallet on your floor
G   **B7**   **C**
Make it soft make it low so my good gal will never know
G   **D**   **G**
Make me a pallet on your floor.

I'm goin' to the country through the cold rain, sleet and snow.
I'm goin' to the country through the cold rain, sleet and snow.
I'm goin' to the country through the cold rain, sleet and snow, ain't no tellin how far I will go.

Come all you good time friends of mine
Come all you good time friends of mine
When I had a dollar you treated me just fine
Where'd you go when I only had a dime.   *Chorus*

I'd be more than satisfied
If I could catch a train and ride
When I reach Atlanta and have no place to go
Won't you make me a pallet on your floor.   *Chorus*

Pig in a Pen

Traditional Old-Time and Bluegrass Song; **DATE**: Late 1800's; **CATEGORY**: Early Country and Bluegrass Songs; **RECORDING INFO**: Fiddlin' Arthur Smith & his Dixieliners; Bill Monroe; Camp Creek Boys; Wilma Lee Cooper; Pine River Boys with Maybelle; Round Peak Band; **OTHER NAMES**: Pig at Home in a Pen (Arthur Smith-1937); **NOTES**: Classified under Hard To Love-1873 (Little Turtle Dove) by Meade, *Pig in a Pen,* is close related to Little Turtle Dove-1856 and Shady Grove songs.

G   **C**
I got a pig at home in a pen, Corn to feed him on
G   **D**   **G**
All I need's a pretty little girl, To feed him when I'm gone.

Going up on a mountain,
To sow a little cane
Put that old gray bonnet on,
Sweet little Liza Jane.

Going up on a mountain,
To sow a little cane
Raise a barrel of sorghum,
Sweet little Liza Jane.

Black smoke arising,
Sure sign of rain
Put that old gray bonnet,
On little Liza Jane.

Bake them biscuits baby,
Bake 'em good and brown
When you get them biscuits baked,
We're Alabama bound.

Poor Wayfaring Stranger

Traditional Gospel Song; **DATE:** 1858; **CATEGORY:** Early Gospel Songs; **RECORDING INFO:** Vaughan's Texas Quartet- 1929; Bill Monroe-1958; Roscoe Holcomb; **OTHER NAMES:** Poor Wayfaring Pilgrim; I Am a Poor Wayfaring Pilgrim; **NOTES:** The hymn text (tune as *Judgement* in Kentucky Harmony-1816) was first published in Bever's 1858 *Christian Songster*. Versions printed in Dett 1927 (and Jackson 1933), in Hymns for The Camp, 1862; and The Southern Zion's Songster, 1864. This tune, set with these words, continues in the present editions of both the Cooper and the Denson Sacred Harps and the Primitive Baptist songbook *Old School Hymnal*. Related to Lady of Carlisle; John Riley.

Am   **E**   **Am**   **Dm**   **E7**
I know dark clouds will gather 'round me, I know my way is rough and steep;
     Am E   **Am**   **Dm E**   **Am**
But beauteous fields lie just beyond me, Where souls redeemed their vigil keep.

     F   **G**   **C**
Chorus: I'm going there to meet my father
   F   **G**   **E**
I'm going there no more to roam
   Am E   **Am**
I'm just a-going over Jordan
   Dm E   **Am**
I'm just a-going over home.

I'm going there to meet my mother
She said she'd meet me when I come
I'm just a-going over Jordan
I'm just a-going over home.

I'm going there to meet my Saviour
To sing His praises forevermore
I'm only going over Jordan
I'm only going over home.

I want to wear a crown of glory
When I get home to that bright land
I want to shout Salvation's story
In concert with that bloodwashed band.

PRECIOUS MEMORIES

Southern Gospel Song J. B. F. Wright; **DATE:** Early 1900's ca. 1920; **CATEGORY:** Early Gospel Songs; **RECORDING INFO:** Bill Monroe; Stanley Brothers; Emmylou Harris; **NOTES:** J. B. F. Wright, author-composer of "Precious Memories" was born in Tennessee, February 21, 1877. In contrast to the majority of modern day writers and composers, Mr. Wright has never taught nor does he claim a great amount of music education. He writes from inspiration, and in his own words, "... when words came spontaneously, flowing into place when I feel the divine urge." Mr. Wright is a member of the Church of God, and his writing, as did his church work, began at a very early age.

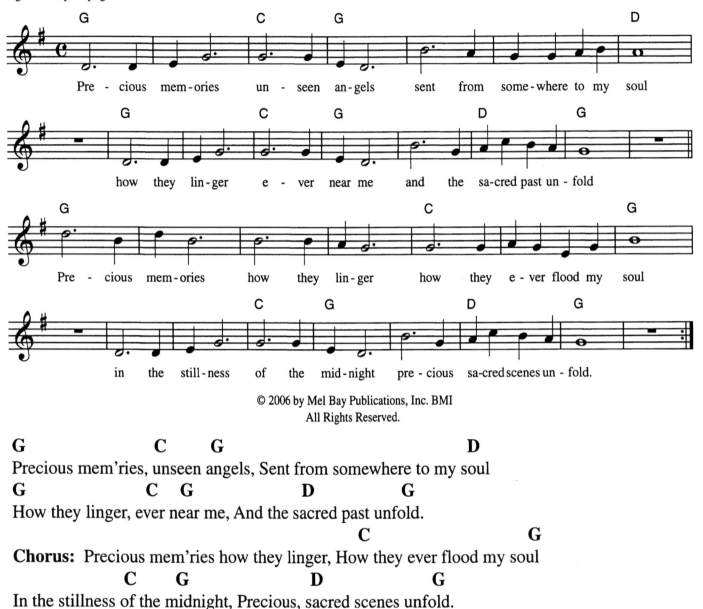

G   C G   D
Precious mem'ries, unseen angels, Sent from somewhere to my soul
G   C G   D   G
How they linger, ever near me, And the sacred past unfold.

                              C   G
Chorus: Precious mem'ries how they linger, How they ever flood my soul
          C G   D   G
In the stillness of the midnight, Precious, sacred scenes unfold.

Precious father, loving mother, Fly across the lonely years
And old home scenes of my childhood, In fond memory appear.

In the stillness of the midnight, Echoes from the past I hear
Old-time singing, gladness bringing, From that lovely land somewhere.

I remember mother praying, Father, too, on bended knee
Sun is sinking, shadows falling, But their pray'rs still follow me.

As I travel on life's pathway, Know not what the years may hold
As I ponder, hope grows fonder, Precious mem'ries flood my soul.

PRETTY POLLY [LAWS P36B/SH 49]

Traditional Old-Time and Bluegrass Song; DATE: 1800's; **CATEGORY:** Early Country and Bluegrass Songs; **RECORDING INFO:** Dock Boggs-1927; B.F. Shelton-1927; Coon Creek Girls-1938; Dillards; Erik Darling; Country Pardners; Red Fox Chasers; Stanley Brothers; Hedy West. **RELATED TO:** Cruel Ship's Carpenter; The Gosport Tragedy. **NOTES:** On January 15th, 2000, Ralph was honored by the Grand Ole Opry by becoming its newest member. Patty Loveless then joined Ralph to perform a hair-raising version of "Pretty Polly," which she recorded for the Clinch Mountain Country album. This is one the old popular mountain ballads-Cecil Sharp found 21 Appalachian versions in the early 1900's.

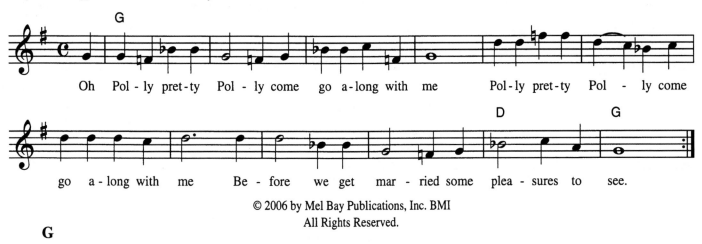

G

Oh, Polly, pretty Polly, would you take me unkind

                                                             D   **G**

Polly, pretty Polly, would you take me unkind, You to sit beside me, and tell me your mind

Well my mind is to marry and never to part
My mind is to marry and never to part, First time I saw you, you wounded my heart

Well Polly, pretty Polly, come and go along with me
Polly, pretty Polly come go along with me, Before we get married, Some pleasure we'll see

Well he led her over mountains and valleys so deep
He led her over mountains and valleys so deep, Polly mistrusted and then began to weep

Say Willie, little Willie I'm afraid of your ways
Willie, little Willie I'm afraid of your ways, The way you've been rambling and leadin' me astray

Now Polly, pretty Polly your guess is about right
Polly, pretty Polly your guess is about right, I dug on your grave the biggest part of last night

Well he led her little farther and what did she spy
He led her little farther and what did she spy, New dug grave with a spade lyin' by

Then she knelt down before him a pleadin' for her life
She knelt down before him a pleadin' for her life, Let me be a single girl if I can't be your wife

Now Polly, pretty Polly that never can be
Polly, pretty Polly that never can be, Your past reputation's been troublin' to me

Well he opened up her bosom as white as any snow
He opened up her bosom as white as any snow, He stabbed through the heart and the blood did overflow

Then he went down to the jailhouse and what did he say
He went to the jailhouse and what did he say, Killed pretty Polly and tryin' to get away.

RED APPLE JUICE

Traditional Old-Time and Bluegrass Song; **DATE:** Early 1900's; **CATEGORY:** Early Country and Bluegrass Songs; **RECORDING INFO:** Dock Boggs, "Sugar Baby" (Brunswick 118B, 1927); Clarence Ashley "Honey Babe Blues," Charlie Monroe & the Kentucky Pardners; Frank Proffitt, "Got No Sugar Baby Now;" Bascom Lamar Lunsford "Little Turtle Dove" 1928; Country Gentlemen "Red Rocking Chair." **OTHER NAMES:** "Ain't Got No Honey/Sugar Babe," "Sugar Baby," "Red Rocking Chair;" "Red Apple Juice." **NOTES:** Part of a large family of white blues songs in the Sugar Baby/Red Rocking Chair/Red Apple Juice group. Floating lyrics are also found in "Pay Day"; "Cold Rain and Snow"; "Storms Are on the Ocean, The" (False True Lover, The True Lover's Farewell, Red Rosy Bush, Turtle Dove).

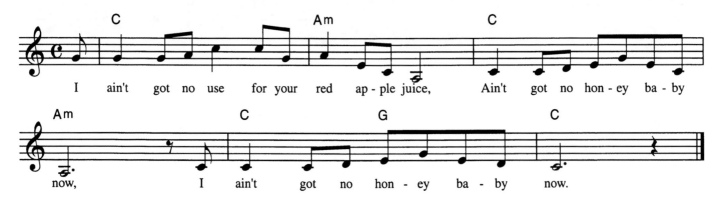

      C   **Am**   **C**
Well I ain't got no use for your red apple juice.
               Am
Ain't got no honey baby now,
C   **G**   **C**
Ain't got no honey baby now.

It's who'll rock the cradle, and who'll sing this song,
And it's who'll be your honey when I'm gone?
It's who'll be your honey when I'm gone?

I'll rock the cradle, and I'll sing this song,
I'll rock the cradle when you're gone,
I'll rock the cradle when you're gone.

It's all I can do, it's all I can say.
I'll send you to your Mama next payday
I'll send you to your Mama next payday.

I've drawed in my check, give her every dime I made.
What more could a poor boy do?
What more could a poor boy do?

RED WING

Old-Time and Bluegrass Song by Thurland Chattaway and Kerry Mills **DATE:** 1907; **CATEGORY:** Fiddle and Instrumental Tunes; **RECORDING INFO:** Norman Blake and Red Rector; Wilma Lee Cooper; Riley Puckett; Don Reno and Bill Harrell; Reno & Smiley Chubby Wise; **NOTES:** "Red Wing" was composed by Kerry Mills in the early years of Tin Pan Alley and published in 1907. Jim Kimball explains it was subtitled "An Indian Fable" or "An Indian Intermezzo" and was part of a fad for things Native-American that swept the country in the first decade of the 20th century.

    C   **F**   **C**
There once lived an Indian maid, a shy little prairie maid,
  Dm   **G**   **C**   **Am**   **D**   **G**
Who sang alay, a love song gay, as on the plain she'd while away the day;
  C   **F**   **C**
She loved a warrior bold, this shy little maid of old,
  Dm   **G**   **C**   **Am**   **D** **G** **C**
But brave and gay, he rode one day to battle far away.

               F   **C**
Chorus: Now the moon shines tonight on pretty Red Wing,
          G   **C**
The breeze is sighing, the night bird's crying,
 F   **C**
For afar 'neath his star her brave is sleeping
          G   **C**
While Red Wing's weeping her heart away.

She watched for him day and night, she kept all the campfires bright,
And under the sky, each night she would lie, and dream about his coming by and by;
But when all the braves returned, the heart of Red Wing yearned,
Far, far, far away, her warrior gay fell bravely in the fray.   *Chorus*

Reuben's Train

Traditional Old-Time and Bluegrass Song; **DATE:** Early 1900's; **CATEGORY:** Early Country and Bluegrass Songs; **RECORDING INFO:** Bill Monroe; J.D. Crowe; Blue Mountain Boys; Cockerham, Jarrell and Jenkins; Dillards; Flatt & Scruggs & the Foggy Mountain Boys; Wade Mainer and the Sons of the Mountaineers; Frank Proffitt; Tony Rice; Roscoe Holcomb and Wade Ward; Doc Watson; **OTHER NAMES:** Train 45; Ruben/Reuben's Train; **RELATED TO:** Long Steel Rail; Train 45; Ruby (Are You Mad at Your Man?); Seventy Four; Nine Hundred Miles/One Hundred Miles; Longest Train I Ever Saw; **NOTES:** A banjo tune and song which Frank Proffitt pronounced as "one of the oldest simple banjo tunes...it was the first tune generally learned. There are about fifty different verses to this, as everybody added them all along" [Warner]. G.B. Grayson, born in 1887 in Ashe County, North Carolina 1928 cut the first recording of "Train 45" derived from "Reuban's Train." The old-timey song "Keep My Skillet Good and Greasy" is also a related tune.

D
Reuben had a train, he put it on the track
                          A   **D**
You could hear the whistle blow a hundred miles.
              D
Chorus: Oh me, oh my
                      A   **D**
You can hear the whistle blow a hundred miles.

I'm going to the East, I'm going to the West
I'm going where them chilly winds don't blow.   *Chorus*

Oh, you ought to been uptown and seen that train come down
You could hear the whistle blow a hundred miles.   *Chorus*

I'm walking these old ties with tears in my eyes
I'm trying to read a letter from my home.   *Chorus*

If that train runs right, I'll be home tomorrow night
Arriving on that Train 45.   *Chorus*

ROCK ABOUT MY SARO JANE

Traditional Old-Time and Bluegrass Song; **DATE**: Early 1900's; **CATEGORY**: Early Country and Bluegrass Songs; **RECORDING INFO**: Uncle Dave Macon-1927; New Lost City Ramblers; Kingston Trio; Red Clay Ramblers; Red Smiley and the Bluegrass Cut-Ups; **OTHER NAMES**: Saro Jane; My Sarah Jane; **NOTES**: The song has been adapted by Bob Dylan and also others in the bluegrass category including the Kingston Trio, Red Clay Ramblers, Red Smiley and the Bluegrass Cut-Ups. Uncle Dave Macon's classic 1927 version indicates an earlier Civil War origin. Macon learned it from black stevedores on the Cumberland River in the 1880s.

Em   **G**   **Em**
I've got a wife and a five little chillun, Believe I'll make a trip on the big MacMillan, oh Saro Jane!

       G   **C**   **G**   **Em**   **G**   **D** **G**
Chorus: Oh there's nothing to do but to sit down and sing, and rock about my Saro Jane.
                 C   **G**
Oh rock about, my Saro Jane, oh rock about, my Saro Jane.
       C   **G**   **Em**   **G**   **D** **G**
Oh there's nothing to do but to sit down and sing, and rock about my Saro Jane.

Boiler busted and the whistle done blowed, The head captain done fell overboard, Oh Saro Jane! *Chorus*

Engine gave a crack and the whistle gave a squall, The engineer gone to the hole in the wall, Oh Saro Jane!

Yankees build boats for to shoot them rebels, My musket's loaded and I'm gonna hold her level, Oh Saro Jane!

ROCKY TOP

Old-Time and Bluegrass Song by B. & F. Bryant; **DATE:** Copyright 1967; **CATEGORY:** Early Country and Bluegrass Songs; **RECORDING INFO:** Lynn Anderson; Osborne Brothers; Dillard & Clark; Jim and Jesse; Rose Maddox and the Vern Williams Band; **NOTES:** Written by Boudleaux Bryant and Felice Bryant in 1967, this is a country song written to be a bluegrass song. A classic version is by the Osborne Brothers on Yesterday and Today, Decca DL-74993.

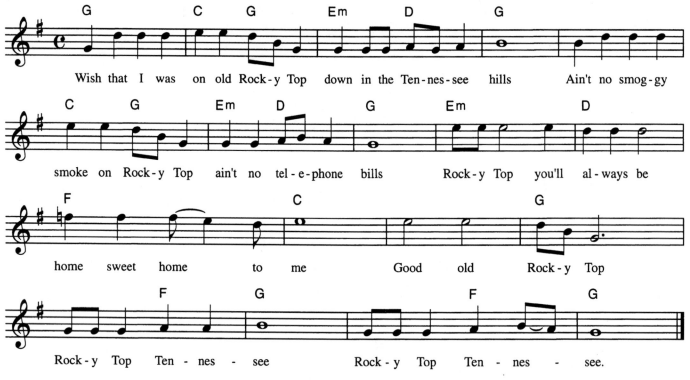

G		**C**	**G**	**Em**	**D**	**G**

Wish that I was on ol' Rocky Top, Down in the Tennessee hills;

		C	**G**	**Em**	**D**	**G**

Ain't no smoggy smoke on Rocky Top, Ain't no telephone bills.

	Em	**D**	**F**	**C**

Chorus: Rocky Top, you'll always behome sweet home to me;

	G		**F**	**G**	**F**	**G**

Good ol' Rocky Top, Rocky Top, Tennessee, Rocky Top, Tennessee.

Once I had a girl on Rocky Top, Half bear, other half cat
Wild as a mink and sweet as soda pop, I still dream about that.

Once two strangers climbed ol' Rocky Top, Lookin' for a moonshine still,
Strangers ain't come down from Rocky Top, Reckon they never will. *Chorus*

Corn won't grow at all on Rocky Top, Dirt's too rocky by far;
That why all the folks on Rocky Top, Get their corn from a jar. *Chorus*

I've had years of cramped-up city life, Trapped like a duck in a pen
All I know is it's a pity life, Can't be simple again. *Chorus*

ROLL IN MY SWEET BABY'S ARMS

Traditional Old-Time and Bluegrass Song; **DATE**: Early 1900's; **CATEGORY:** Early Country and Bluegrass Songs; **RECORDING INFO**: The Monroe Brothers-1936; Flatt and Scruggs-1950; The Stanley Brothers; Doc & Merle Watson; **OTHER NAMES:** Rollin' In My Sweet Baby's Arms; **NOTES:** A bluegrass standard originating from the textile mills area in the mountains of NC and Va., Roll In My Sweet Baby's Arms was popularized by the Monroe Brothers in 1936. This song is now performed by everyone from parking lot pickers to Buck Owens and Leon Russell.

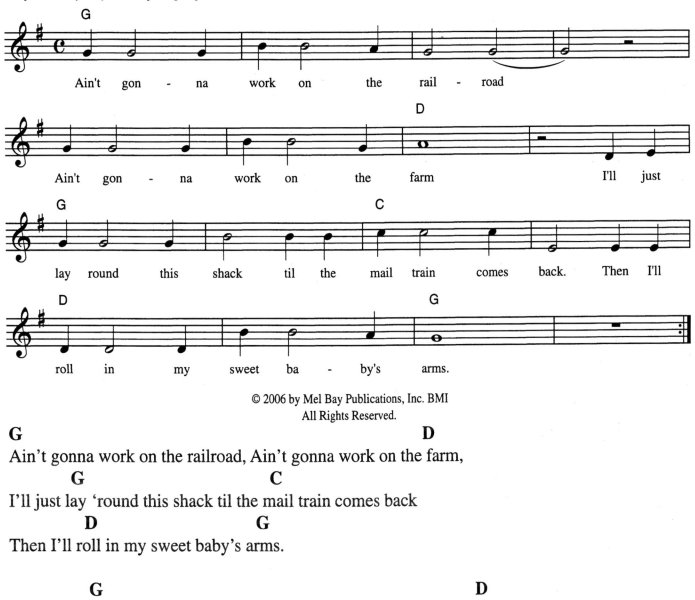

   G   **D**

Ain't gonna work on the railroad, Ain't gonna work on the farm,

         G   **C**

I'll just lay 'round this shack til the mail train comes back

       D   **G**

Then I'll roll in my sweet baby's arms.

          G   **D**

Chorus: Roll in my sweet baby's arms, Roll in my sweet baby's arms,

G   **C**   **D**   **G**

Lay round this shack til the mail train gets back, Then I'll roll in my sweet baby's arms.

Now where were you last Friday night, While I was layin' in the jail?

Were you walkin' the streets with another man? You wouldn't even go my bail. *Chorus*

Sometimes there's a change in the ocean, Sometimes there's a change in the sea,

Sometimes there's a change in my own true love, But there's never a change in me. *Chorus*

I know your parents don't like me, They turn me away from your door,

If I had my life to live over, Oh well, I'd never go back anymore. *Chorus*

ROLL ON BUDDY

Traditional Old-Time and Bluegrass Song; **DATE:** Early 1900's; **CATEGORY:** Early Country and Bluegrass Songs; **RECORDING INFO:** Al Hopkins and his Bucklebusters-1927; Jack Elliot and Derroll Adams; Roscoe Holcomb; Aunt Molly Jackson; McGee Brothers and Arthur Smith; Monroe Brothers; Doc Watson; **RELATED TO:** Black Dog Blues; Pea Fowl; Don't Go Ridin' Down That Old Texas Trail; Roll On, John; Mole in the Ground; **OTHER NAMES:** Roll on Buddy, Roll On; **NOTES:** Closely related to Tempy/I Wish I Was A Mole in the Ground, Roll on Buddy is a different song than the Nine Pound Hammer songs having only the lyrics "roll on buddy" in common.

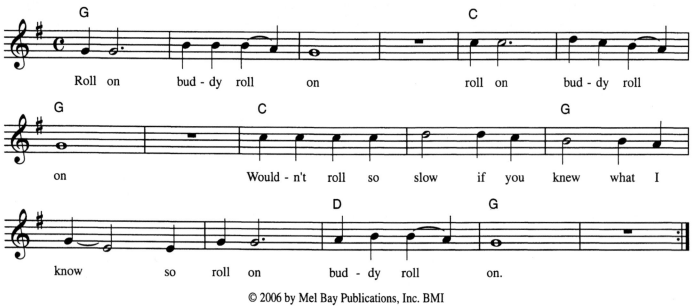

G   **C**   **G**
Roll on buddy, roll on , Roll on buddy, roll on
C   **G**   **D**   **G**
You wouldn't roll so slow, if you knew what I know, Roll on buddy, roll on.

I've got a home in Tennessee
I've got a home in Tennessee
I've got a home, down in Sunny Tennessee,
Roll on buddy, roll on.

My baby wants a nine dollar shawl
My baby wants a nine dollar shawl
I come over the hill, with a hundred dollar bill
And it's baby where you been so long.

Baby where you been so long
Baby where you been so long
I've been down in the pen, with some rough and rowdy men
And baby where you been so long.

ROVING GAMBLER [LAWS H 4]

Traditional Old-Time and Bluegrass Song; **DATE:** 1886; **CATEGORY:** Early Country and Bluegrass Songs; **RECORDING INFO:** Kelly Harrell-1925; Vernon Dalhart- 1925; Wade Mainer; Hedy West; Mac Wiseman; Stanley Brothers; **OTHER NAMES:** Gambling Man; **NOTES:** The Roving Gambler is related to and possibly originated from Roving Irishman (1854). It's the melody for *Gambler's Dying Words*, *Mary Phagan* and the gospel song *Little Black Train*. In some versions the last line is repeated twice.

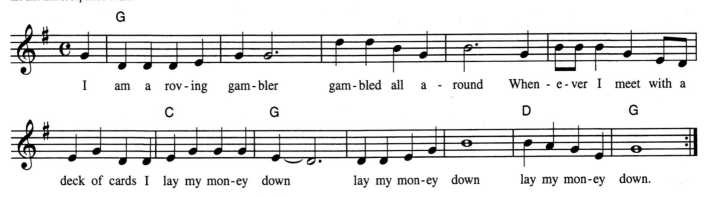

G
I am a roving gambler, gambled all around
                               C   **G**
Whenever I meet with a deck of cards I lay my money down
           D   **G**
Lay my money down, lay my money down.

I had not been in Frisco many more weeks than three
I met up with a pretty little gal, she fell in love with me
Fell in love with me, fell in love with me.

She took me in her parlor, cooled me with her fan
Whispered low in her momma's ear, I love this gamblin man...

Oh daughter oh dear daughter how can you treat me so
Leave your dear old momma, and with a gambler go...

My mother oh my mother you can not understand
If you ever see me a comin back, I'll be with a gamblin man...

I left her there in Frisco and I wound up in Maine
I met up with a gamblin man, got in a poker game...

We put our money in the pot and dealt the cards around
I saw him deal from the bottom of the deck, and I shot that gambler down...

Well, now I'm in the jailhouse got a number for my name
Jailer said as he locked the door, you've gambled your last game...

195

RYE WHISKEY

Traditional Old-Time and Bluegrass Song; **DATE:** Late 1800's; **CATEGORY:** Early Country and Bluegrass Songs; **RECORDING INFO:** Fiddlin' John Carson-1925; Jules Allen, "Jack O' Diamonds" (Victor 21470, 1928); Frank Proffitt; Tex Ritter; **OTHER NAMES:** "Drunkard's Hiccups/Hiccoughs;" "Jack of Diamonds," "Way Up on Clinch Mountain," **NOTES:** The tune is from an old and distinguished family originating in the British Isles, but well-known in America. The tune features pizzicato, or plucked, notes on the fiddle. Arizona fiddler Kartchner called it a "favorite from the South." Mt. Airy, North Carlolina, fiddler Tommy Jarrell knew the melody as a show piece in a repertoire heavy with dance tunes, having learned it from his father, Ben Jarrell (who recorded it with Frank Jenkins in 1927). Ben Jarrell, according to Tommy, had the tune from "old man" Houston Galyen at Low Gap, North Carolina. Bayard (1981) states it was a vocal piece before it was an instrumental one.

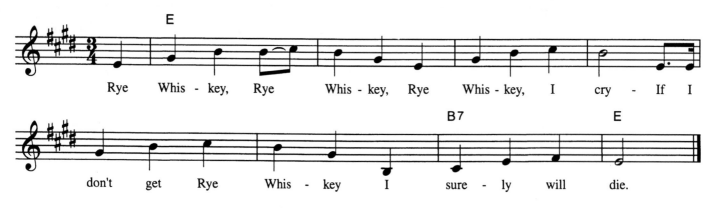

E
Rye whiskey, Rye whiskey, Rye whiskey I cry,
                  B7   **E**
If I don't get rye whiskey I surely will die.

I'll eat when I'm hungry, I'll drink when I'm dry;
If the hard times don't kill me I'll live till I die.

Beefsteak when I'm hungry, red liquor when I'm dry,
Greenbacks when I'm hard up and religion when I die.

Oh Whiskey, you villian, you've been by downfall;
You've kicked me, you've cuffed me, but I love you for all.

If the ocean was whiskey and I was a duck,
I'd dive to the bottom and get one sweet suck.

But the ocean ain't whiskey and I ain't a duck,
So we'll round up the cattle and then we'll get drunk.

Sail Away Ladies

Traditional Old-Time and Bluegrass Song; **DATE**: Late 1800's; **CATEGORY:** Early Country and Bluegrass Songs; **RECORDING INFO**: Sid Harkreader & Uncle Dave Macon- 1925; Kenny Baker; Joan Baez; Erik Darling; John Hartford; David Holt; New Lost City Ramblers; Slate Mountain Ramblers; **NOTES:** The tune is related to the numerous versions of "Sally Ann" and "Great Big Taters in Sandy Land." According to Guthrie Meade (1980), the tune is identified with the south central Kentucky and middle Tennessee locals. Recorded by Uncle Dave Macon, the song was collected around the turn of the 20th century and seems to have been common to both black and white traditions. Wolfe (1991) finds the song in several older collections: Brown, Brewer and a 1903 collection by William W. Newell, Games and Songs of American Children.

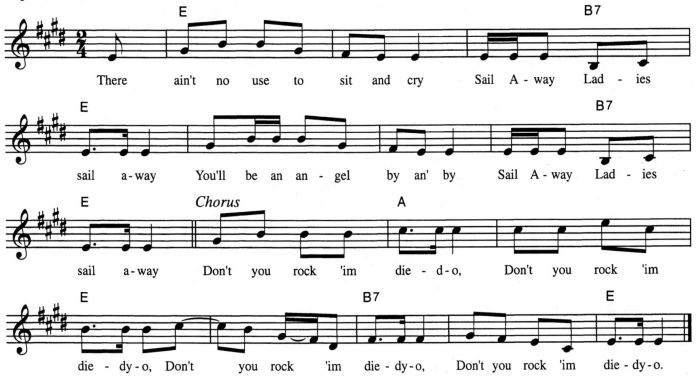

E
There ain't no use to sit and cry
    B7   **E**
Sail away, ladies, sail away.

You'll be an angel by an' by,
    B7   **E**
Sail away, ladies, sail away,
      E   **A**
Chorus: Don't you rock 'im die-dy-o
      E
Don't you rock 'im die-dy-o,
      B7
Don't you rock 'im die-dy-o,
      E
Don't you rock 'im die-dy-o.

Come along, girls, and go with me.
Sail away, ladies, sail away.
We'll go back to Tennessee
Sail away, ladies, sail away.

If ever I get my new house done,
Sail away, ladies, sail away.
I'll give my old one to my son
Sail away, ladies, sail away.

I got the news from Charlotte Town.
Sail away, ladies, sail away.
Big St. Louis is a-burning down
Sail away, ladies, sail away.

I asked that girl to be my beau
Sail away, ladies, sail away.
She hacked at me with a garden hoe
Sail away, ladies, sail away.

I asked that girl to be my wife,
Sail away, ladies, sail away.
She took at me with a butcher knife.
Sail away, ladies, sail away.

SALLY ANN

Traditional Old-Time and Bluegrass Song; **DATE:** Late 1800's; **CATEGORY:** Early Country and Bluegrass Songs; **RECORDING INFO:** Hill Billies 1925; Fiddlin' John Carson-1925; Frank Blevins & his Tar Heel Rattlers- 1927; Doc Roberts- 1931; Camp Creek Boys; Flatt & Scruggs & the Foggy Mountain Boys; Hollow Rock String Band; Wade Mainer; Roscoe Holcomb and Wade Ward; **NOTES:** Lomax says that this is the same melody as the fiddle piece "Sandy Land (actually Great Big Taters in Sandy Land)" in turn related to "Sally Goodin." Although I don't consider it closely related to *Sally Goodin*, *Sally Ann* is related to "Sail Away Ladies" and "Great Big Taters in Sandy Land" and appears in the Journal of American Folklore in 1915. John McCutcheon notes it could easily be called "Scott County's Anthem" and was fiddler Beachard Smith's (1911-1981) signature tune. The *Hound Dog Song*, also in this collection, has a similar melody.

D	**Bm**	**D**	**A**

Goin' to the wedding, Sally Ann, goin' to the wedding, Sally Ann

D	**A7**	**D**

Sift that meal and save your bran, I'm goin' home with Sally Ann.

D	**A7**	**D**

Chorus: I'm gonna marry you, Sal, Sal, I'm gonna marry you, Sally Ann.

Did you ever see a muskrat, Sally Ann? Pickin' a banjo, Sally Ann,
Draggin' his slick tail through the sand? I'm gonna marry you, Sally Ann.   *Chorus*

Shake that little foot, Sally Ann, shake that little foot, Sally Ann,
Great big wedding up, Sally Ann, I'm goin' home with Sally Ann.   *Chorus*

Pass me the brandy, Sally Ann, pass me the brandy, Sally Ann,
I'm goin' 'way with Sally Ann, great big wedding up, Sally Ann.   *Chorus*

Sally's in the garden sifting sand, Susie's upstairs with the hog-eyed man;
I'm goin' home with Sally Ann, I'm goin' home with Sally Ann.   *Chorus*

SALLY GOODIN

Traditional Old-Time and Bluegrass Song; **DATE:** Late 1800's; **CATEGORY:** Fiddle and Instrumental Tunes; **RECORDING INFO:** Eck Robertson-1922; Fiddlin' John Carson-1923; Uncle Dave Macon-1925; Clark Kessinger-1929; Skillet Lickers-1929; J. E. Mainer's Mountaineers; Kenny Baker; Sam Bush; Flatt & Scruggs & the Foggy Mountain Boys; Ricky Skaggs; Doc Watson; **OTHER NAMES:** Sally Goodwin; Sallie Gooden; **NOTES:** *Sally Goodin* is one of the popular fiddle tunes of upland south. According to North Carolina fiddler Bruce Green, the tune was originally called *Boatin' Up Sandy* (referring to the Big Sandy River in eastern Kentucky) and was renamed by Civil War Confederate soldiers in Morgan's Raiders while they were camped on the Big Sandy in Pike County, Kentucky. Sally Goodin ran a boarding house there and allowed the soldiers to camp and play music. Eck Robertson's 1922 recording (reissued on County CO CD 5515) popularized the tune across America.

G   **D**   **G**

Had a piece of pie, had a piece of puddin', Give it all away to see Sally Goodin'. (repeat)

I love pie, I love puddin', Crazy 'bout the gal they call Sally Goodin'. (repeat)

Looked up the road, seen Sally comin',
Thought to my soul she'd break her neck a-runnin'. (repeat)

An' I dropped the 'tater pie an' I left the appie puddin',
But I went across the mountain to see my Sally Goodin. (repeat)

Sally is my doxy an' Sally is my daisy,
When Sally says she hates me I think I'm goin crazy. (repeat)

I'm goin up the mountain an' marry little Sally,
Raise corn on the hillside an' the devil in the valley. (repeat)

Had five dollars, now I've got none, Give it all away to see Sally Goodin.
Hey, ho, old Sally Goodin, Hey, ho, old Sally Goodin.

Raspberry pie, blackberry puddin', Give it all away to kiss Sally Goodin.
Hey, ho, old Sally Goodin, Hey, ho, old Sally Goodin.

SALTY DOG BLUES

Traditional Old-Time and Bluegrass Song; **DATE:** Early 1900's; **CATEGORY:** Early Country and Bluegrass Songs; **RECORDING INFO:** Allen Brothers 1927; Flatt & Scruggs & the Foggy Mountain Boys; Erik Darling; Mississippi John Hurt; Osborne Brothers; Morris Brothers; Don Reno and Bill Harrell; **OTHER NAMES:** Salty Dog Blues; Old Salty Dog Blues; **NOTES:** The first commercially successful self-accompanied artist in the "race field" was African-American Papa Charlie Jackson, who played a banjo strung like a guitar. The classic Morris Brothers recording "Let me Be Salty Dog" in 1938 was based on Papa Charlie Jackson's 1924 recording. Flatt & Scruggs based their version on the earlier Morris Brothers version. The term 'salty dog' suggests an off-color meaning for the chorus.

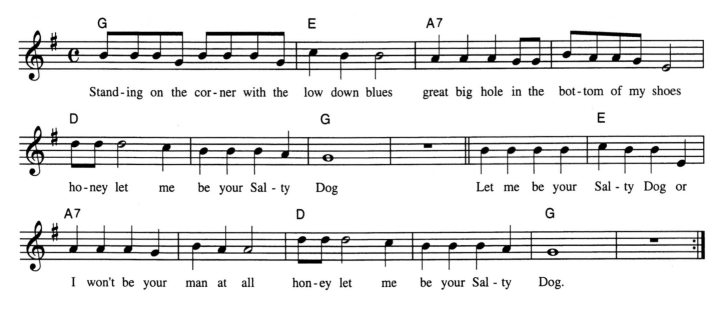

G   **E**
Standing on the corner with the low down blues
A7
Great big hole in the bottom of me shoes
D   **G**
Honey, let me be your salty dog.
               G   **E**   **A7**
Chorus: Let me be your salty dog, Or I won't be your man at all
D   **G**
Honey let me be your salty dog.

Now look a hear Sal, I know you
Run down stocking and worn out shoes
Honey let me be your salty dog.   *Chorus*

I was down in the wildwood setting on a log
Finger on the trigger and an eye on the hog
Honey let me be your salty dog.   *Chorus*

I pulled the trigger and the gun said go
Shot fell over in Mexico
Honey let me be your salty dog.   *Chorus*

SHADY GROVE (MAJOR KEY)

Traditional Old-Time and Bluegrass Song; **DATE:** Late 1800's; **CATEGORY:** Early Country and Bluegrass Songs; **RECORDING INFO:** Henry Whittier (Western Country)- 1924; Kentucky Thorobreds- 1927; Clarence Tom Ashley; David Grisman and Jerry Garcia; Kentucky Colonels; Kingston Trio; Charlie Moore; New Lost City Ramblers; Doc Watson; Jean Ritchie; **OTHER NAMES:** Western Country; **NOTES:** Categorized by Meade under *Fly Around my Pretty Little Miss*, this bluegrass favorite is usually played up-tempo in a major key. Doc Watson and others do a version in a minor key that is slower. The song first appears under the Shady Grove title in Journal of American Folklore in 1915. First recorded as Shady Grove by Kentucky Thorobreds in 1927, the song was recorded as Western Country by Henry Whittier in 1924. Shady Grove has floating lyrics with many similar songs.

```
G              C        G
```
Shady Grove, my little love, Shady Grove I say
```
G              C        G        D        G
```
Shady Grove, my little love, I'm bound to go away.

When I was a little boy, I wanted a Barlow knife
Now I want little Shady Grove to say she'll be my wife.

Cut a banjo from a gourd, string it up with twine
The only song that I can play is "Wish that gal was mine".

Apples in the summer time, peaches in the fall
If I can't have the girl I love, I don't want none at all.

Cheeks as red as a bloomin rose, Eyes of the deepest brown,
You are the darlin of my heart, Stay till the Sun goes down.

Shady Grove, my little love, Shady Grove my darlin,
Shady Grove, my little love, I'm going away to Harlan.

Went to see my Shady Grove, she was standing in the door,
Shoes and stockings in her hand, little bare feet on the floor.

Shady Grove (Minor Key)

Traditional Old-Time and Bluegrass Song; **DATE:** Late 1800's; **CATEGORY:** Early Country and Bluegrass Songs; **RECORDING INFO:** Henry Whittier (Western Country)- 1924; Kentucky Thorobreds- 1927; Clarence Tom Ashley; David Grisman and Jerry Garcia; Kentucky Colonels; Kingston Trio; Charlie Moore; New Lost City Ramblers; Doc Watson; Jean Ritchie; **OTHER NAMES:** Western Country; **NOTES:** Categorized by Meade under *Fly Around my Pretty Little Miss*, this bluegrass favorite is usually played up-tempo in a major key. Doc Watson and others do a version in a minor key that is slower. The song first appears under the Shady Grove title in Journal of American Folklore in 1915. First recorded as Shady Grove by Kentucky Thorobreds in 1927, the song was recorded as Western Country by Henry Whittier in 1924. Shady Grove has floating lyrics with many similar songs.

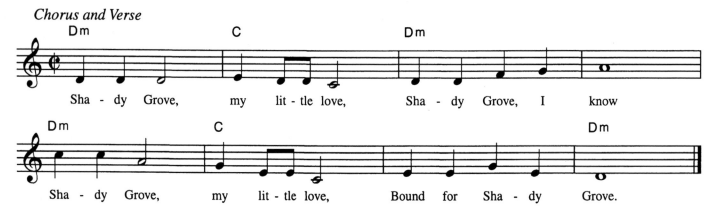

Dm   **C**   **Dm**
Shady Grove, my little love, Shady Grove I know
Dm   **C**   **Dm**
Shady Grove, my little love, I'm bound for Shady Grove

When I was a little boy, I wanted a Barlow knife
Now I want little Shady Grove to say she'll be my wife

Cut a banjo from a gourd, string it up with twine
The only song that I can play is "Wish that gal was mine"

Apples in the summer time, peaches in the fall
If I can't have the girl I love, I don't want none at all

Cheeks as red as a bloomin rose, Eyes of the deepest brown,
You are the darlin of my heart, Stay till the Sun goes down.

Shady Grove, my little love, Shady Grove my darlin,
Shady Grove, my little love, I'm going away to Harlan.

Went to see my Shady Grove, she was standing in the door,
Shoes and stockings in her hand, little bare feet on the floor.

SHALL WE GATHER AT THE RIVER

Gospel Song by Robert Lowry (1826-1899); **DATE:** 1865; **CATEGORY:** Early Gospel Songs; **RECORDING INFO:** Alcoa Quartet-1925; Dixie Sacred Singers-1927 with Uncle Dave Macon and the McGee Brothers; Carter Family; Chuck Wagon Gang; Lost And Found; Peter Rowan; Mac Wiseman; **OTHER NAMES:** The Beautiful River; **NOTES:** First recorded in 1925 by the Alcoa Quartet, Shall We Gather At the River was one of Uncle Dave Macon's favorite hymns and a gospel standard. There's a great version by the Carter Family on Border Radio, County 550.

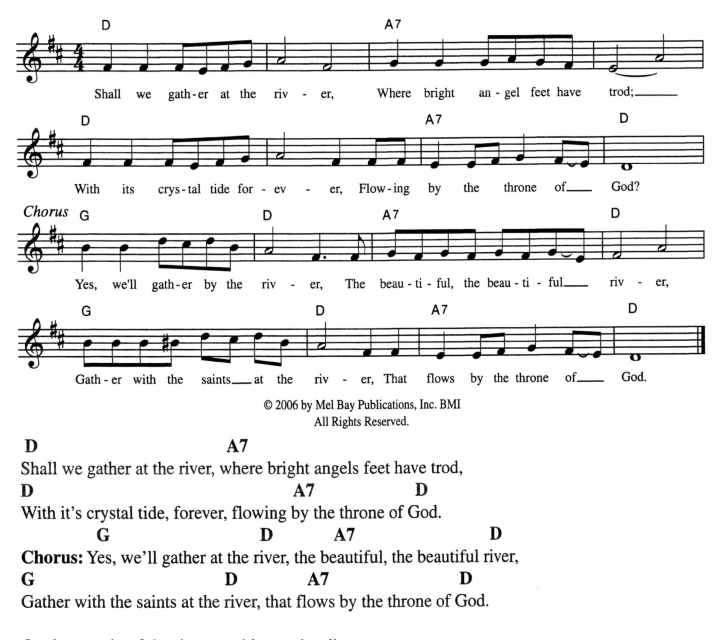

D   **A7**
Shall we gather at the river, where bright angels feet have trod,
D   **A7**   **D**
With it's crystal tide, forever, flowing by the throne of God.
      G   **D**   **A7**   **D**
Chorus: Yes, we'll gather at the river, the beautiful, the beautiful river,
G   **D**   **A7**   **D**
Gather with the saints at the river, that flows by the throne of God.

On the margin of the river, washing up its silvery spray,
We shall walk and worship ever, all the happy golden day. *Chorus*

Ere we reach the shining river, lay we every burden down,
Grace our spirits will deliver and provide a robe and crown. *Chorus*

Soon we'll reach the shining river, soon our pilgrimage will cease,
Soon our happy hearts will quiver, with the melody of peace. *Chorus*

Silver Dagger [Laws G21]

Traditional Old-Time and Bluegrass Song; **DATE:** Earliest text: Drowsy Sleeper- Bodelian Library 1817; Appears in The Social Harp 1855 (first verse only); Earliest complete version in US "Awake Awake!" sung by Mary Sands at Allanstand, NC Aug 1, 1916; **CATEGORY:** Early Country and Bluegrass Songs; **RECORDING INFO:** Oh Molly Dear (BVE 35667-3) Kelly Harrell-1926; Oh Molly Dear (BVE 39725-2) B. F. Shelton-1927; Sleepy Desert (Paramount 3282)- Wilmer Watts & the Lonely Eagles-1929; Wake Up You Drowsy Sleeper (BE 62575-2) Oaks Family-1930; Katie Dear (14524-2) Callahan Brothers (vcl duet w.gtrs)- 1934; Katie Dear (BS 018680-1) - Blue Sky Boys (vcl duet w/mdln & gtr)- 1938; Sarah Ogan Gunning; Joan Baez; Old Crowe Medicine Show; Dave Van Ronk; **OTHER NAMES:** Oh Molly Dear (Go Ask Your Mother); Katie Dear; Awake, Awake; Julianne; **RELATED TO:** "Greenback Dollar," "Old Virginny/East Virginia Blues/Dark Holler Blues," "Darling Think of What You've Done;" **NOTES:** "Silver Dagger" has the same basic plot as "Drowsy Sleeper" but the silver dagger is used as the suicide weapon. The relationship of "Drowsy Sleeper" with "Old Virginny/ East Virginia Blues/ Dark Holler Blues/ Man of Constant Sorrow" has been well documented. The Callahan Brothers learned Katie Dear (Silver Dagger) from their mother. This would probably bring the date back to the late 19th century at least.

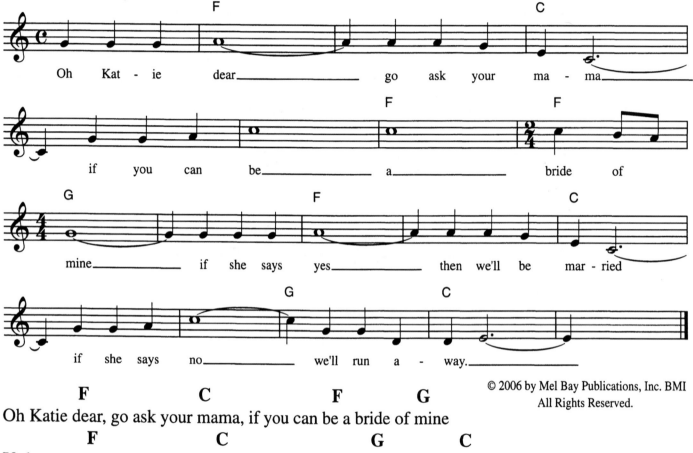

>   **F**   **C**   **F**   **G**
> Oh Katie dear, go ask your mama, if you can be a bride of mine
>   **F**   **C**   **G**   **C**
> If she says yes, then we'll be married, if she says no, we'll run away.

Oh Willie dear, there's no need in asking, she's in her room taking her rest
And by her side is a silver dagger, to slay the one that I love best.

Oh Katie dear, go ask your papa, if you can be a bride of mine
If he says yes, come back and tell me, if he says no, we'll run away.

Oh Willie dear, there's no need in asking, he's in his room taking a rest
And by his side is a silver dagger, to slay the one that I love best.

So he picked up that silver dagger, and plunged it through his troubled heart
Saying, 'Goodbye Katie, goodbye darlin', it's now forever we must part.'

So she picked up that bloody dagger, and plunged it through her lily-white breast
Saying, 'Goodbye papa, goodbye mama, I'll die for the one that I love best.'

SITTIN' ON TOP OF THE WORLD

Traditional Old-Time, Blues, Bluegrass Song; **DATE**: Early 1900's; **CATEGORY**: Early Country and Bluegrass Songs; **RECORDING INFO**: Mississippi Sheiks, 1930; Charlie Patton "Some Summer's Day" 1930; Two Poor Boys (Joe Evans and Arthur McClain), 1931; Milton Brown, 1934; Bob Wills, 1935; The Carter Family On Border Radio 1938-1942, Bill Monroe, 1957; Whole Lotta Shakin', Carl Perkins, 1958; Doc Watson, 1964; Chester Burnette A.K.A. Howlin' Wolf, Howlin' Wolf, 1972; Top Of The World, Earl Scruggs, 1983; Jimmy Martin; **OTHER NAMES**: I'm Sittin' on Top of the World; **NOTES:** Generally attributed to Walter Vincson (Walter Jacob) and Bo Chatman (Lonnie Carter) from the Mississippi Shieks who recorded "I'm Sittin' on Top of the World" in 1930. For the Mississippi Shieks Walter Vinson played both guitar and fiddle, Sam Chatman played guitar, Bo Chatman played guitar and fiddle with Charlie McCoy on banjo and mandolin. It is probable that Walter Vincson (also Vinson) adapted the song from folk sources or from Chatman's half brother- Charlie Patton.

    G   **C**   **G**

It was in the spring, one sunny day, my good gal left me, now she's gone away

                                  Em   **G**   **D**   **G**

Chorus: Now she's gone and I don't worry, cause I'm sitting on top of the world.

She called me up from El Paso
Said, "Come back, Daddy, Lord I need you so."   *Chorus*

Ashes to ashes, dust to dust
Show me a woman a man can trust.   *Chorus*

Mississippi River long, deep, and wide
The woman I'm loving is on the other side.   *Chorus*

You don't like my peaches, don't you shake my tree
Get out of my orchard, let my peaches be.   *Chorus*

Don't you come here running, poking out your hand
I'll get me a woman like you got your man.   *Chorus*

SKILLET GOOD AND GREASY

Traditional Old-Time and Bluegrass Song; **DATE**: Early 1900's (Uncle Dave Macon- 1924); **CATEGORY:** Early Country and Bluegrass Songs; **RECORDING INFO**: Uncle Dave Macon, "" (Vocalion 14848, 1924); Henry Whitter "Keep My Skillet Good and Greasy" (OK 40296- 1924); John Henry Howard "Gonna Keep My Skillet Greasy" (Gnt 3124- 1925); Don Stover& the White Oak Mountain Boys; Doc Watson; **OTHER NAMES:** Bootlegger's Blues; Gonna Keep My Skillet Greasy; Keep My Skillet Good and Greasy; **RELATED TO:** Gonna Have a Feast Here Tonight (Rabbit in a Log); Salty Dog; **NOTES:** This song is recognized primarily by the line "(Gonna) keep my skillet (good and) greasy all the time." It is related to Rabbit in a Log/ Feast Here Tonight and has floating lyrics with "Salty Dog." Uncle Dave first recorded this song acoustically in 1924 and it was his first hit. It continued to be a favorite so it was redone in better sound in 1935. According to Charles Wolfe, Sid Harkreader always said Uncle Dave got it from 'an old colored man' who worked at the Readyville Mill near where Macon worked. The song was part of that 'common stock' of banjo and fiddle tunes and songs in the black and white traditions.

G

I'se gwine down town gonna get me a sack of flour

Gwine cook it every hour

Keep my skillet good and greasy all the time, time, time

D   **G**

Keep my skillet good and greasy all the time.

Honey, if you say so, I'll never work-a no more
I'll bed down on the floor.
I'll lay round your shanty all the time, time, time
I'll lay round your shanty all the time

I'se gwine to the hills for to buy me a jug of brandy
Gwine give it all to Mandy
Keep her good and drunk and boozy all the time, time, time
Keep her good and drunk and boozy all the time

SOLDIER'S JOY

Traditional Old-Time and Bluegrass Song; **DATE**: Aird's 1778 collection (Vol. 1, No. 109); In the US- 1851; **CATEGORY:** Fiddle and Instrumental Tunes; **RECORDING INFO**: Fiddlin' John Carson-1925; Gid Tanner and His Skillet Lickers-1929; Hillbillies; Camp Creek Boys; Curly Ray Cline; Clark Kessinger; Earl Scruggs; Doc Watson and Bill Monroe; **OTHER NAMES**: "I Am My Mamma's Darlin' Child," "John White," "Love Somebody," "Payday in the Army," "Rock the Cradle Lucy."**NOTES**: One of, if not the most popular fiddle tune in history, widely disseminated in North America and Europe in nearly every tradition. Tommy Jarrell, the influential fiddler from Mt. Airy, North Carolina, told Peter Anick in 1982 that it was a tune he learned in the early 1920's when he first began learning the fiddle, at which time it was known as "I Love Somebody" in his region. Soon after it was known in Mt. Airy as "Soldier's Joy" and, after World War II, as "Payday in the Army." Doc Watson and Bill Monroe do a ripping version (live) that's hard to beat.

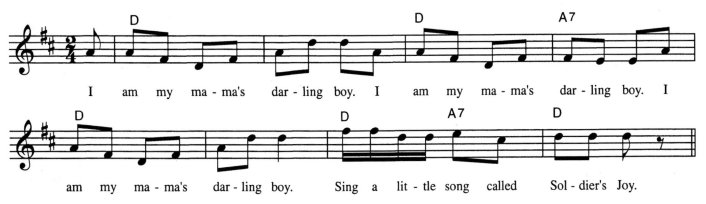

D   **D**   **A7**

I am my mama's darling boy. I am my mama's darling boy.

D   **D**   **A7**   **D**

I am my mama's darling boy. Sing a little song called Soldier's Joy.

Fifteen cents for the morphine. Twenty five cents for the beer
Fifteen cents for the morphine. They're gonna take me away from here

Grasshopper sitting on a sweet potato vine.
Grasshopper sitting on a sweet potato vine.
Grasshopper sitting on a sweet potato vine.
Along comes a chicken and says "you're mine!"

I love somebody, yes I do. I love somebody, yes I do.
I love somebody, yes I do. And I bet you five dollars, you can't guess who.

I'm gonna get a drink, don't you want to go.
I'm gonna get a drink, don't you want to go.
I'm gonna get a drink, don't you want to go
All for the Soldier's Joy.

Chicken in the bread tray scratchin' out dough,
Granny will your dog bite? No, child, no.
Ladies to the center and gents to the bar, Hold on you don't go too far.

SOURWOOD MOUNTAIN

Traditional Old-Time and Bluegrass Song; **DATE:** Late 1800's; Journal of American Folklore 1909; Wyman-Brockway 1916; **CATEGORY:** Early Country and Bluegrass Songs; **RECORDING INFO**: Uncle Am Stuart-1924; Uncle Dave Macon-1926; Bradley Kincaid-1928; Curly Ray Cline; Tommy Jarrell; Wade Mainer and the Mainers Mountaineers; Charlie Monroe and the Kentucky Pardners; Frank Proffitt; Mac Wiseman; **NOTES:** Although the banjo song has been widely collected in the South, Sourwood Mountain is located in the state of Massachusetts, and the ballad is said by some to have originated in that state. Mrs. Betty Jane Dodrill writes to say that family lore has it that the song was composed by her ancestor William Combs (1840-1924), a fiddler and farmer from Russell County, Virginia. The tune was mentioned by William Byrne who described a chance encounter with West Virginia fiddler 'Old Sol' Nelson during a fishing trip on the Elk River. The year was around 1880, and Sol, whom Byrne said was famous for his playing "throughout the Elk Valley from Clay Courthouse to Sutton as...the Fiddler of the Wilderness," had brought out his fiddle after supper to entertain (Milnes-1999). Sourwood is also the name for chestnut or other bark used in tanning leather. Version below collected by my Grandfather, Maurice Matteson, on Beech Mountain, NC.

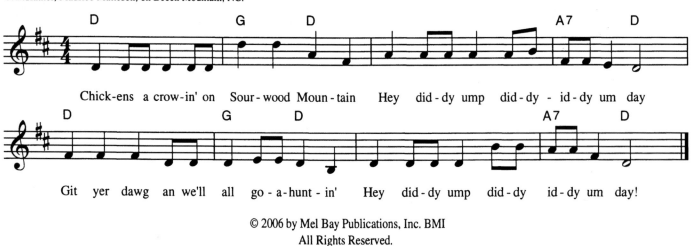

D   **G**   **D**   **A7**   **D**
Chickens a-crowin' on Sourwood Mountain, Hey, diddy ump diddy-iddy-um day.
D   **G**   **D**   **A7**   **D**
Git yer dawg an' we'll all go a-huntin', Hey, diddy ump diddy-iddy-um day.

My true love's a blue-eyed daisy, Hey, diddy ump diddy-iddy-um day.
She won't come and I'm too lazy. Hey, diddy ump diddy-iddy-um day.

Big dog bark and little one bite you, Hey, diddy ump diddy-iddy-um day.
Big girl court and little one spite you. Hey, diddy ump diddy-iddy-um day.

My true love's a blue-eyed daisy, Hey, diddy ump diddy-iddy-um day.
If I don't get her, I'll go crazy. Hey, diddy ump diddy-iddy-um day.

My true love lives at the head of the holler, Hey, diddy ump diddy-iddy-um day.
She won't come and I won't foller. Hey, diddy ump diddy-iddy-um day.

My true love lives over the river, Hey, diddy ump diddy-iddy-um day.
A few more jumps and I'll be with her. Hey, diddy ump diddy-iddy-um day.

Ducks in the pond, geese in the ocean, Hey, diddy ump diddy-iddy-um day.
Devil's in the women if they take a notion. Hey, diddy ump diddy-iddy-um day.

STEWBALL [LAWS Q22]

Traditional Old-Time and Bluegrass Song; **DATE:** 1784; **CATEGORY:** Early Country and Bluegrass Songs; **RECORDING INFO:** Joan Baez; Greenbriar Boys; Memphis Slim; Leadbelly & Golden Gate Quartet; Country Gentlemen; **OTHER NAMES:** Skew Ball; **NOTES:** The facts are that sometime around 1790 a race took place near Dublin between a skewbald horse owned by Sir Arthur Marvel and "Miss Portly", a gray mare owned by Sir Ralph Gore. Skewball appeared as broadside ballad in 1784. In America, the Stewball ballad was "...most popular in the South, where the winning horse is known variously as 'Stewball' or 'Kimball," and was apparently one of the chain-gang songs. The song was recorded by Leadbelly in 1940 and then by Memphis Slim, whose slower bluesy rendition is echoed in this version.

   G   **C7**   **G**
There's a big day in Dallas and I wish I a-were there
                        C7   **G**
Spend my last hundred dollars on that iron gray mare
                     C   **G** **C7** **G** **C7**   **G**
See her travel, all day long, long, long. See her travel all day long, all day long.

Well I don't mind horse racing if it wasn't for my wife.
Old Stewball may stumble and away with my life
Wife and baby, left behind, yeah yeah . Wife and baby, left behind, left behind.

Old Stewball was a black horse jus' as slick as a mole,
Had a ring 'round his fore-shoulder, and it shined just like gold.
Shined like gold, shined like gold, Lord, Lord
Shined like gold, shined like gold, shined like gold.

Old Stewball was a racehorse, but the poor horse was blind.
He ran so fast in Texas, left his shadow behind
Behind, behind, Left his shadow behind, left behind.

Old Stewball was a racehorse and old Molly, she was too.
Old Molly, she stumbled and Old Stewball, he just flew.
Round the track, round the track, yeah, yeah. Round the track, round the track, round the track.

STORMS ARE ON THE OCEAN

Traditional Old-Time and Bluegrass Song; **DATE**: 1800's; Journal of American Folklore- 1926; **CATEGORY:** Early Country and Bluegrass Songs; **RECORDING INFO**: Carter Family-1927; Delmore Brothers-1940; Flatt & Scruggs & the Foggy Mountain Boys; New Lost City Ramblers; Jeanie West; Jean Ritchie and Doc Watson; **NOTES:** *The Storms Are on the Ocean* is part of a large family of songs classified under *The True Lover's Farewell* by Cecil Sharp. This tune was popular in both England and in America. Sharp collected nine variants in the Appalachian Mountains from 1916 to 1918 which were published in *English Folk Songs from the Southern Appalachians*. Variants and alternate titles include *The Turtle Dove* and *Ten Thousand Miles*. *True Lover's Farewell* appeared in *Roxburghe Ballads* dated 1710. It was also in *Five Excellent New Songs* a collection printed in 1792. The song is similar to a song *Queen Mary's Lament*, that was printed in Johnson's *Scots Musical Museum* (1787-1803). The *Who Will Shoe your Pretty Little Foot* songs are closely related and use interchangeable "floating" lyrics. The typical lyrics are: "Oh who will shoe your pretty little foot, And who will glove your hand...." "(Papa) will shoe my pretty little foot, (Mama) will glove my hand...." Charlie Poole and the North Carolina Ramblers, "When I'm Far Away" is a good local North Carolina version of the song. *The Storms Are on the Ocean* by the Carter Family is another variant of the *False True Lover, The True Lover's Farewell, Red Rosy Bush, Turtle Dove* family so commonly found in the Appalachians after the early 1900's. *My Dearest Dear* is another branch of songs in this family.

D   **G**   **D**   **A7**   **D**
Now who will shoe your pretty little feet? And who will glove your hand?
      G   **D**   **A7**   **D**
Who will kiss your red rosy cheek, till I come back again?   *Chorus*

Poppa will shoe my pretty little feet, Momma will glove my hand.
And you can kiss my red rosy cheeks, when you return again.   *Chorus*

See that lonesome turtle dove as he flies from pine to pine.
He's mourning for his own true love, just the way I mourn for mine.   *Chorus*

I'll never go back on the ocean love, I'll never go back on the sea.
I'll never go back on the blue-eyed girl, till she goes back on me.   *Chorus*

SWEET BUNCH OF DAISIES

Traditional Old-Time Waltz and Bluegrass Song by Anita Owen; **DATE**: 1894; **CATEGORY**: Early Country and Bluegrass Songs; **RECORDING INFO**: Richard Matteson, American Fiddle Tunes for Acoustic Guitar- Mel Bay Pub. CD; Kenny Baker; Chubby Wise; Oscar Whittington; Uncle Dave Macon; Clark Kessinger; **NOTES**: There are two versions of Sweet Bunch of Daisies, one is a breakdown in common time the other is a waltz (the Kenny Baker/ Chubby Wise) version that is included here. The earliest fiddle citation for this tune is from Arizona fiddler Kenner C. Kartchner who learned it as one of his first, in 1898 (Shumway). It was remembered by north Georgia fiddler Lowe Stokes (1898-1982) as having been fiddled by his father. "Sweet Bunch of Daisies" was recorded in 1924 for Gennett and in 1929 for Columbia by fiddler Jess Young (Chattanooga, Tenn.), and apparently popularized by him among fiddlers (C. Wolfe, The Devil's Box, Dec. 1981, Vol. 15, #4). It appears in the repertoires of both the Stripling Brothers (Ala.) and Freeny's Barn Dance Band (twin fiddle band from Leake County, Mississippi), 1930. Tommy Magness (1911-1972), born in north Georgia near the southeastern Tennessee border, knew the tune and recorded it for Roy Acuff on a home recorder in 1948. Only the chorus lyrics are included since it is usually the fiddle melody.

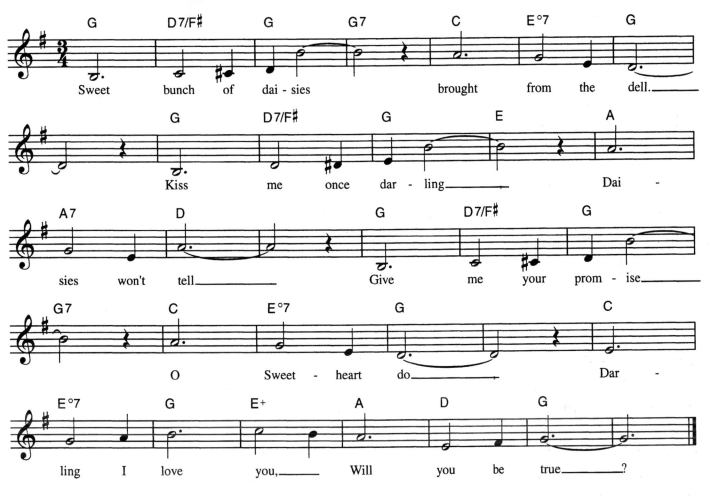

```
G      D7       G   C    E°7    G
```
Sweet bunch of daisies, brought from the dell,
```
G    D7      G E  A           D
```
Kiss me once, darling, daisies won't tell.
```
G    D7       G   C   E°7   G
```
Give me your promise, oh sweetheart do,
```
C   E°7  G  E+  A   D     G
```
Darling I love you, will you be true?

SWEET BYE AND BYE

Traditional Old-Time and Bluegrass Song by S. Fillmore Bennet and J.P. Webster; **CATEGORY:** Early Country and Bluegrass Songs; **RECORDING INFO:** Carter Family; Curly Ray Cline; Stanley Brothers; George Pegram; Jean Ritchie; Elizabeth Cotten

    G   **C**   **G**   **D**
There's a land that is fairer than day, and by faith we can see it afar;
    G   **C**   **G**   **D7**   **G**
For the Father waits over the way to prepare us a dwelling place there.
          G   **D**   **G**
Chorus: In the sweet bye and bye, we shall meet on that beautiful shore
  G7   **C**   **G**   **D7**   **G**
In the sweet bye and bye, we shall meet on that beautiful shore.

We shall sing on that beautiful shore, the melodious songs of the blessed,

And our spirits shall sorrow no more, not a sigh for the blessing of rest.

To our bountiful Father above, we will offer the tribute of praise,

For the glorious gift of his love, and the blessings that hallow our days.

SWEET SUNNY SOUTH

Traditional Old-Time and Bluegrass Song; **DATE**: 1800's; **CATEGORY**: Early Country and Bluegrass Songs; **RECORDING INFO**: Da Costa Woltz's Southern Broadcasters [GE 12779] - ca 1927; Red Patterson's Piedmont Log Rollers [Vi 21132] - 1927, issued 1928; Charlie Poole & The North Carolina Ramblers [Co 15425-D] –1929. There were also recordings by Tennessee Ramblers [1929], Arkansas Woodchopper [1931] and J.E. Mainer's Mountaineers [1936]. Jerry Garcia and David Grisman; Tommy Jarrell; Tim & Molly O'Brien; Kimble Family; **NOTES**: "Sweet Sunny South" is a sentimental song about the South that seems to have struck the right chord with Southerners, for it has turned up often in the repertory of traditional singers in the twentieth century. Kinney Rorrer notes sheet versions of this dating back at least to the Civil War period, and possibly to several decades before that, but gives no details. The tune is akin to the older "Hicks's Farewell" tune that appears in nineteenth-century shape-note hymnals. For twentieth-century sets, see Sharp, *English Folk Songs from the Southern Appalachians*, vol. 2, 262 (#186 "The Sunny South"), vol. 2, 142-143. A well-known hillbilly recording of the song and tune from the 1920's is by Charlie Poole and the North Carolina Ramblers, reissued on County 505. "The Bright Sunny South, words by F. M. Prince and music by A. Scherzer," printed by Klemm and Bro., (1848) sung by Doc Watson and others (Doc Boggs) is a different song.

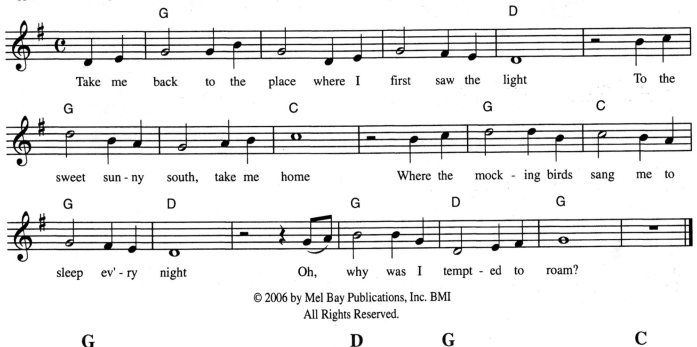

    G   **D**   **G**   **C**
Take me back to the place where I first saw the light, to the sweet sunny south take me home

   G   **C**   **G**   **D**   **G**   **D**   **G**
Where the mockingbirds sang me to sleep ev'ry night, oh why was I tempted to roam?

I think with regret of the dear home I left, of the warm hearts that sheltered me there
Of wife and of dear ones of whom I'm bereft, for the old place again do I sigh.

Take me back to the place where the orange trees grow, to my plot in the evergreen shade
Where the flowers from the river's green margin did grow
And spread their sweet scent through the glade.

The path to our cottage they say has grown green, and the place is quite lonely around
Where the flowers from the river's green margin did grow
And spread their sweet scent through the glade.

But yet I'll return to the place of my birth, for the children have played round the door
Where they gathered wild blossoms that grew round the path
They will echo our footsteps no more.

Take me back, let me see what is left that I knew, can it be that the old house is gone?
Dear friends of my childhood indeed must be few, and I must face death all alone.

Swing Low, Sweet Chariot

Traditional Gospel Song; **DATE:** 1800's (Cabin and Plantation Songs – 1874); **CATEGORY:** Early Gospel Songs; **RECORDING INFO:** Bill Monroe and his Blue Grass Boys (1951) Lucky Chapman and John Duffey; Seldom Scene; Jim and Jesse and the Virginia Boys (1964) Clyde Moody (1989); Jethro Burns (1995); Red Allen and Frank Wakefield (1994); Bruce Jones and the Southern Blue Grass Boys; **OTHER NAMES:** Swing Low, Chariot; **NOTES:** Swing Low, Sweet Chariot is originally a black spiritual in repertoire of the Fisk Jubilee Singers in 1909. It was first recorded by Vaughan Quartet in 1924. Early print versions include Printed in Fenner, 1874, Cabin and Plantation Songs, as The Danville Chariot, p. 11 and Swing Low, Sweet Chariot p. 179 with sheet music. Bascom Lamar Lunsford thinks Swing Low Chariot, a forerunner of Swing Low, Sweet Chariot he recorded in 1925, is an early mountain version.

   G   **C**   **G**   **D**
I looked over Jordan and what did I see, coming for to carry me home

   G   **C**   **G**   **D**   **G**
A band of angels coming after me, coming for to carry me home.

         G   **C G**   **D**
Chorus: Swing low sweet chariot, coming for to carry me home

   G   **C G**   **D**   **G**
Swing low sweet chariot, coming for to carry me home.

If you get there before I do, coming for to carry me home
Tell all my friends I'm coming, too, coming for to carry me home. *Chorus*

I'm sometimes up and sometimes down, coming for to carry me home
But still my soul feels heavenward bound, coming for to carry me home. *Chorus*

TALK ABOUT SUFFERING

Traditional Old-Time and Bluegrass Song; **DATE:** 1900's; **CATEGORY:** Early Country and Bluegrass Songs; **RECORDING INFO:** Doc Watson; Ricky Skaggs and Tony Rice; Edgar Meyer; John Renbourn Group; Eric Schoenberg; **NOTES:** Frequently sung a cappella (vocals only), the classic version of *Talk about Suffering* is Skaggs and Rice rendition on their 1980 Sugar Hill album- *Family & Friends*. Another good version was arranged and recorded by the Renborn Group, an English traditional-music group.

Talk about Suffering here below,
and let's keep a-loving Jesus
Talk about suffering here below
and let's keep following Jesus.

Oh don't you hear it mother?
and don't you want to go?
and leave this world of trials
and troubles here below.

Talk about Suffering here below,
and talk about loving Jesus
Talk about suffering here below
and let's keep following Jesus.

Oh don't you hear it brothers?
and don't you want to go?
and leave this world of trials
and troubles here below.

Oh don't you hear it sister?
and don't you want to go?
and leave this world of trials
and troubles here below.

Talk about Suffering here below,
and talk about loving Jesus
Talk about suffering here below
and let's keep following Jesus.

TENNESSEE HOUND DOG

Bluegrass Song by B. & F. Bryant; **DATE:** 1969; **CATEGORY:** New Bluegrass Songs; **RECORDING INFO:** The Osborne Brothers; Roger Ball; **NOTES:** "Tennessee Hound Dog" was written by husband and wife team, Boudleaux and Felice Bryant. It was written in room number 9, in the Gatlinburg Inn, on the strip in Gatlinburg, Tennessee. Rocky Top and 8 more national chart songs for us there in the same room. They also wrote many other hits including *"Bye Bye Love," "Wake Up Little Susie,"* Boudleaux sang bass on Bill Monroe's *"Walking In Jerusalem Just Like John."*

    A   **F#m**   **A**   **F#m**
He looks like skin on a bone pile, a cat wouldn't give him a glance
    A   **C**   **F**   **C**
But when he stretches his long legs out a fox ain't got a chance
      Am   **(2-4) A G F#m Em**
Tennessee hound dog, Tennessee hound dog.   *(See lyrics chorus above)

Sad faced moon-eyed creature, his ears hang down to his knees
The she-hounds call him a has-been, an old-aged home for fleas
Tennessee hound dog, Tennessee hound dog

He looks like ugly warmed over, some dog lovers have said;
But he's got more sense in the end of his nose, than they've got in their head
Tennessee hound dog, Tennessee hound dog.

There'll Be No Distinction There

Old-Time and Bluegrass Song by Blind Alfred Reed; **DATE:** 1920's; **CATEGORY:** Early Country and Bluegrass Songs; **RECORDING INFO:** Blind Alfred Reed-1929; Carter Family-1940; New Lost City Ramblers; **OTHER NAMES:** No Distinction There; **NOTES:** There'll Be No Distinction comes from Blind Alfred Reed. He was an extremely religious man and many of his secular pieces have a hymn-like austerity. This is one of the few early recordings, black or white, on the subject of discrimination and was subsequently recorded twice by the Carter Family. There is also a version in the Brown Collection of NC Folklore. Reed kept rattlesnake rattles in his fiddle in hopes of improving the tone.

E
There'll be no sorrow on that heavenly shore
                    B7
There'll be no woes at the cabin door
      E
We will all be wealthy and the poor will all be there
A   **E**
We'll all be rich and happy in that land bright and fair
  B7   **E**
There'll be no distinction there.

(Chorus: See page 218)

THERE'LL BE NO DISTINCTION THERE (ADDITIONAL VERSES)

             E
Chorus: There'll be no distinction there
                 B7
There'll be no distinction there
        E
For the Lord is just and the Lord is right
      A   E
And we'll all be white in that heavenly light
    B7   E
There'll be no distinction there.

In the same kind of raiment and the same kind of shoes
We'll all sit together in the same kind of pews
The whites and the black folks, the gentiles and the Jews
We will praise the Lord together and there'll be no drinking booze
There'll be no distinction there.

Oh when we get to heaven we will know and understand
No woman will be flirting with another woman's man
We will all be wealthy in that holy happy land
We will play on golden instruments and shout to beat the band
There'll be no distinction there.

We are never blue in heaven, nothing there to wreck the mind
Everybody is our neighbor, all the folks are good and kind
No aggravatin' women there to boss the men around
When we enter into heaven we will wear a golden crown
There'll be no distinction there.

THIS LITTLE LIGHT OF MINE

Gospel Song; Words and music by Harry Dixon Loes; **DATE:** Early 1900's; **CATEGORY:** Early Gospel Songs; **RECORDING INFO:** Bluegrass Messengers on Diggin' Up Roots; Marty Stuart; Alan Munde; Casey Anderson; Blind James Campbell and his Nashville Street Band; Gateway Singers; **NOTES:** This song is attributed to Harry Dixon Loes (1895-1965), who studied at Moody Bible Institute, Chicago, Illinois; the American Conservatory of Music; the Metropolitan School of Music; and the Chicago Musical College. From 1927-1939, he served in musical positions in Baptist churches in Okmulgee and Muskogee, Oklahoma. From 1939 to retirement, he served on the music faculty at the Moody Bible Institute. This Little Light of Mine originated from African American sources and was probably arranged by Loes. Olivia and Jack Solomon in *"Honey in the Rock"*: The editors seem to think this originated among African Americans: "Widely performed by choirs and gospel groups during the 1930's, a favorite on gospel radio shows, 'Let hit shine' is now also in white folk tradition." (p. 5). Lomax collected a version from Doris McMurray, Goree Farm, Huntsville, TX. in his 1939 Southern States recording trip.

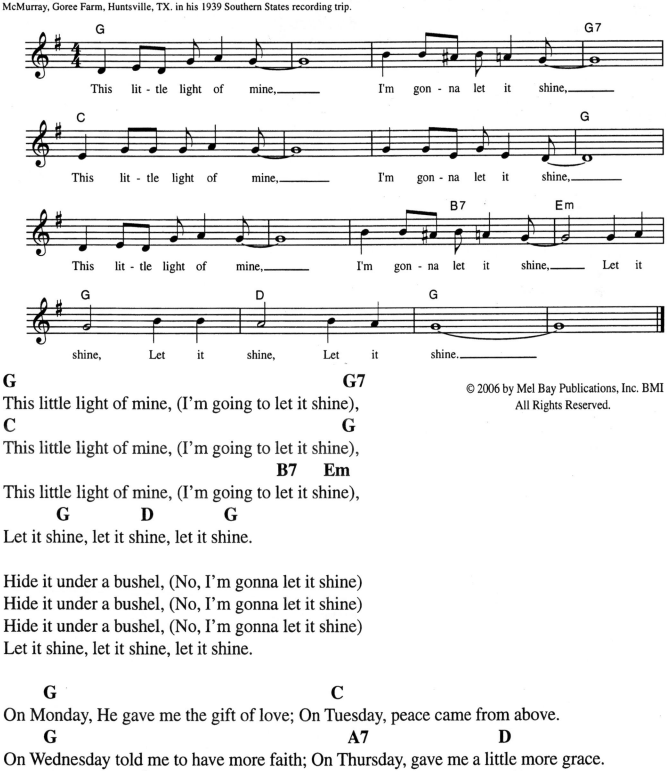

G   **G7**
This little light of mine, (I'm going to let it shine),
C   **G**
This little light of mine, (I'm going to let it shine),
                                                           B7   **Em**
This little light of mine, (I'm going to let it shine),
        G   **D**   **G**
Let it shine, let it shine, let it shine.

Hide it under a bushel, (No, I'm gonna let it shine)
Hide it under a bushel, (No, I'm gonna let it shine)
Hide it under a bushel, (No, I'm gonna let it shine)
Let it shine, let it shine, let it shine.

        G   **C**
On Monday, He gave me the gift of love; On Tuesday, peace came from above.
        G   **A7**   **D**
On Wednesday told me to have more faith; On Thursday, gave me a little more grace.
        G   **C**   **G**
On Friday, told me to watch and pray; On Saturday, told me just what to say,
                E   **A7**   **D**   **G**
On Sunday, gave power divine, to let my little light shine.   *Repeat 1st verse*

TOM DOOLEY [LAWS F36A]

Traditional Old-Time and Bluegrass Song; **DATE:** Late 1800's; **CATEGORY:** Early Country and Bluegrass Songs; **RECORDING INFO:** First recorded Grayson and Whitter- 1929; Frank Proffitt; Doc Watson; Kingston Trio; **OTHER NAMES:** Murder of Laura Foster; Tom Dula; **NOTES:** In 1866 Laura Foster was murdered by Thomas C. Dula and his sweetheart Ann Melton. On May 1, 1868 Tom Dula is hanged for the murder. The details and various versions about this famous love triangle could fill a short book. After Frank Warner collected the song from Frank Proffitt in NC, The Kingston Trio picked up Warner's version, and made a huge hit of it in 1958.

G   **D**
Verse 2: Hang your head, Tom Dooley. Hang your head and cry.

                                                         G
You killed poor Laura Foster. You know you're bound to die.

You took her on the hillside, as God Almighty knows.
You took her on the hillside, and there you hid her clothes.

You took her by the roadside, where you begged to be excused.
You took her by the roadside, where there you hid her shoes.

You took her on the hillside, to make her your wife.
You took her on the hillside, where there you took her life.

Take down my old violin, play it all you please.
This time tomorrow, it'll be no use to me.

I dug a grave four foot long. I dug it three foot deep.
Poured cold clay o'er her, and tromped it with my feet.

This world one more morning, then where you reckon I'll be?
Hadn't 'a been for Grayson, I'd 'a been in Tennessee.

[Here is the Kingston Trio's version]
Met her on the mountain, there I took her life.
Met her on the mountain, stabbed her with my knife.

This time tomorrow, reckon where I'll be?
Hadn't have been for Grayson, I'd been in Tennessee.

This time tomorrow, reckon where I'll be?
Down in some lonesome valley, hanging from a white oak tree.

TROUBLES UP AND DOWN THE ROAD

Old-Time and Bluegrass Song by W.E. Myers; **DATE:** 1920's; **CATEGORY:** Early Country and Bluegrass Songs; **RECORDING INFO:** Blue Highway; Dock Boggs; **OTHER NAMES:** Old Rub Alcohol Blues; Rub Alcohol Blues; **NOTES:** "Troubles Up And Down The Road" is a remake by Blue Highway and others of "Old Rub Alcohol Blues" by W.E. Myers sung by Dock Boggs in 1929.

Trou - bles up and down the road and trials all the way a round

Ne - ver knew what trou - ble was till my dar - ling threw me down.

Em   **G**
Troubles up and down the road, And trials all the way around;
      A   **Em** **B7** **Em**
Never knew what trouble was, 'Til my darling threw me down.

With nothing but old ragged clothes, My heart strings broken to shreds;
Blues creepin' over my body, Queer notions flyin' to my head.

If ever I meet that girl again, Our troubles will all be o'er;
I'll steal her out away from home, We will sail for some foreign shore.

When my worldly trials are over, And my last goodbye I've said;
Bury me near my darling's doorstep, Where the roses bloom and fade.

My pockets are all empty, Like they've often been before;
If I ever reach my home again, I'll walk these ties no more.

The easiest thing I ever done, Was lovin' and drinkin' wine;
The hardest thing I ever done, Was workin' out a judge's fine.

The cheapest thing I ever done, Was sleepin' out amongst the pines;
The hardest thing I ever tried, Was keeping pork chops off of my mind.

Have never worked for pleasure, Peace on earth I cannot find;
The only thing I surely own, Is a worried and troubled mind.

If wine and women don't kill me, There's one more plan to find;
Soak up the old rub alcohol, Ease all troubles off my mind.

When my worldly trials are over, And my last goodbye I've said;
Bury me near my darling's doorstep, Where the roses bloom and fade.

TURKEY IN THE STRAW

Old-Time and Bluegrass Song; **DATE:** Early 1800's; **CATEGORY:** Fiddle and Instrumental Tunes; **RECORDING INFO:** Doc Roberts; New Lost City Ramblers; Clark Kessinger; The Tweedy Brothers (1924. W.Va. string band). Bill Monroe- "Bluegrass Time." Eck Robertson; **OTHER NAMES:** Old Zip Coon; Natchez Under the Hill; **NOTES:** "Turkey In the Straw" was one of the earliest American minstrel songs appearing as Zip Coon by J. B. Farrell in 1834. It originated from the fiddle tune "Natchez Under the Hill." Nearly all the best fiddlers recorded it including Doc Roberts, Clark Kessinger, Eck Robertson in the 1920's to 1940's. It was also recorded on Bill Monroe's "Bluegrass Time." According to Linscott, the tune is derived from the ballad "My Grandmother Lived on Yonder Little Green" which in turn derived from the Irish ballad "The Old Rose Tree."

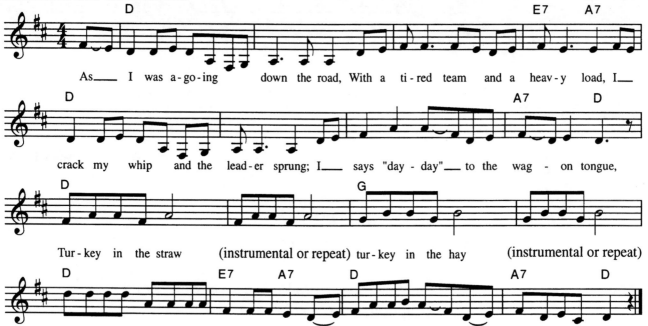

D   **E7   A7**
As I was a-going on down the road, With a tired team and a heavy load,
D   **A7   D**
I crack'd my whip and the leader sprung, I says day-day to the wagon tongue.
D   **G**   **D**   **E7   A7**
Turkey in the straw(Fill), turkey in the hay(Fill), Roll 'em up and twist 'em up a high tuckahaw
D   **A7**   **D**
And twist 'em up a tune called Turkey in the Straw.

Went out to milk, and I didn't know how, I milked the goat instead of the cow.
A monkey sittin' on a pile of straw, A-winkin' at his mother-in-law.

Met Mr. Catfish comin' down stream. Says Mr. Catfish, "What does you mean?"
Caught Mr. Catfish by the snout, And turned Mr. Catfish wrong side out.

Came to a river and I couldn't get across, Paid five dollars for a blind old hoss;
Wouldn't go ahead, nor he wouldn't stand still, So he went up and down like an old saw mill.

As I came down the new cut road, Met Mr. Bullfrog, met Miss Toad
And every time Miss Toad would sing, Old Bullfrog cut a pigeon wing.

Oh I jumped in the seat and I gave a little yell, The horses ran away, broke the wagon all to hell
Sugar in the gourd and honey in the horn, I never been so happy since the day I was born.

TURN YOUR RADIO ON

Gospel Song by Albert E. Brumley (1905-1977); **DATE:** 1938; **CATEGORY:** Early Gospel Songs; **RECORDING INFO:** Chris Hillman; Johnnie and Jack; Rose Maddox; Mill Run Dulcimer Band; Jean Redpath and Lisa Neustadt; **NOTES:** "Turn Your Radio On" is one of the favorite gospel songs written by Albert E. Brumley (born in Spiro, OK in 1905) who wrote over 800 gospel and sentimental songs. Brumley songs have been estimated to have been printed 15 million times in sheet music and songbooks.

G   G7   C   G

Come and listen in to a radio station,Where the mighty host of heaven sing

G   D

Turn your radio on (Turn your radio on), Turn your radio on (Turn your radio on)

G   G7   C   G

If you want to hear the songs of Zion, Coming from the land of endless spring

D

Get in touch with God (Get in touch with God)

G

Turn your radio on (Turn your radio on)

Turn Your Radio On (Additional Verses)

                G   **C**   **G**
Chorus: Turn your radio on (Turn your radio on), And listen to the music in the air
                                A7   **D**
Turn your radio on (Turn your radio on), Heaven's glory share (Heaven's glory share)
                G   **C**   **G**
Turn the lights down low (Turn the lights down low) And listen to the Master's radio
                            D
Get in touch with God (Get in touch with God)
                G
Turn your radio on (Turn your radio on)

Listen to the songs of the fathers and the mothers
And the many friends gone on before
Turn your radio on (Turn your radio on), Turn your radio on (Turn your radio on)
Some eternal morning we shall meet them, Over on the hallelujah shore
Get in touch with God (Get in touch with God)
Turn your radio on (Turn your radio on)

Brother listen in to the gloryland chorus, Listen to the glad hosannahs roll
Turn your radio on (Turn your radio on), Turn your radio on (Turn your radio on)
Get a little taste of joys awaiting, Get a little heaven in your soul
Get in touch with God (Get in touch with God)
Turn your radio on (Turn your radio on)

UNCLOUDY DAY

Gospel Bluegrass Song by J. K. Alwood,1828-1909; **DATE:** 1890; **CATEGORY:** Early Gospel Songs; **RECORDING INFO:** Elmer Bird; Mill Run Dulcimer Band; Simmons Family; Hobart Smith; Stanley Brothers; Willie Nelson; Doc Watson. **OTHER NAMES:** Unclouded Day; **NOTES:** First recorded by Homer Rodeheaver in 1914 and then by the Old Southern Sacred Singers in 1927, Uncloudy Day (or Unclouded Day) is a favorite bluegrass gospel song. *Born* July 15, 1828, near Cadiz, Harrison County, Ohio. Alwood was a circuit riding preacher in the Midwest, and later an elder in the North Ohio Conference of the United Brethren Church.

    G   **C**   **D**
Oh they tell me of a place where my friends have gone, And they tell me of that land far away
   G   **C**   **G**   **D**   **G**
And they tell me of a place where no storm clouds fly, Oh, they tell me of an uncloudy day.

   G   **C**   **G**   **D**
Chorus: Oh, the land of a cloudless day, Oh, the land of an uncloudy sky
   G   **C**   **G**   **D**   **G**
Oh they tell me of a place where my friends have gone, Oh, they tell me of an uncloudy day.

Oh they tell me that he smiles on his children's face, Oh, his smile drives their sorrow away
And they tell me that no tears ever come again, Oh, they tell me of an uncloudy day. *Chorus*

Oh, they tell me of a home far beyond the sky, And they tell me of a home far away
And they tell me of a home where no storm clouds fly, Oh, they tell me of an uncloudy day.
Chorus

WABASH CANNONBALL

Traditional Old-Time and Bluegrass Song; **DATE:** 1800's; **CATEGORY:** Early Country and Bluegrass Songs; **RECORDING INFO:** Norman and Nancy Blake; Kimble Family; Doc Watson; **NOTES:** Wabash Cannonball first appeared in print in 1904 copyrighted by William Kindt and based on "Great Rock Island Route." Meade references an earlier version by J.A. Roff in 1882. Made popular by the Carter Family in 1930's it first became a hit in 1938 for Roy Acuff (Vocalion 4466). The Wabash Cannonball Trail runs on the two lines originally established by the Wabash Railroad. The southwestern leg was built in 1855, running from Fort Wayne, Indiana to Toledo, Ohio, making it one of the oldest rail lines in northwest Ohio.

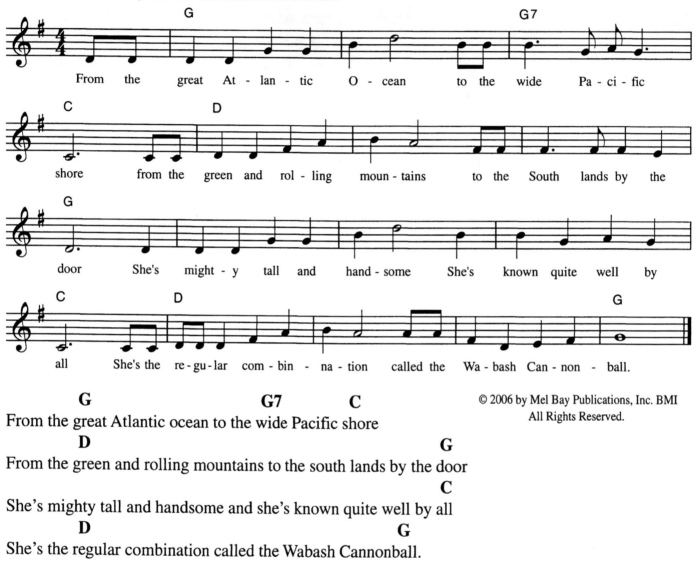

    G   **G7**   **C**
From the great Atlantic ocean to the wide Pacific shore
    D   **G**
From the green and rolling mountains to the south lands by the door
                                          C
She's mighty tall and handsome and she's known quite well by all
    D   **G**
She's the regular combination called the Wabash Cannonball.

Listen to the jingle, the rumble and the roar
As she glides along the woodland through the hills and by the shore
Hear the mighty rush of the engine, hear the lonesome hobos call
You're traveling through the jungles on the Wabash Cannonball.

Our eastern states are dandy, so the people always say
From New York to St. Louis with Chicago by the way
From the hills of Minnesota where the rippling waters fall
No changes can be taken on the Wabash Cannonball.

Now here's to Daddy Claxton, may his name forever stand
And always be remembered through the courts throughout the land
His earthly race is over, now the curtains round him fall
We'll carry him home to victory on the Wabash Cannonball.

WALKING IN JERUSALEM, JUST LIKE JOHN

Traditional Gospel Song; **DATE:** Early 1900's; **CATEGORY:** Early Gospel Songs; **RECORDING INFO:** Bill Monroe & His Blue Grass Boys Decca 28608, 1953; Country Gentlemen; Round Town Girls; Doc Watson, Clint Howard and Fred Price; Hotmud Family; **OTHER NAMES:** Walk in Jerusalem; **NOTES:** The classic recording is Bill Monroe & His Blue Grass Boys, "Walking In Jerusalem Just Like John" (Decca 28608, 1953). The Biblical references here are a bit confused. The New Jerusalem is said to be descending in Rev. 21:2, and is said to be foursquare in Rev. 21:16 but there is no promise to meet John there. The coming of the Spirit at Pentecost is told in Acts 2 — but the Spirit came before this, upon a large group, and only then did Peter preach about it. The song is related to "Bear the News, Mary," "Heaven and Hell," "Hand Me Down My Walking Cane."

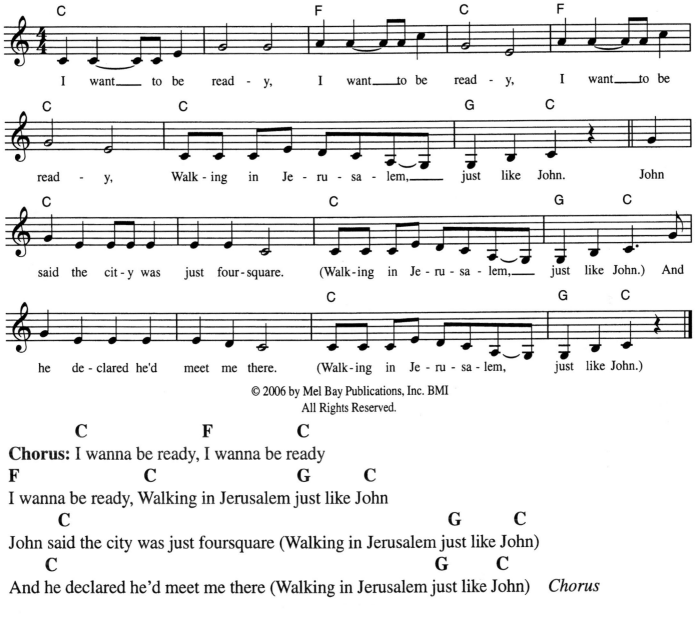

	C		F	C
Chorus: I wanna be ready, I wanna be ready

F		C		G	C
I wanna be ready, Walking in Jerusalem just like John

    C   G   C
John said the city was just foursquare (Walking in Jerusalem just like John)

    C   G   C
And he declared he'd meet me there (Walking in Jerusalem just like John) *Chorus*

Oh John oh John oh didn't you say (Walking in Jerusalem just like John)
You'd be there on that great day (Walking in Jerusalem just like John) *Chorus*

Some came crippled and some came lame (Walking in Jerusalem just like John)
Some came walking in Jesus' name (Walking in Jerusalem just like John) *Chorus*

Now brother, better mind how you step on the cross
(Walking in Jerusalem just like John)
Your feet might slip and your soul get lost (Walking in Jerusalem just like John) *Chorus*

WAY DOWNTOWN

Traditional Old-Time and Bluegrass Song; **DATE:** Early 1900's; **CATEGORY:** Early Country and Bluegrass Songs; **RECORDING INFO:** Uncle Dave Macon-1926; Frank Blevins and His Tar Heel Rattlers-1927; Roy Acuff "One Old Shirt" -1938; Dickel Brothers; New Lost City Ramblers Doc Watson; Tony Rice; Jody Stecher; **OTHER NAMES:** Late Last Night (When Willie Came Home); **NOTES:** "Way Downtown" or "Late Last Night When Willie Came Home" is grouped by Meade under "Ain't It Hell"- A. It's related to "Slippin' and A-Sliding with My New Shoes On," "To Love One Who Don't Love You" ("Hard Ain't It Hard" by Woody Guthrie) and includes the *Hard for to Love* songs. One of the great versions is Doc Watson with Clint Howard and Fred Price (1962).

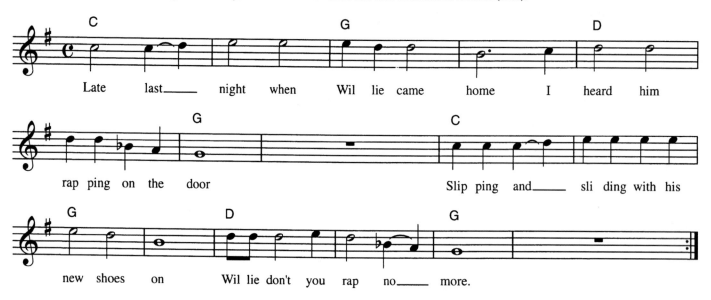

> **C**   **G**
> It was late last night when Willie came home
> **D**   **G**
> I heard him rapping on the door
> **C**   **G**
> Slipping and sliding with his new shoes on
> **D**   **G**
> Willie don't you rap no more.

Chorus: Way downtown just foolin' around, Took me to the jail
It's oh me and it's oh my, No one to go my bail

I wish I was over at my sweet Sally's house
Sittin' in that big armed chair
One arm around this old guitar
And the other one around my dear.   *Chorus*

Now, its one old shirt is all that I got
And a dollar is all that I crave
I brought nothing with me into this old world
Ain't gonna take nothing to my grave.   *Chorus*

WE'LL UNDERSTAND IT BETTER BYE AND BYE

Gospel Song by Charles A. Tindley; **DATE:** Ca. 1905; **CATEGORY:** Early Country and Bluegrass Songs; **RECORDING INFO:** Frank and James McCravy-1927; Kentucky Mountain Choristers; Morris Brothers and Homer Sherrill-1938; Pinder Family & Joseph Spence; Preservation Hall Jazz Band; **OTHER NAMES:** We'll Understand it Better; **NOTES:** Charles Tindley 1851-1933, is known as one of the "founding fathers of American Gospel music." The son of slaves, he taught himself to read and write at age 17. In 1902, he became pastor of the Calvary Methodist Episcopal Church in Philadelphia, Pennsylvania. Tindley's "I'll Overcome Some Day" was the basis for the American civil rights anthem "We Shall Overcome," popularized in the 1960's.

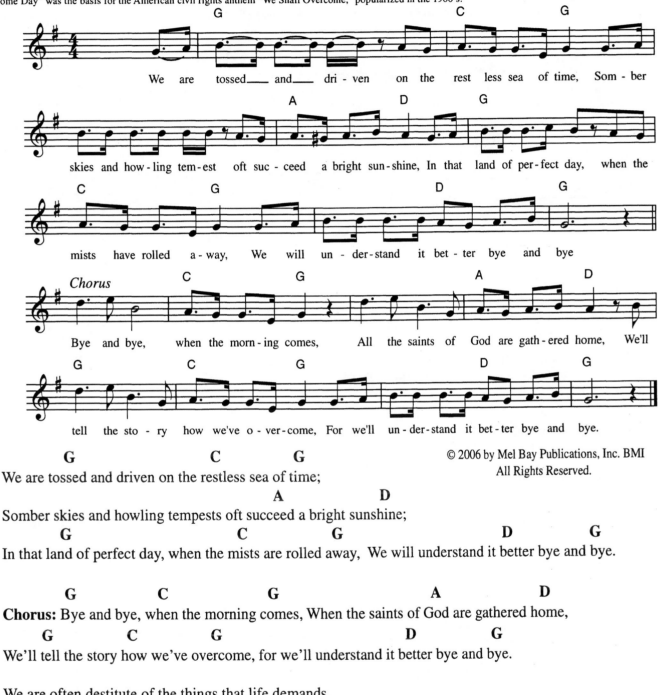

    G   **C**   **G**
We are tossed and driven on the restless sea of time;
                  A   **D**
Somber skies and howling tempests oft succeed a bright sunshine;
    G   **C**   **G**   **D**   **G**
In that land of perfect day, when the mists are rolled away, We will understand it better bye and bye.

      G   **C**   **G**   **A**   **D**
Chorus: Bye and bye, when the morning comes, When the saints of God are gathered home,
    G   **C**   **G**   **D**   **G**
We'll tell the story how we've overcome, for we'll understand it better bye and bye.

We are often destitute of the things that life demands,
Want of food and want of shelter, thirsty hills and barren lands;
We are trusting in the Lord, and according to God's word, We will understand it better bye and bye. *Chorus*

Trials dark on every hand, and we cannot understand
All the ways of God would lead us to that blessed promised land;
But he guides us with his eye, and we'll follow till we die, for we'll understand it better bye and bye. *Chorus*

Temptations, hidden snares often take us unawares,
And our hearts are made to bleed for a thoughtless word or deed;
And we wonder why the test when we try to do our best, But we'll understand it better bye and bye. *Chorus*

WEEVILY WHEAT

Traditional Old-Time and Bluegrass Song; **DATE:** Referenced to the 1700's by William Newell in Games and Songs of American Children-1883; **CATEGORY:** Early Country and Bluegrass Songs; **RECORDING INFO**: Kelly Harrell and the Virginia String Band "Charley, He's a Good Old Man" (Victor 21069, 1927; on KHarrell02, CrowTold02); Erik Darling; Granville Bowlin; New Lost City Ramblers; **OTHER NAMES:** Charley He's a Good Old Boy/Man; Charlie's Neat; **NOTES:** Described by Botkin in *The American Play-Party Song*, p. 345, as "A Virginia reel related to the Scotch Weaving Game based on a Jacobite song of Bonnie Prince Charles Stuart, the Pretender." Alan Lomax derives it from the Scots "Charlie Over the Water." There's a resemblance and floating lyrics to "Roll the Tater" and "Fly Around, My Pretty Little Miss."

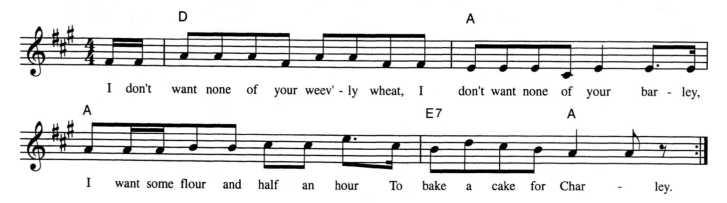

I don't want none of your weev' - ly wheat, I don't want none of your bar - ley,

I want some flour and half an hour To bake a cake for Char - ley.

  D   **A**
I don't want none of your weev'ly wheat, I don't want none of your barley,
A   **E7**   **A**
I want some flour and half an hour, To bake a cake for Charlie.

Chorus: Oh Charley, he's a fine young man
And Charley he's a dandy
And Charlie loves to kiss the girls
Whenever they come handy.

Charley he's a handsome man, Oh, Charley he's a dandy
Charley he's the very man, That sold his hat for brandy.

Over the river and through the trees, Over the river to Charlie,
Over the river to feed my sheep, On buckwheat cakes and barley.

Coffee grows on white oak trees, Rivers flow with brandy,
I've got a pretty little blue-eyed gal, Sweet as 'lasses candy.

WERE YOU THERE

Traditional Gospel Song; **DATE:** 1800's; **CATEGORY:** Early Gospel Songs; **RECORDING INFO:** Uncle Dave Macon-1930; Wade Mainer-1938; Roy Acuff and the Smoky Mountain Boys-1949; Bill Monroe-1941; Seldom Scene; **OTHER NAMES:** Were You There When They Crucified My Lord? **NOTES:** The first version in print is "When I Think How They Crucified My Lord" found in John Work's *Songs of the American Negro* #134, 1907. It was in the repertoire of the Fisk Jubilee Singers in 1920.

   D   **G**   **G**
Were you there when they crucified my Lord, were you there,
                     D
Were you there when they crucified my Lord, were you there
  G   **C**
Well sometimes it causes me to tremble, tremble
       G   **D**   **G**
Where you there when they crucified my Lord?

Were you there when they nailed Him to the cross, were you there,
Were you there when they nailed Him to the cross, were you there,
Well sometimes it causes me to tremble, tremble
Were you there when they nailed Him to the cross?

Were you there when they laid Him in the tomb, were you there,
Were you there when they laid Him in the tomb, were you there,
Well sometimes it causes me to tremble, tremble
Were you there when they laid Him in the tomb?

WHEN THE ROLL IS CALLED UP YONDER

Gospel Song by James M. Black; **DATE: 1893; CATEGORY:** Early Country and Bluegrass Songs; **RECORDING INFO:** Jenkins Family- 1924; Carter Family; Virginia Squires; The Harvesters Bluegrass Gospel Band; Mountain Therapy; **NOTES:** James M. Black, a Methodist Sunday school teacher in Williamsport, Pennsylvania, was calling roll one day for a youth meeting. Young Bessie, daughter of a drunkard, did not show up, and he was disappointed at her failure to appear. Black made a comment to the effect, "Well, I trust when the roll is called up yonder, she'll be there." He tried to respond with an appropriate song, but could not find one in his song book: "This lack of a fitting song caused me both sorrow and disappointment. An inner voice seemed to say, "Why don't you write one?" I put away the thought. As I opened the gate on my way home, the same thought came again so strongly that tears filled my eyes. I entered the house and sat down at the piano. The words came to me effortlessly. The tune came the same way—I dared not change a single note or word."

G   C   G

On that bright and cloudless morning when the dead in Christ shall rise,

D

And the glory of His resurrection share;

G   C   G

When His chosen ones shall gather to their home beyond the skies,

G   D   G

And the roll is called up yonder, I'll be there.

                 D

Chorus: When the roll, is called up yon-der, When the roll, is called up yon-der,

G   C   G   D   G

When the roll, is called up yonder, When the roll is called up yonder I'll be there.

Let us labor for the Master from the dawn till setting sun,

Let us talk of all His wondrous love and care;

Then when all of life is over, and our work on earth is done,

And the roll is called up yonder, I'll be there.

WHEN THE SAINTS GO MARCHING IN

Traditional Old-Time and Bluegrass Song; **DATE:** Late 1800's; **CATEGORY:** Early Country and Bluegrass Songs; **RECORDING INFO:** Fiddlin' John Carson-1934; Monroe Brothers-1936; Lester Flatt & Earl Scruggs; Kingston Trio; Lilly Brothers; Clyde Moody; **OTHER NAMES:** Saints Go Marching In; Saints Go Marching Home; **NOTES:** First recorded as "When All The Saints Go Marching In" by the Paramount Jubilee Singers in 1923, and best known through Louis Armstrong, this song was published twice in 1896 by J. M. Black and once with words credited to Katherine E. Purvis and music by Black. The song may have originated in the Bahamas as it was collected in Nassau by the McCutcheons in 1917.

     G   **D**
And when the stars begin to shine, And when the stars begin to shine,
     G   **C**   **G**   **D**   **G**
Then Lord, let me be in that number, When the stars begin to shine

When Gabriel blows in his horn, When Gabriel blows in his horn,
Oh Lord I want to be in that number, When Gabriel blows in his horn.

And when the moon has turned to blood, And when the moon has turned to blood,
Oh Lord I want to be in that number, When the moon has turned to blood.

And when the sun refuse to shine, And when the sun refuse to shine,
Oh Lord I want to be in that number, When the sun refuse to shine.

And when they gather round the throne, And when they gather round the throne,
Oh Lord I want to be in that number, When they gather round the throne.

And on that Halleluja Day, And on that Halleluja Day
Oh Lord I want to be in that number, On that Halleluja Day.

WHEN THEY RING THE GOLDEN BELLS

Traditional Gospel Song- Words Unknown, music by Dion De Marbelle 1818-1903; **DATE:** 1887; **CATEGORY:** Early Gospel Songs; **RECORDING INFO:** Country Gentlemen; Emmylou Harris; Mac Wiseman; **OTHER NAMES:** When They Ring Those Golden Bells; **NOTES:** Born in Seville, France, Daniel de Marbelle (sometimes called Dion De Marbelle) worked on a whaling ship in the early 1800's, then joined the American Navy and served during the Mexican War (1847). After that, he toured America as a musician and actor with an opera company, later organizing his own theatrical troupe. At the invitation of Bailey (of Barnum and Bailey fame), he became the very first circus clown. Later, he managed his own circus, but lost everything in a fire while touring Canada. Then, he helped Buffalo Bill Cody set up his famous Wild West Show. De Marbelle could play almost any instrument, and wrote many songs. He was a ventriloquist, organized a brass band, and sang in a Methodist choir in Elgin, Illinois. He also called the figures in local square dances. He claimed he could make an eloquent speech on any subject, without preparation! The royalties from all his songs were stolen from him, and he died penniless, near starvation. This version can be played in 6/8 time also. Alfred G. Karnes version from 1928 is in 6/8 time.

There's a land be-yond - the riv-er, That we call the sweet for-ev-er, And we on-ly reach that shore by faith's de-cree, One by one we'll gain the por-tals, There to dwell with the im-mor-tals, When they ring the gol-den bells for you and me. yond the shin-ing riv-er, When they ring the gol-den bells for you and me.

Chorus
Don't you hear the bells now ring-ing? Don't you hear the an-gels sing-ing? 'Tis the glo-ry Hal-le-lu-jah Ju-bi-lee, In that far - off sweet for-ev-er, Just be

When our days shall know their number, And in death we sweetly slumber,
When the King commands the spirit to be free;
Nevermore with anguish laden, We shall reach that lovely aiden,
When they ring the golden bells for you and me.   *Chorus*

WHERE THE SOUL OF MAN NEVER DIES

Gospel Song by W. M. Golden; **DATE:** 1914; **CATEGORY:** Early Gospel Songs; **RECORDING INFO:** Blue Sky Boys-1936; Arthur Smith- 1938; Wry Straw; Harry and Jeanie West; Ricky Skaggs and Tony Rice; **OTHER NAMES:** Where the Soul Never Dies; To Canaan's Land I'm On My Way; **NOTES:** W. M. Golden , author of Where The Soul of Man Never Dies, was *born* January 28, 1878 and died and was buried in Spring Valley Cemetery, Webster County, Mississippi on May 13,1934. This is one of the more difficult gospel duets to sing.

G   **D**
To Canaan's land I'm on my way, Where the soul of man never dies;
G   **D**   **G**
My darkest night will turn to day, Where the soul of man never dies.

Refrain: Dear friends, there'll be no sad farewells, There'll be no tear dimmed eyes,
Where all is peace and joy and love, And the soul of man never dies.

A rose is blooming there for me, Where the soul of man never dies;
And I will spend eternity, Where the soul of man never dies. *Refrain*

My life will end in deathless sleep, Where the soul of man never dies;
And everlasting joys I'll reap, Where the soul of man never dies. Refrain

I'm on my way to that fair land, Where the soul of man never dies;
Where there will be no parting hand, Where the soul of man never dies. *Refrain*

WHERE WE'LL NEVER GROW OLD

Gospel Song- James C. Moore; **DATE:** 1923; **CATEGORY:** Early Gospel Songs; **RECORDING INFO:** Jenkins Family-1926; Vernon Dalhart-1927; Carter Family–1932; Maddox Brothers & Rose; Bill Clifton & the Dixie Mountain Boys; Jean Redpath and Lisa Neustadt; **OTHER NAMES:** Land Where We'll Never Grow Old; **NOTES:** James C. Moore was a Missionary Baptist minister, and a singing teacher in Spaulding County, Georgia. He attended Draketown Baptist Institute, Mercer University, and the University of Florida. After being ordained a Baptist minister, he served at Funstron, Alma, Moultree, Glenwood, Willacoochee, and Abbeville, Georgia, Hawthrone, Florida. He also served for two years as president of the Georgia-Florida-Alabama Tri-State Singing Convention, and was president of the Southern Singers's Association of Georgia. He estimated that he wrote over 500 songs.

	D		**G**	**D**	**A7**

I have heard of a land on the far away strand, 'Tis a beautiful home of the soul;

D　　　　　　　　　　　　　　　**G**　　**A7**　　**D**

Built by Jesus on high, where we never shall die, 'Tis a land where we never grow old.

Chorus:
D　　　　**G**　　**D**　　　　　　**E**　　**A**

Never grow old, never grow old, In a land where we'll never grow old;

D　　**G**　　**D**　　　　　　**A7**　　**D**

Never grow old, never grow old, In a land where we'll never grow old.

In that beautiful home where we'll never more roam, We shall be in the sweet bye and bye;
Happy praise to the King through eternity sing, 'Tis a land where we never shall die. *Chorus*

When our work here is done and the life crown is won, And our troubles and trials are o'er;
All our sorrow will end, and our voices will blend, With the loved ones who've gone on before.
Chorus

WHITE HOUSE BLUES

Traditional Old-Time and Bluegrass Song; **DATE:** Early 1900's; **CATEGORY:** Early Country and Bluegrass Songs; **RECORDING INFO:** Charlie Poole and the North Carolina Ramblers- 1926; Flatt & Scruggs & the Foggy Mountain Boys; Greenbriar Boys; Wade Mainer; Satanley Brothers-1947; Bill Monroe-1954; Charlie Monroe & the Kentucky Pardners; Muleskinner; Don Reno, Bill Harrell and the Tenn. Cutups; Stoneman's Dixie Mountaineers; Doc Watson; **OTHER NAMES:** Mister McKinley; Road to Washington; **NOTES:** White House Blues is based on the shooting death of President William McKinley by anarchist Leon Czolgosz on Sept 6, 1901. MacKinley's wounds should not have been serious, but his inept doctor decided to operate immediately rather than wait for a specialist. The same tune is used for the old-time song, "Battleship of Maine."

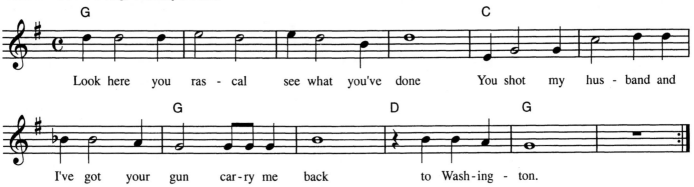

G
Look here you rascal, see what you've done
C   **G**
You shot my husband and I've got your gun
                D   **G**
Carry me back   to Washington.

McKinley hollered , McKinley squalled
Doctor said, "McKinley, I can't find the cause
You're bound to die, you're hound to die."

He jumped on his horse, he pulled on his mane
Said, "Listen you horse, you got to out run this train
From Buffalo to Washington."

The doctor come a running, took off his specs
Said, "Mr. McKinley, betteincash in your cheeks
You're bound to die, you're bound to die."

Roosevelt's in the White House, doing his best
McKinley's in the graveyard, taking his rest
He's gone, he's gone.

WHOA MULE

Traditional Old-Time and Bluegrass Song; **DATE:** Early 1900's; Journal of American Folklore 1911; **CATEGORY:** Early Country and Bluegrass Songs; **RECORD-ING INFO:** Riley Puckett- 1924; The Hill Billies- 1924; Uncle Dave Macon-1926; Chubby Parker- 1927; Clarence Tom Ashley; Georgia Yellow Hammers; Kimble Family; J. E. Mainer's Mountaineers; Smokey Valley Boys; **OTHER NAMES:** Hold on to that Sleigh; Whoa Mule Whoa; Buckin' Mule; Kickin' Mule; **NOTES:** One of the popular old-time songs, it has even been sung as "Flop-Eared Mule" on "Andy Griffith Sings Favorite Old Time Songs."

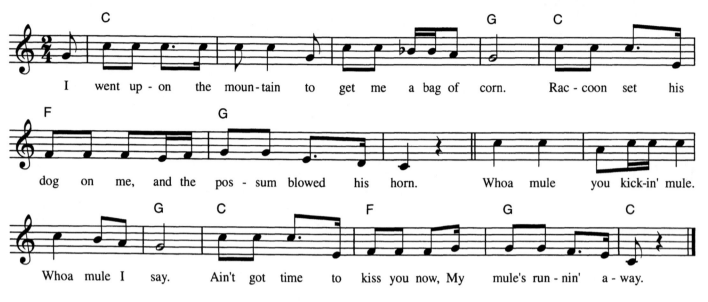

    C   **G**
I went up on the mountain, To get a bag of corn.
C   **F**   **G**   **C**
Raccoon set his dog on me, And the possum blowed his horn.

                   C   **G**
Chorus: Whoa mule, you kickin' mule, Whoa mule I say.
C   **F**   **G**   **C**
I ain't got time to kiss you now, My mule's runnin' away.

Mary had a little cat, It swallowed a ball of yarn.
When those little cats came out, They all had sweaters on.

Now grandma had a yeller hen, Yeller as pure gold.
She set her on three buzzard eggs; She hatched out one old crow.

Your face is like a coffee pot, Your nose is like a spout.
Your mouth is like a fireplace, With all the ashes out.

Wildwood Flower

Old-Time and Bluegrass Song by J. P. Webster and Maud Irving; **DATE:** 1859; **CATEGORY:** Early Country and Bluegrass Songs; **RECORDING INFO:** Joan Baez; Norman Blake; Carter Family; Roy Clark; Flatt & Scruggs; New Lost City Ramblers; Stanley Brothers; Keith Whitley & Ricky Skaggs; **OTHER NAMES:** I'll Twine Mid the Ringlets; Frail Wildwood Flower; **NOTES:** Autoharpist Sara Carter sang lead when the Carter Family made "Wildwood Flower" the #3 hit in the nation in 1928. As a parlor tune, the piece went back at least to 1859, as Maud Irving's "I'll Twine Midst the Ringlets." Music historian Charles Wolfe hears "The Pale Amaryllis" entangled in it as well. The actual flower (aronatas) has never been identified.

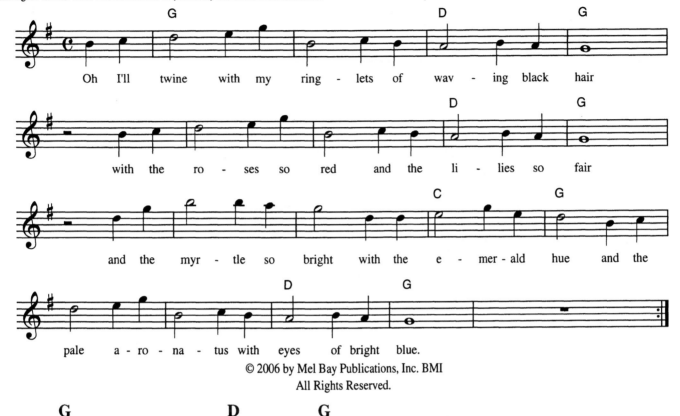

```
     G                    D          G
Oh, I'll twine with my ringlets of waving black hair
                         D        G
With the roses so red and the lilies so fair
                           C        G
And the myrtles so bright with emerald hue
                         D          G
And the pale aronatus with eyes of bright blue.
```

Oh, I'll dance, I will sing and my laugh shall be gay
I will charm ev'ry heart, in his crown I will sway
When I woke from my dreaming, idols were clay
All portions of love then had all flown away.

Oh, he taught me to love him and promised to love
And to cherish me over all others above
How my heart now is wond'ring misery can tell
He's left me no warning, no words of farewell.

Oh, he taught me to love him and called me his flow'r
That was blooming to cheer him through life's dreary hour
Oh, I'm longing to see him through life's dark hour
He's gone and neglected this pale wildwood flower.

WILL THE CIRCLE BE UNBROKEN

Old-Time and Bluegrass Gospel Song by Jennie Wilson and F.L. Eiland; **DATE:** 1905; **CATEGORY:** Early Gospel Songs; **RECORDING INFO:** Frank and James McCravy-1927; Frank Welling & John McGhee-1930; The Carter Family- 1935); Monroe Brothers-1936; Morris Brothers-1939; Blue Sky Boys; Curly Ray Cline; Lester Flatt & the Nashville Grass; Doc Watson, Clint Howard and Fred Price; **OTHER NAMES:** "Can The Circle Be Unbroken"; **NOTES:** One of the great old-time gospel songs popularized by The Carter Family's 1935 recording "Can the Circle Be Unbroken," on Conqueror 8529.

Will the cir - cle be un - bro - ken bye and bye Lord bye and bye There's a bet - ter home a wait - ing in the sky Lord in the sky.

        G   **C**   **G**
Chorus: Will the circle be unbroken, Bye and bye, Lord, bye and bye?
                                              D   **G**
There's a better home a-waiting, In the sky, Lord, in the sky.

  G   **C**   **G**
I was standing by the window, On one cold and cloudy day;
                                  D   **G**
And I saw the hearse come rolling, For to carry my mother away.

Lord, I told the undertaker, "Undertaker, please drive slow;
For this body you are hauling, Lord, I hate to see her go"

I followed close behind her, tried to hold up and be brave
But I could not hide my sorrow, When they laid her in the grave.

Went back home, Lord, my home was lonesome, Since my mother, she was gone;
All my brothers, sisters crying, What a home so sad and lone.

WORKING ON A BUILDING

Traditional Old-Time and Bluegrass Song; **DATE:** Early 1900's; **CATEGORY:** Early Country and Bluegrass Songs; **RECORDING INFO:** Carter Family-1934; J.E. Mainer-1946; Bill Monroe-1954; Old & In The Way; **OTHER NAMES:** I'm Working On a Building; **NOTES:** The spiritual song " Working On a Building" recorded in Odum & Johnson, *The Negro and His Songs* (1925, p. 72): "I'm workin' on the building fer my Lord/Fer my Lord, fer my Lord" seems to be on of the earliest versions. Charles K. Wolfe says in notes to *The Carter Family: Longing for Old Virginia* (Rounder CD): Another "Holiness song" [in addition to "Hello Central, Give Me Heaven"] was "I'm Working on a Building," still current in gospel repertoires today. Bill Monroe recorded this gospel song, with origins in African American spiritual traditions, for Decca in 1954 on the same day he cut "On and On.".

D

If I was a sinner, I'll tell you what I would do
(2nd verse gambler)   **A**   **D**

I'd quit my sinning and I'd work on the building too
 (2nd verse gambling)

Chorus: I'm working on a building, I'm working on a building,
                    A   **D**

I'm working on a building for my Lord, for my Lord!

It's a Holy Ghost building, it's the Holy Ghost building,
                    A   **D**

It's a Holy Ghost building, for my Lord, for my Lord!

Worried Man

Traditional Old-Time and Bluegrass Song; **DATE:** Early 1900's; **CATEGORY:** Early Country and Bluegrass Songs; **RECORDING INFO:** Carter Family-1930; Blue Sky Boys; Wade Mainer and the Mainers Mountaineers-1936; Wilma Lee and Stoney Cooper; Kingston Trio; Don Reno and Bill Harrell with the Tennesse Cutups; **OTHER NAMES:** Worried Man Blues; **NOTES:** First recorded by John Fox in 1927, *Worried Man Blues* is related to *My Long Journey Home* and *Haunted Road Blues*. It was popularized first by the Carter Family in 1930 and then was a hit (peak Billboard position # 20) in 1959 for the Kingston Trio.

It takes a wor-ried man to sing a wor-ried song It takes a wor-ried man to sing a wor-ried song It takes a wor-ried man to sing a wor-ried song I'm wor-ried now but I won't be wor-ried long.

G   **C**   **G**
It takes a worried man to sing a worried song, It takes a worried man to sing a worried song
                                                        D   **G**
It takes a worried man to sing a worried song, I'm worried now, but I won't be worried long

I went across the river and I laid down to sleep, I went across the river and I laid down to sleep
I went across the river and I laid down to sleep, When I woke up, there were shackles on my feet

Twenty one links of chain around my leg, Twenty one links of chain around my leg
Twenty one links of chain around my leg, And on each link, the initials of my name

I asked the judge what's gonna be my fine, I asked the judge what's gonna he my fine
I asked the judge what's gonna be my fine, Twenty one years on the Rocky Mountain Line

If anyone should ask you who composed this song, If anyone should ask you who composed this song
If anyone should ask you who composed this song, Tell him it was I and I sing it all day long

WRECK OF THE OLD 97 [LAWS G 2]

Traditional Old-Time and Bluegrass Song; **DATE:** Early 1900's; **CATEGORY:** Early Country and Bluegrass Songs; **RECORDING INFO:** G. B. Grayson and Henry Whitter-1927; Stoneman Family Don Reno, Red Smiley and the Tennessee Cut Ups; Kelly Harrell; Norman and Nancy Blake; **OTHER NAMES:** Wreck of the Southern Old 97; **NOTES:** No ballad composition has touched more Americans than the song describing the wreck of mail train No.97. "Old 97," which consisted of four cars and locomotive No.1102, crashed on September 27, 1903. Engineer Joseph A. Broady was trying to make up time as his train approached Danville down a three-mile grade. He realized he did not have enough air pressure to slow the train for an upcoming curved trestle, and in vain he reversed the engine to lock the wheels. "Old 97" vaulted off the trestle, and 11 people were killed. "The Wreck of the Old 97" was initially recorded commercially by Virginia musicians G. B. Grayson and Henry Whitter, but when it was released by singer Vernon Dalhart, it became the first million-selling record in the United States. David G. George, a Pittsylvania telegraph operator who was at the accident scene, was the song's original author. George composed the ballad by adding new lyrics to the altered tune of an older song, Ship That Never Returned.

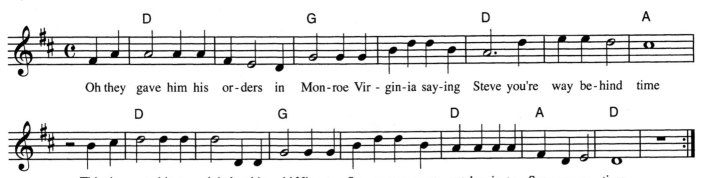

    D   **G**   **D**   **A**
Well, they give him his orders at Monroe Virginia, Saying: Pete, you're way behind time
    D   **G**   **D**   **A**   **D**
This ain't thirty-eight, but it's old ninety-seven, And you've got to be in Danville on time.

But he turned around to his black greasy fireman, Said: Shovel in a little more coal
When we cross the White Oak Mountain, You can watch old ninety-seven roll.

It's a mighty rough road from Lynchburg to Danville, On a line on a three mile grade
It is on this grade that he lost his airbrakes, And you see what a jump he made.

He was a-going down the grade making ninety miles an hour
And his whistle broke out in a scream
It is on that grade that he lost his airbrakes, And you see what a jump he made.

He was a-going down the grade making ninety miles an hour, And his whistle begin to scream
And they found him in the wreck
With his hand on his throttle and scalded to death by the steam.

Well, ladies, you can all take warning, From this time now and on
Never speak harsh words to your true loving husband, He might leave you and never return.

YOUNG MAN WHO WOULDN'T HOE CORN

Traditional Old-Time and Bluegrass Song; **DATE:** 1916 (Cox); **CATEGORY:** Early Country and Bluegrass Songs; **RECORDING INFO:** Buster Carter & Preston Young, "A Lazy Farmer Boy " (Columbia 15702, 1931); Possum Hunters; Canebreak Rattlers; Oscar Brand; Ritchie Family of Kentucky; Alison Krauss and Union Station; **OTHER NAMES:** A Lazy Farmer Boy; The Lazy Man; Harm Link; Lazy Young Man, Georgia Boy. **NOTES:** The first recording of "Young Man Who Wouldn't Hoe Corn" is entitled "A Lazy Farmer Boy" by Buster Carter & Preston Young on Columbia 15702 (1931) with Preston Young- vocal and guitar; and Posey Rorer- fiddle. Bluegrass versions by Richard Greene and lately by Alison Krauss and Union Station. It is related to 'Wind Blew the Bonnie Lassie's Plaidie Awa'.

    G   **D**   **Em**
I'll sing you a song and it's not very long, It's about a young man who wouldn't hoe corn
      G   **B7**   **Em**   **D**   **Em**
The reason why I cannot tell, For this young man was always well.

He planted his corn in the month of June, And by July it was knee-high
First of September there came a big frost, And all this young man's corn was lost.

He went to the fence and there peeked in, The weeds and the grass grew up to his chin;
The weeds and the grass they grew so high, It caused this young man for to sigh.

He went down to his neighbor's door, Where he had often been before,
Saying "Pretty little miss, will you marry me? Pretty little miss what do you say?"

"Here you are a-wanting for to wed, And cannot make your own cornbread
Single I am and single I'll remain, A lazy man I won't maintain."

Well he went down to a pretty little widder, And I hope by heck that he don't get her.
She gave him the mitten as sure as you're born, And all because he wouldn't hoe corn.

GUITAR CHORDS

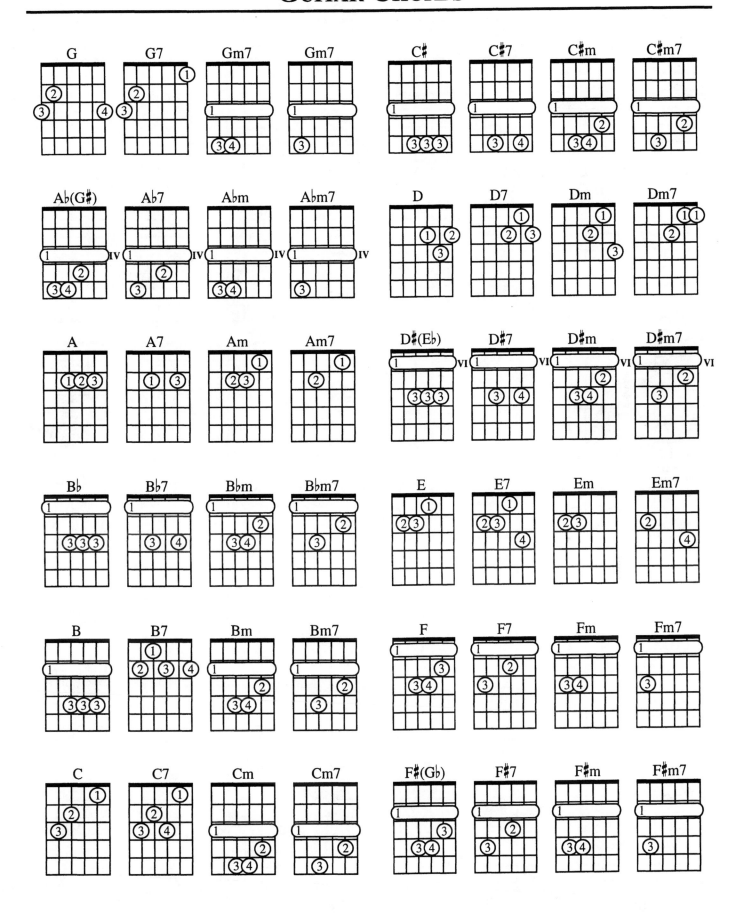

MANDOLIN CHORDS

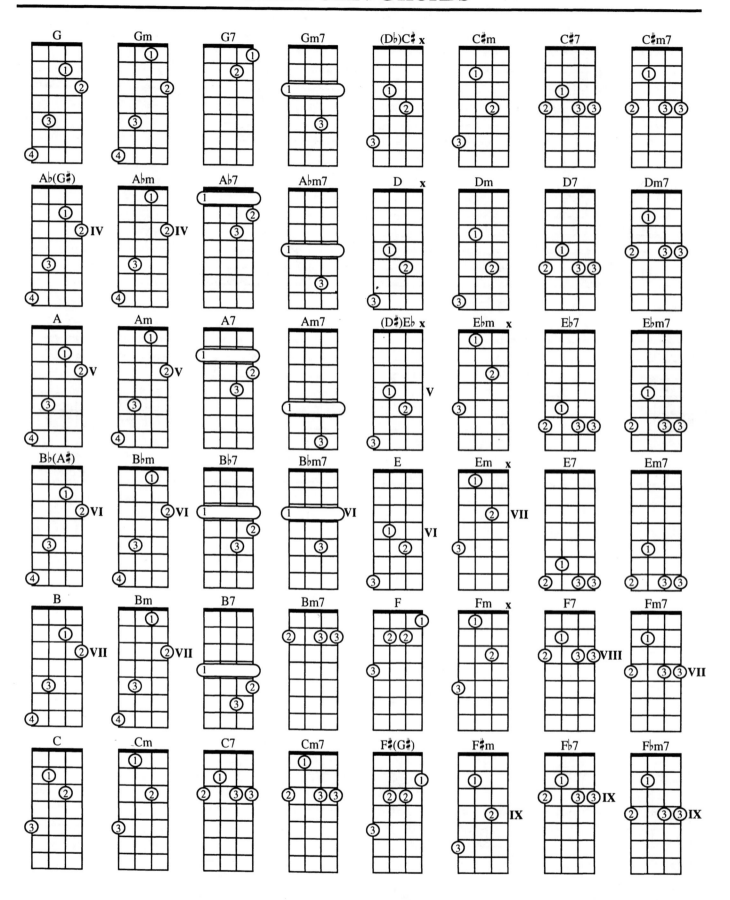

Banjo Chords

G

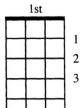 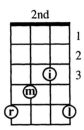 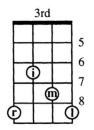

G7

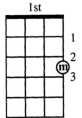 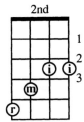 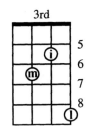

C

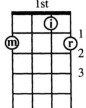 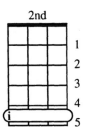 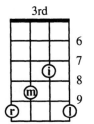

D

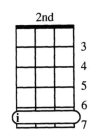 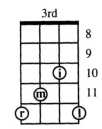

D7

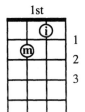 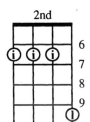 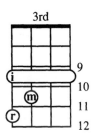

Em

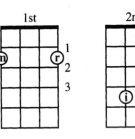 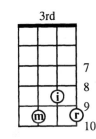

E

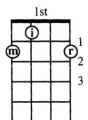 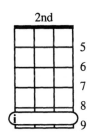 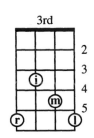

F

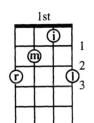 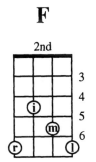 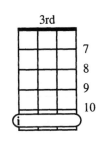

A

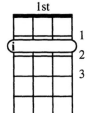 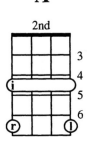 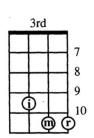

Am

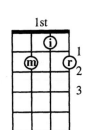 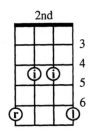 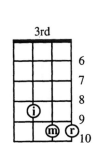